NEGRO LABOR
A National Problem

NEGRO LABOR

A National Problem

ROBERT C. WEAVER

NEW YORK
HARCOURT, BRACE AND COMPANY

TO ELLA

PREFACE

SINCE the beginning of the defense effort there have been many changes in the economic status of Negroes. Most of these were preceded by an insistent drive on the part of colored Americans to achieve greater equality of opportunity. And as changes were forced by wartime necessity, the Negro became more insistent. Because we have accepted stereotyped notions about our color minorities (often as a means of justifying our undemocratic treatment of them), these developments have been viewed with alarm. From the start, there were those who were opposed to making any concessions to the demands of Negroes. Others found their real or imaginary vested interests theatened by impending change. Both groups combined in resisting those developments which would narrow the differential in status between white and colored Americans. There were tensions; then in the summer of 1943, Detroit burst forth into a bloody race riot. The forces of reaction said, "I told you so," and advocated a cessation in progressive action.

But there could be no going back. War—and a global war in particular—is a social revolution. Preparation and execution of programs for defensive and offensive military action have affected all aspects of community life. To the average citizen this found its expression in the departure of loved ones, the scarcity of consumers' goods, price and commodity controls, and an increased tempo of living and working. It occasioned the dislocation of temporary adjustments incident to fundamental social problems. In this period, the basic unsolved social issues came to the fore and demanded attention.

Race relations was such an issue. Prior to the war it was our habit to generalize about the progress which had been made. There was some basis for this optimism in the rise of new programs for social welfare which brought federal benefits down to

Mr. and Mrs. Average American—including the black citizen. Although the basic evils in the interracial problem remained, some concrete action was being carried on to ameliorate them.

Then came the war. It was a war of ideologies. It was dedicated to achieving the Four Freedoms for peoples everywhere. It was a struggle of the democracies against the fascist states; it was an attack upon foreign theories and practices of racialism. In such a conflict our native racialism was sure to come out into the open. It could no longer be ignored; nor did those who suffered from it fail to see the world-wide implications of their struggle.

Segregation and discrimination in the armed forces, insults to the groups which suffer from them in peacetime, became open and painful wounds in time of war. The maltreatment of black boys in the uniform of the United States in the South became a national problem when these soldiers and sailors were drawn from all sections of the country, sections in which they had not been exposed to the cruder forms of racial bigotry. Inability to serve in certain branches and divisions of the armed services, an evidence of less than full citizenship status in time of peace, became a practical problem affecting the lives and families of a million citizens during the war. The Harlem riot of August, 1943, was set off by rumors of an incident which typified the true reports of abuses against Negro servicemen in the South. Its basic causes, however, were the frustrations and the confusions which inevitably come from living in America's largest ghetto.

Job discrimination was an important factor in the disillusionment of Negroes in New York and elsewhere. Denial of the right to work is always tragic for those who experience it. In a rapidly expanding economy where every citizen was urged to enter essential work, this denial became an ever-present, additional evidence of not belonging, occasioning at the same time economic privation. It had implications for the future, too, for if in such a period Negro labor could not find full utilization, the submerged status of the black worker seemed to be set for all time.

These ills, and others, such as increasingly overcrowded housing at high rents, the spread of southern color attitudes to other sections of the nation by white migrants, and general community hostility faced our identifiable color minorities in World War II. At the same time the general population was inconvenienced and harassed by certain developments: all were affected by wartime restrictions on spending; all suffered from an inadequate supply of housing; all felt the inconveniences of overtaxed transportation systems and the inadequacies of recreational facilities which had suddenly become terribly overcrowded. People contracted "war nerves." Many were without roots in the community. All were troubled by a multiplicity of large and small irritations. They were looking for a scapegoat. Color minorities offered a ready outlet for the general dissatisfaction and pent-up resentment.

Community defects, under the strain of wartime living, resulted in short tempers and fights. On many occasions, local police were most inept in handling potentially explosive situations involving Mexicans or Negroes and whites, and the press often stressed inflammatory material. Out of such situations came the "zoot suit" riot in Los Angeles and the Beaumont riot in Texas, victimizing the Mexican-American in the former and the Negro in the latter.

These factors figured in Detroit's tragic race riot of 1943. But in that highly industrial city none was as important as the reaction of the community to the changes in the economic status of the Negro which were inevitable at the outbreak of the war—changes which became imperative as we faced a serious shortage of manpower. Resistance to advances in the economic and occupational status of the Negro persisted in Detroit and elsewhere in the wartime period of full employment, for better jobs for him represented a direct and fatal challenge to the accepted color-caste system.

At the same time, the entrance of the Negro into new spheres of activity brought the "race problem" into the experience of hundreds of thousands of Americans who never before had had any real contact with it. These citizens were poorly prepared to meet the situation. Most of them accepted the popular misconceptions about race; many of them had been conditioned to look for undesirable racial characteristics; almost all of them became disturbed about the so-called militancy of the Negro, whom many had come to regard as their potential economic competitor.

Labor, management, and government faced new and difficult problems. It is about them that this book is written. In Part I there is a brief description of over-all developments. Part II interprets these events and describes the roles of government, management and labor. Part III is devoted to a discussion of the future of the Negro in our economy.

Throughout the book, there are constant references to labor unions and their influence upon the Negro's right to work. The reader should be forewarned that there can be no sound generalization about unions' contribution, since organized labor is made up of many units. Policies vary greatly from one unit to another; practices are even more diverse, and nowhere are there greater differences than in matters involving racial groups. On the one hand, the most effective wartime programs for intergroup understanding and co-operation have been developed in certain labor unions. On the other hand, some of the most persistent barriers to Negro employment and up-grading are found in other labor unions. Four principal factors have determined Negro-union relationships: the announced racial policies and practices of unions, the attitudes and actions of responsible labor leaders and union officials, the efficacy of educational programs for interracial understanding within unions, and the extent and intelligence of Negro participation in the affairs of organized labor. Each of these factors has been influential to the extent that it has ultimately reached the rank and file membership of the unions.

This book was completed just after V-E Day. Since that time, many things have happened; the most important, of course, was the unexpected cessation of the war in the Pacific. None the less, what is set forth in Part III of the text seemed as pertinent in September as it had seemed in May. The problems of reconversion and the post-war economy were no different, although they had become more immediate than anyone could have foreseen in the early summer of 1945.

V-J Day brought a deeper appreciation for these problems. This was reflected in the widespread discussion of the Murray-Wagner Full Employment Bill, the introduction of the Wagner-Ellender Housing Bill, and the announcement of a fifteen-point reconversion program sponsored by New Dealers in the Senate. Yet the war was over and we still had no adequate legislative program for reconversion. The Committee on Fair Employment Practice was still a temporary agency, with less than half its previous year's appropriation. There was no legislation for a permanent FEPC, and only three states had set up machinery for encouraging or securing fair employment practices.

Congress reconvened early in September. But the nation was in grave danger of having too little planning and acting too late to meet the problems of post-war adjustment. Despite President Truman's advocacy of a sound legislative program for reconversion and post-war economic reforms, there was no immediate acceptance of his proposals by Congress. Mass unemployment in the post-war economy was a live possibility in September, 1945, and nothing in the record of the Congress which reconvened indicated that it would legislate a program adequate to meet the problems of reconversion. In such a situation, race relations, unstable throughout the war, seemed explosive in the peace.

What will happen in the months following V-J Day depends upon the understanding and the organized will of the American people. Those concerned with human relations should concentrate upon creating the kind of local and national economy which will assure job opportunities for the maximum number of employable individuals of all colors, creeds, and national origins in the peace for which we have all fought.

The basic materials for this book were secured by field investigations, personal interviews, and correspondence. I am particularly indebted to those men who assisted me during the period, from 1940 to 1944, when I was in various government agencies assigned the task of encouraging fuller utilization of Negro labor in defense and war industries. Throughout that period their knowledge of events was of great assistance to me, and I have now drawn upon this for assistance in presenting and interpreting events. Most of the factual materials contained in the first two sections of this book have been presented elsewhere in periodicals (mentioned in the bibliography), and since references have been noted in most of the articles, footnotes have been dispensed with in the hope that their absence will make reading less arduous.

The published works from which materials have been drawn are cited in the text and are included among those listed in the bibliography.

I am indebted to Dr. Herbert R. Northrup for materials contained in the sections on coal mining and railroad firemen in Chapter VII. The events contained therein were drawn from his book, "Organized Labor and the Negro," Harper and Brothers graciously granting permission to use the materials.

Chapter X, Local Transportation—a Special Case, originally appeared as a pamphlet of the American Council on Race Relations, under the title, "Negro Platform Workers." The materials for the pamphlet were gathered principally by Joseph Weckler, formerly of the staff of the American Council and now of the University of Southern California. The Council has been kind enough to permit my reproducing much of the material contained in its bulletin prepared by Mr. Weckler and me.

Chapter XVI, Seniority—a Special Problem in Reconversion, is the result of a project undertaken and financed by the American Council on Race Relations. I am especially indebted to William Prince, who did field work on that project, and to J. Lawrence Duncan, who helped in the planning, collection of material, and interpretation of the seniority survey.

The editors and publishers of the periodicals listed below have kindly permitted reproduction of some of the materials which originally appeared in their journals: Annals of the American Academy of Political and Social Science, International Labour Review, Journal of Negro Education, Journal of Political Economy, Opportunity, Phylon, Quarterly Journal of Economics, Social Forces, The Atlantic Monthly, and The Crisis.

Two of my former associates in government, Clarence M. Mitchell and Austin H. Scott, have read the manuscript and offered suggestions and corrections. Miss Ruth Warren, my secretary, has assisted me in the final preparation of the text. Many sections of the manuscript were read by my wife who has done much to make this book readable. For the faults, the author alone is responsible.

R. C. W.

Hull-House,
Chicago, Illinois.

CONTENTS

PART I: OVER-ALL DEVELOPMENT

PART II: INTERPRETATION

PART III: IMPLICATIONS FOR THE FUTURE

PART I

OVER-ALL DEVELOPMENT

CHAPTER I

THE NEGRO WORKER'S PAST

MOST of the diverse peoples who make up America voluntarily migrated to the New World. Negroes, however, were brought here expressly and involuntarily to furnish cheap labor. When large-scale cotton production and the plantation system became extremely profitable in the South, the importation of slave labor grew appreciably. It continued long after the slave trade had been officially banned, becoming the basis for one of the most extensive bootlegging businesses in the United States. It furnished the South with an ever-expanding source of labor; it sustained the shipping interests of the New England states; it offered the basis for large fortunes in the North and Middle Atlantic states. But slavery did more. It occasioned color attitudes and patterns of inferior status for Negroes which still haunt and harass the nation.

The plantation system, with its abundance of slave labor, had little need for agricultural wage-earners. When whites were employed by the large planters, they were used to do hazardous jobs which exposed the workers to sickness, injury, or death. The plantation owners soon captured most of the desirable land as well as a large segment of the market for cotton. And as time went on, Negro slaves obtained the majority of the domestic service jobs in the towns and cities of the South and captured an ever-growing proportion of the skilled work. The poor white wage-earner was pushed out in this economy; he found little work; he was insecure; he developed deep animosity toward the plantation system. This animosity was not always directed against the institution of slavery, for the injection of color concepts and the rationalization and defense of slavery on the basis of imputed racial characteristics of inferiority often prevented such results. It encouraged many of the propertyless whites to identify themselves with the master classes and find compensation for their insecurity in the support of a racial and economic system which relegated the Negro to a permanent sub-human status. The poor whites' hatred for the plantation system was transferred to a hatred for their fellow victims of it—the Negro slaves.

This animosity was inevitable once a concept of status based on race and color was introduced. It was extremely useful for those who benefited from slavery because it confused an economic issue with a racial one. That confusion has persisted and is still basic to any discussion of the economic status of colored minorities in America. And the animosities of the poor white against the Negro became bilateral; the slave developed contempt for the propertyless white. That too has persisted and finds its current expression in the disdain of many southern Negroes for "poor white trash."

Slavery has long been abolished, although instances of peonage occasionally remind us that forced labor still exists in our Southland. In the place of slavery we have substituted a color occupational system. That system perpetuates the concept of the Negro as an inferior being and establishes institutions to assure his inferior status. It serves to conceal the basic nature of economic problems and covers them with color situations. Whenever necessity or national policy dictates modifications in color occupational patterns, the resulting changes are sure to be opposed violently by those who have a real or assumed vested interest in maintaining the color line.

The history of the Negro in American industry is as old as our economic life. Plantations of the old South were totally dependent upon slave labor, and the Negro still forms a large segment of the agricultural workers of that region. In urban centers of the South, Negroes have been and are the traditional servants and casual laborers. In heavy, dirty industries, such as coal mining, iron and steel, tobacco processing, and fertilizer, the southern Negro has a long and successful history.

It is in the construction industry, however, that the black worker has his firmest traditions as an artisan, for he has a long but little-known past as a skilled mechanic in construction. Much of the historically important architecture of the old South—the

ironwork in the old French section of New Orleans, the fine old
residences of Charleston, the impressive buildings throughout the
rural South which symbolize the plantation system—stands as a
monument to the dexterity which the Negro slave quickly developed in the building trades. Many of these black artisans used
their skills as a means of buying their freedom, and so formed a
large segment of the free Negroes in the cities of the deep South.
Consequently, many of the early craft unions of the old South
were organized by colored mechanics. Local 1 of the bricklayers
in New Orleans is over fifty years old, and its membership has
always been predominantly colored. The local plasterers' union,
about ten years younger, has always had an appreciable Negro
membership. In the trowel trades unions in Charleston, there is
a corresponding record of Negro participation.

But with the economic reconstruction of the South, there came
a distinct decline in the proportion of colored workers in the
building industry. New materials and large-scale construction
modified the operations performed by carpenters. The older
skills which the Negro carpenter knew were supplanted by new
methods employed in large-scale construction. At the same time,
plumbing, steamfitting, and electrical work became essential in
many types of building. The Negro slave was never taught these
trades; the free Negro rarely had a chance to learn them. Labor
unions placed their emphasis upon organizing workers who were
in large-scale construction. The black artisan, despite his early
start in home construction, knew only the skills of small-scale
building and could maintain a favorable competitive position only
in those of his inherited skills which carried over into large-scale
building, such as the skills of the trowel trades in which the techniques remained substantially unchanged. The Negro continued
to work in those operations which he had learned until the white
artisan—who entered many occupations in the building industry
with the advent of large-scale building—used his political power
(after Reconstruction) and Jim Crow unionism to capture new
occupations and new expressions of old operations. This meant
a continuing displacement of Negro carpenters and monopoly
of the mechanical building trades by white workers who were

newcomers into the older building trades which the Negroes once dominated in the South.

Outside capital which promoted the South's industrialization adhered closely to the color-caste system of the region. The occupational patterns which evolved were in accord with this basic principle: clean, light, well-paid jobs for whites and heavy, dirty, lower paid jobs for Negroes. The prime requirement for most Negro workers was that they have strong backs and, it was assumed, weak minds. In light of this development, the black worker received many jobs in iron and steel where the operations were hot and heavy, but most of the higher paid skilled jobs (even if they were both hot and heavy) were exclusively for the white worker. In order to preserve and follow the dictates of the color-caste system, management in the textile industry developed an entirely different pattern. This was a comparatively light and clean industry which symbolized the rise of the factory system in the South; consequently, Negroes were assigned to outside cleaning and other unskilled work. Operation of machinery in such an industry became a white job exclusively. In tobacco production, an intermediate color occupational pattern devolved. For the most part, Negroes and whites were both assigned to machine operations. But the majority of the colored workers were in unskilled jobs, and those on machines were concentrated in the stemming departments where there were dust hazards and lower rates of pay. Thus, the departure from the color-caste system in tobacco processing was only superficial.

During the last two decades of the nineteenth century and until World War I, a somewhat similar racial occupational pattern evolved in the North where the Negro population in most industrial centers was extremely small. Colored persons were usually employed as servants, porters, and janitors; a few were engaged as common laborers. In many cities, the only Negro families in the community were those who had come with the railroads and were employed as Pullman porters and dining-car waiters. Then, as labor disputes occurred and harassed employers, Negroes were often imported to break strikes and weaken labor organization. It was via the road of strike-breaking that the first colored workers got into the northern branches of iron and steel, meat-packing, and other heavy industry.

The first World War occasioned a radical change in the geographic and industrial distribution of Negroes. It led to the first mass migration from the South to the North. It also accelerated at a rapid rate the urbanization of colored Americans. Most important, it offered the Negro a chance to enter the basic industries of the North in large numbers.

At the outbreak of World War I, there was a general shortage of unskilled workers. Negroes were brought into the industrial centers of the North to meet this need. They found employment in iron and steel, meat-packing, shipbuilding, automobile and associated industries. This time, as contrasted to their earlier sporadic migration, they came in by the tens of thousands and established a permanent place for themselves in the heavy industries of the region. They inherited many of the domestic service jobs from earlier migrant groups. Negro men became a significant element in the unskilled labor force for construction and street maintenance. By the close of the war, it had been demonstrated that when labor shortages forced their employment in new industries and new occupations, Negroes were found to be satisfactory workers. The results were perhaps most outstanding in shipbuilding, where the labor market was the tightest. In Philadelphia, for example, a gang of Negro pile drivers established a new world record; and at Sparrows Point, just outside Baltimore, a colored riveter broke the existing record.

The black worker had become accepted as a part of the industrial reserve in the North. He was, however, almost exclusively employed in unskilled capacities. Further, his high visibility made it easy to identify him with common labor. The earlier color antagonisms occasioned by strike-breaking and the general spread of segregation when Negroes arrived suddenly in large numbers, during World War I, contributed toward the establishment of an occupational color line in the North. But the pattern was not an exact duplicate of that in the South. First, in contrast to the South, there was no general system of wage differentials based on race in northern industrial employment. In addition, in a few industries and in some plants, Negroes were occasionally able to get into higher skills. Although the vast majority of Negro skilled workers in the North were in foundry and other hot, disagreeable, or relatively low-wage work, a few were in jobs which were absolutely inconsistent with southern racial occupational patterns in large industrial plants. For in the South, when a Negro held a skilled job, it was usually in a trade in which the black worker had inherited a place from the slave era or it was on the basis of a personal relationship and the employment was generally in a small plant.

When industry came with unprecedented speed to the South in the post-war period, colored labor was already in such industries as iron and steel, fertilizer, tobacco, turpentine, and furniture production. Expansion in over-all industrial employment created additional job opportunities for the urban Negro in the region. It expanded his participation in the service industries as the population expanded and greater hotel and restaurant facilities were developed. He shared appreciably in the resulting demand for hotel and restaurant workers (in menial capacities); he received a major part of the newly created domestic service jobs which developed. Other positions, such as those of janitors, delivery boys and garage and other attendants, increased, and he participated widely in them. A similar development occurred in those urban areas to which Negroes migrated. Since most of these service jobs are dependent upon the earnings of others—in the sense that wage- and salary-earners and those who receive dividend payments are the principal employers and customers—the state of industrial activity determines the volume of employment. Thus, during the industrial expansion of World War I and the 1920's, there were many jobs for Negroes in the service industries and in domestic service in the South and in the North.

Then came the depression. The Northern Negro worker had little seniority and only the beginnings of skilled status in a few basic industries. He felt doubly the throes of the depression and the devastating influence of unemployment which typified the period. Racial attitudes intensified the impact of these economic developments. In a few industries, such as meat-packing, where the demand for the finished product was more stable than in the heavy industries, the colored worker was able to maintain some of his earlier gains in occupational status. But, in general, he suffered extreme unemployment and lost much of the little ground which he had won in semi-skilled and skilled employment. In the southern states, where Negro artisans were more firmly established (via a wage structure involving racial differentials), there was the least amount of occupational shifting and unemployment. But depression also took its toll in the South, where the displacement of Negro skilled workers in the building and hand trades had gradually been in process for some time. Extreme competition for jobs in a contracting economy accelerated these trends and gave a new economic basis for antagonism between white and black labor.

Almost a half of the skilled Negro males in the nation were displaced from their usual types of employment during the period 1930 to 1936; a third of those outside their usual occupations were in unskilled work, and over 17 per cent were unemployed. The degree of occupational shifting varied from region to region, reflecting sectional differences in job opportunities for colored workers.

Few industries illustrate these developments better than construction, where most skilled Negroes were concentrated. Although the decline in building preceded the general slump of 1929, unemployment in the industry was greatest during the first four years of the 1930's. When there was a small upswing, it was dominated by programs of government-financed construction, and in 1932 and 1933 public construction involved greater expenditure than private construction. This meant that an increasingly large proportion of construction workers were employed on large-scale public building. This emphasis upon large-scale construction created a new pattern of demand for skilled workers in the industry. It was most pronounced in the South, where frame construction and brick veneer are so important in home building. In the South, as in no other part of the nation, technological processes and types of material differ greatly between public, large-scale, fireproof construction and private, small-scale building. When it is remembered that the Negro's entrance into the building industry occurred during a period when residential construction was the typical building and that his position in the industry has aiways been dependent largely upon the traditional methods in small-scale construction in the South, the importance of this development becomes apparent. There was an additional factor: in the South, Negro workers usually received lower wage rates than whites, but federal projects did not allow racial wage differentials. Thus, the initial effort of New Deal construction programs was to hasten the displacement of Negro skilled workers.

Although the program of public construction financed and executed by the Public Works Administration was not the first of its kind, it was by far the most extensive. Before the New Deal there had always been some federal construction, usually new government buildings or post offices. Until the depression of 1929, however, employment on these projects had not represented an appreciable proportion of all work in the building industry, and Negroes had usually found a chance to get jobs in the trowel trades in those areas of the nation where colored artisans were concentrated. After 1930 the situation changed. There was extreme competition for any and all jobs in construction; labor unions strengthened their control over these projects; outside contractors were usually low and successful bidders.

These trends were already developing when PWA initiated its vast new program of building. Under this program, more outside contractors entered the South, there was continuing competition for jobs, and labor unions secured wider acceptance and greater influence over employment. There had, of course, been discrimination against Negroes on public works in the past. But it was not until 1932 that government had been pressed to do anything about it. In October of that year, Ogden Mills, then Secretary of the Treasury, issued a communication to construction engineers stating that race discrimination in employment was not to be tolerated. In accord with this precedent, Secretary Ickes, in the capacity of Administrator of PWA, issued an order to state engineers on September 21, 1933, to the effect that "there be no discrimination exercised against any person because of color or religious affiliation."

Neither order was effective. It was humanly impossible to define discrimination (much less prove it) in a situation where a borrower, a contractor, and a labor union were involved. When discrimination was clearly apparent, as in instances where no colored artisans were employed, the hiring of a few skilled Negroes would correct the obvious abuse, but there was no criterion which could be used to indicate when discrimination had been abolished. In addition, PWA projects were usually constructed by state, county, or municipal governments; the federal agency issued loans and grants but was not a direct party to the construction contract.

When the public housing program of PWA was launched, this contractual relationship changed. The Housing Division of PWA directly undertook the construction of projects, and it was a party to contracts. At the same time, about a third of the low-rent housing projects were designed for Negro occupancy. They had been planned with the co-operation of local advisory boards on which colored members often sat, and some had been designed by architectural firms which included Negroes. It was natural that colored people expected to participate in their construction.

Public housing became the guinea pig for experimenting with developing techniques for assuring the employment of skilled Negro labor on public financed projects during a period of general unemployment. Many problems arose. Should there be an attempt to secure the use of all Negro labor, skilled, semi-skilled and unskilled, on projects located in Negro areas? There was, especially in the South, a large body of Negro opinion which supported this position. PWA decided against such a program for several reasons: it would establish an unfortunate and dangerous precedent; it would mitigate against the use of Negro workers in the bulk of public works designed to benefit all groups in the population; it was doubtful if there were sufficient numbers of Negroes in the various crafts to man the projects completely. But experience had shown that a simple non-discrimination clause was not enough. There had to be a definition of discrimination. This was finally provided by establishing a prima facie basis of discrimination, the failure to pay Negro skilled workers (regardless of trades) a minimum percentage of the skilled payroll. The percentage was based upon the latest occupational census with slight variations adjusted to current population movements.

This machinery proved more effective. It was adopted by the United States Housing Authority when it succeeded the Housing Division of PWA in administering the public housing program. As of December, 1940, over $2,250,000 or 5.8 per cent of the total payroll to skilled workers on public housing projects in 95 cities had been paid to Negro artisans. This represented a proportion of the total skilled payroll larger than the proportion of Negro artisans reported in the occupational census of 1930. Three-quarters of the skilled Negroes employed were engaged in the trowel trades.

One of the complications incident to this experiment was the status of Negro building trades craftsmen in labor unions. In the South, Negroes were either excluded from the local unions of the carpenters or assigned to separate locals. Most of the Negro locals were small and relatively ineffectual in negotiating with large contractors for job opportunities, and by 1932, it had become the custom in the region for white carpenters to refuse to work on the same job with their darker brothers in the union. In all building trades, there was unprecedented unemployment after 1930. The first job opportunities to open were concentrated in large-scale public building, which, because of its technological nature and the federal policy of using the lowest qualified builder, depended upon large contractors who were often unfamiliar with local Negro skilled labor. These contractors usually secured their labor from unions and were responsive to local political pressures which urged the employment of white mechanics only.

During the depression both white and colored union members got behind in their union dues. Where there were small colored locals, the membership which remained in good standing was insufficient to keep the local active, and charters were lost. When work was revived, the availability of white union members, their greater familiarity with methods of large-scale production, and the fact that they were white contributed to their employment. Because many locals had been able to keep going through the activity, and often sacrifice, of a few dues-paying white members, this group insisted that they have first preference on union jobs. This was, of course, most prevalent in instances where there had been a white and a Negro union, and the latter had lost its charter. In locals where the Negro membership was a minority, white business agents usually gave preference to white workers. The neglect of Negro employment and the discouragement of Negroes to re-enter unions followed. Related to this, too, was the fact that Negroes had been fired earlier and had been out of work in construction longer than white mechanics. They often lost tools, and occasionally they lost dexterity.

Any effective device to assure non-discrimination in employment had to meet the union problem realistically. The New Deal had been dedicated to protecting labor's right to organize, and, at the same time, it was interested in protecting the Negro's right to work. In the past these two had been conflicting interests, and job opportunities for the Negro had usually been secured at the price of weakening labor organization. Indeed, the employment of colored labor had often been initiated expressly for this purpose. In order to avoid such results, PWA began to negotiate for the co-operation of local unions and in many localities secured union clearance through the issuance of work permits or the acceptance of Negroes as union members.

This mechanism for defining and enforcing non-discrimination in employment was a significant development, although not a definitive solution of discrimination on public financed construction. It almost lost its usefulness by being pushed too far. The minimum percentage clauses were designed to meet a peculiar situation. Their objective was to retain past occupational advances for Negroes in the middle 1930's—a period of slack labor demand. They were frankly a device to regain lost ground; they were not designed to open new types of employment. But as a matter of fact it would have been most unrealistic to have attempted to secure significant occupational gains for a minority group in a period when there was mass unemployment. This philosophy was not universally appreciated. As a result, the minimum percentage clauses were often condemned because they did not open the mechanical trades to Negroes, although they did make some slight advances in this direction. Further, they were criticized because most of the Negroes employed on public housing projects were concentrated in the trowel trades; as a matter of fact, new methods and new materials had made obsolete much of the skill which Negro carpenters possessed, and there were few Negroes trained in the mechanical trades. Only a program of training could have rectified this. But minorities do not enjoy programs of training during periods of mass unemployment. More dangerous, however, was the tendency in 1940 to apply this specialized technique to an entirely different economic situation. At the latter date, the demand for labor was expanding, and the need was not to retain past gains but to achieve new occupational advances. Fortunately, the proposals to apply minimum percentage clauses in such a period were not heeded, and other, more realistic devices were developed.

The New Deal had a profound effect upon the economic status of Negroes. The relief agencies, FERA and WPA, despite certain discriminations, such as lower rates for Negroes or lesser work opportunities for them in skilled and professional capacities, benefited hundreds of thousands of colored Americans. A few were given a chance to continue at their regular skills or learn new ones. But more important was the fact that vast numbers of Negroes were enabled to retain work habits and a minimum of health as a result of federal aid. Programs of the National Youth Administration and the Civilian Conservation Corps had similar effects upon Negro youth. Even the National Recovery Administration had its good influences. At first the establishment of minimum wages under NRA codes threatened the jobs of many Negroes. There were rumors and predictions of mass displacement of colored workers by whites once racial wage differentials were abolished or modified in the South. As a matter of fact, much of this arm-chair theory proved false. There was some displacement, but the extent of it was much less than had been prophesied since in the average establishment it is expensive and troublesome to replace a group of workers who have been employed for some time. More important, however, was the fact that NRA initiated a trend toward weakening the wage differential based on race.

Large programs of public financed construction further weakened the racial wage differential in the South. The operation of the Wages and Hours Act and the growing significance of industrial unions in certain areas of the South had a similar influence. Outside the region even more significant developments were starting. The new, industrial unions of the North were welcoming large numbers of Negroes; this, in turn, was offering the basis for real understanding between Negro and white workers; it was so conditioning the Negro worker and the community from which he came that the danger of the Negro's becoming a strike-breaker again was greatly reduced.

These developments were to have great significance in World War II, but during the 1930's they offered little encouragement to Negroes. It was generally conceded that the Negro was losing in his quest for economic security and occupational advancement. When the defense program was launched the Negro had long been haunted by unemployment. He was harassed by low occupational status and adverse racial attitudes. The proportion of Negroes in manufacturing had grown from 6.2 per cent in 1910 to 7.3 per cent in 1930. By 1940 it was at a new low, 5.1 per cent. Save in domestic service, colored workers had suffered similar losses in other types of employment. Nor was this all; the Negro had little chance to participate in the very industries which were destined to be most important in war production. For example, in 1940, only 2.3 per cent of the workers in apparel were Negroes. Comparable figures for other industries were as follows: rubber products, 2.1 per cent; iron and steel, 5.5 per cent; nonferrous metals and their products, 2.4 per cent; electrical machinery, 0.5 per cent; other machinery, 1.0 per cent; automobile equipment, 3.6 per cent; aircraft and parts, 0.1 per cent; ship- and boat-building, 6.4 per cent.

When the defense program got under way, the Negro was only on the sidelines of American industrial life. He seemed to be losing ground daily. The prospect was dark; he was discouraged. The forces of racial reaction felt that their position was secure. There were few signs to deflate them. The color-caste system seemed to be firmly entrenched.

CHAPTER II

BARRIERS TO NEGRO EMPLOYMENT

"TODAY's urgent need for manpower effectively removes Negro employment in industry from the realm of social reform," said the American Management Association in a pamphlet issued in 1942. This was in striking contrast to employers' attitudes in 1939 and 1940. To understand why a segment of management had reversed itself and come to this conclusion, it is necessary to look into the nature of war production in our modern world. As early as 1940, it should have been clear that we would have to utilize fully every available worker in a total war. The earlier experiences of the British offered ample evidence, but government, management, and labor did not want to face the issue since it involved modifications of the occupational color-caste system. Such modifications would run counter to vested interests, meet stiff opposition, necessitate unpopular decisions and actions, and require planning and resolution. At the beginning of the defense effort, we were not prepared to meet these issues, and we hoped that some unforeseen events would enable us to avoid them.

The Negro community, however, was convinced that the problems had to be met. At the outset of the defense effort this community—and its leaders in particular—viewed with alarm the long-run economic implications of tying the Negro to restricted occupational and industrial patterns. These leaders knew the immediate dangers of having WPA become almost exclusively a group of Negro projects. They were apprehensive of the apathy of Negroes toward the war. Experience had taught them that such developments would haunt colored Americans in the future and become justification for extending patterns of discrimination. They remembered World War I, when Negroes were brought into new areas and introduced into industrial employment only to be generally dismissed in the depression of the thirties. They

16

united in pressing for training, employment, and up-grading in all war industries, and the Negro community was no less dedicated to such a program. The continuing fight for equal job opportunities was not the agitation of a few Negro radicals; it had become the will of the Negro people.

In November of 1942 seven hundred Negroes assembled in a small city of Connecticut to hear a speaker talk about war jobs; most of the Negro men in the town were employed, and the audience was predominantly female. Theirs was an industrial city but few of them were in factories. The vast majority were domestics, and the manager of the local United States Employment Service had been fearful of encouraging their entrance into manufacturing. He stated that such action would occasion the wrath of the wives of the most influential employers in the area. Here was an extreme case of under-employment. Local industries were accepting women and complaining of the fact that female workers could not be recruited fast enough. Many of the local Negro women had finished high school, and the vast majority were capable of training for production work. Industry had made no move to employ them, and these women did not know how to go about getting a defense job. Vital war production was being delayed because a segment of available labor in the community was ignored in the program for recruiting much-needed workers.

In all communities with colored populations, large and small alike, there was serious waste of available Negro manpower and womanpower. Much of it was due to under-employment. The limited number of Negro men who had been admitted to defense training courses were in janitorial or unskilled jobs. Negroes with mechanical experiences or aptitudes were driving delivery trucks or waiting on tables or operating elevators. To an even larger extent, colored women were concentrated in non-essential service jobs. When they attempted to leave this type of employment, some communities saw in their actions the forerunner of racial conflict and manufactured imaginary Eleanor Clubs which were described as subversive organizations among Negro women, designed for a general exodus from their servants' jobs.

At the outset of the defense effort, it was clear that about 75 per cent of the required workers would be in professional, technical, skilled, single-skilled, and semi-skilled jobs. At the same time it was obvious that we did not have a sufficient quantity of trained personnel. Production methods of the past had never required so high a proportion of trained workers, and the depression had depleted our supply of skilled labor and had almost stopped the training of young people. To meet the pressing need for skilled workers, we resorted to two major programs: breaking down skilled operations and initiating mass training for industrial workers. The first was designed to facilitate the use of a large number of persons who knew only one or two operations of a skill, and the second was designed to prepare millions for such operations in a short space of time. America initiated one of the greatest industrial training programs the world has ever known. There was defense training in our schools, training on the job, and supplementary training in both the school and factory.

The most important needs for training were in those occupations from which Negroes had usually been barred. Examples of this were offered by the phenomenal rise in the demand for welders, electrical workers, machinists, and sheet metal workers, types of work in which few Negroes had ever been employed or trained. It was inevitable that there would be resistance to the use of Negroes in these new occupations. That a nation at war would delay the use of its total manpower resources for three long years is the most striking instance of the tenacity with which America has clung to its established color-caste system in occupations. Yet this is just what happened in the United States in World War II. During the earlier phases of the defense effort, the Negro benefited little if at all from the expanding needs for workers, nor was he permitted to prepare himself for future employment in essential war industries. In April, 1940, for example, there were 5,900,000 non-whites (about 95 per cent of whom were Negroes) in the labor market; 1,300,000 or 22 per cent were unemployed. At the same date, 17.7 per cent of the total whites in the labor market were unemployed. By October, total employment had increased by about 2,000,000, and the proportion of whites unemployed had declined to 13 per cent; the proportion of non-whites without jobs had declined by one-tenth of one per cent.

Although most Negroes in the United States had little training and experience in skilled mechanical trades, there were some qualified colored workers in almost every craft. When the nation was tooling up for war production and as defense contractors clamored for more skilled men, Negro artisans applied at the gates of many plants. They were turned away almost to the man. In most instances they were told that "we can't use skilled Negroes"; sometimes more subtle devices were used, but the results were the same. Negro skilled workers in Hartford, Camden, Pittsburgh, Newport News, Houston, Chicago, Cleveland, and Los Angeles were walking the streets while the communities talked of extreme shortages of skilled workers.

Soon after conversion had been initiated, American industry began to recruit large numbers of workers from non-industrial pursuits. Most of them were new to mechanical work; some had never before been in a factory. Plants were training recruits with backgrounds similar to those of most Negroes, but local colored labor was consistently barred. In September, 1941, the Bureau of Employment Security conducted a survey of Negro workers and the national defense program. It reported that past color bars against Negroes in most skilled and industrial work had relaxed but little, if at all. The employment of Negro artisans in the vast defense construction was limited almost exclusively to carpentry, cement finishing, and to some extent, bricklaying. In traditional types of jobs and in traditional occupations, there had been a slight expansion of Negro employment. The survey noted much evidence "to show that even in industries in which Negroes have by custom been accepted, many establishments which have never employed Negroes in the past were refusing to employ Negroes for skilled and semiskilled work." Such practices were helping to accentuate the acute shortage which had developed in some areas in the foundry industry, a branch of war production which was destined to have serious problems of labor supply throughout the war.

Most important war industries were not using Negroes even in those occupations which were essential and in which labor shortages were delaying necessary defense production. During the period January-March, 1941, for example, the United States Employment Service placed 8,769 workers in selected essential occupations in aircraft; only thirteen were Negroes. Of the 1,066 essential placements in electrical equipment, only five were colored. The Employment Service placed almost 35,000 workers in foundry and forging, machine shop and machine tool, and metal processing; 245 were colored. In shipbuilding, where a large proportion of skilled Negroes had been used in World War I, only 1.7 per cent of the 1,500 essential placements were Negroes. The report further stated, "not only are non-white workers not receiving many skilled or semi-skilled jobs in a great many defense establishments, but they are receiving very few jobs of any type, even unskilled." For the period between October, 1940, and March, 1941, the Employment Service placed over 150,000 male workers of all occupational types in twenty major defense industries. Only 6,150 or 4 per cent were Negroes. Some 30,000 of the total placements were in iron and steel, a heavy industry in which it had been traditional to use Negroes; of these, less than 5 per cent were colored. Of the placements in shipbuilding, 14 per cent were colored. This latter figure, when compared with the low percentages of Negroes placed in essential skilled and semi-skilled jobs, indicates that the vast majority of Negro placements were in unskilled work.

In 1941, the color bar in Philadelphia's war industries had not relaxed. The local United States Employment Service office placed only twelve skilled Negroes during the month of January; seven of these were automobile mechanics, and all of them replaced white workers who had entered war plants. None of the skilled Negroes was engaged in war production. In February, the Employment Service placed one skilled and twenty-four semi-skilled colored workers. The remainder of the 550 Negro placements for the month were in unskilled jobs, mostly in domestic service. Negroes were listed indiscriminately as domestics and laborers, regardless of their training or experience. In October, a Negro, Walter J. Archey, went to a local United States Employment Service office to register for defense training. Archey had completed a four-year course as a machinist in a local vocational high school, but the interviewer urged him not to register for a refresher course because there was no future in machinists' work for Negroes. This interviewer's action was a tragic testimony to color discrimination in local defense plants.

Even the two federal establishments in Philadelphia, the Frankford Arsenal and the United States Navy Yard, were far from offering Negroes equal job opportunities. In the spring of 1940, most of the Negroes employed at the Arsenal were in unskilled jobs; there were few if any Negro machinists, and there were no colored guards nor were any Negroes in the apprentice school. When qualified Negro machinists applied for work, they were told that no applications were being received; at the same time whites were examined and employed on the spot. Nor did veteran Negro laborers, qualified for higher work, have a chance for upgrading. Although employment opportunities for Negroes were greater in the local Navy Yard, no colored persons were in the apprentice school.

The situation in Philadelphia was by no means unique. Labor shortages came early to industrial Connecticut. In town after town, there was absorption of most white local labor. Workers began to come into the area from other parts of New England and then from more distant points. Many were raw recruits, uninitiated to industrial employment and usually without any training for mechanical work, but they were white. They were accepted while local Negroes—even the few who were experienced mechanics and those who had completed the defense training courses offered in the local vocational schools—were systematically turned away from the employment offices of war plants. When colored men were employed, they were used as unskilled laborers or janitors; Negro women were not even considered for employment. So blatant was this discrimination in certain establishments that it became the occasion for national publicity. Included among the plants singled out for special comment were the Pratt and Whitney Aircraft Corporation and the Colt Patent Fire Arms Manufacturing Company at Hartford. These firms were by no means exceptional; they became outstanding because they were expanding at a rapid rate and employed large numbers of new workers.

Baltimore, Maryland, too, came in for much publicity relative to its patterns of racial employment. This was due principally to two factors, the great expansion of its industrial payroll and the forward position taken by The Baltimore Sun incident to full utilization of local labor resources. The latter development was not accidental. It was occasioned by the numerical importance of Negroes in the city (about 20 per cent of the labor force) and the activities of the Baltimore Urban League and the Labor Division of OPM.

In the summer of 1941, Baltimore faced a serious manpower problem at the same time that Negroes were generally barred from defense work. More than that, the continuing migration of workers to the city was complicating other local problems. There was insufficient housing, and overcrowding was increasing daily. Other services—transportation, health, public education, police and fire protection, and recreation—were all over-strained and in-adequate. Yet there was a large unused supply of local Negro labor. Colored workers formed approximately 35 per cent of the unemployed reserve in the state and about 40 per cent of the unemployed males under forty-five years of age. There was a shortage of qualified male applicants for defense training, but this was a shortage of white trainees since several thousand male Negroes were available for defense courses in Baltimore.

The Baltimore Sun finally took cognizance of this situation and said in the March 13, 1942, edition that the continued migration of workers into the city while thousands of local Negroes were excluded by management had serious consequences. It greatly intensified the housing shortage; it caused an emergency shortage of school facilities; it occasioned large expenditures for sewer and water connections, new highways and extension of police and fire protection. The Sun concluded its analysis with these pointed observations:

The situation would be less urgent if it were possible to tap a new reservoir of local labor [Negroes], labor which is already housed and serviced (inadequately, to be sure) and requires nothing new beyond what is already under construction or planned.
If this could be done, not only would the city be spared many

problems of the present, but the post-war readjustment in Balti-more would be made just so much easier.

On the West Coast, and particularly at Los Angeles where there was an appreciable Negro population, the same situation existed. Thousands of workers were streaming into the industrial centers of the Coast at the same time that local Negro labor was systematically overlooked and barred from war jobs. As in other sections of the nation, Negro men on the West Coast were either without jobs or were forced into less essential (and lower paid) employment. Where Negroes entered war production, they were in a limited number of lower occupations and in lower paid jobs. In those cities where colored men had been admitted into defense courses, they joined experienced skilled Negro men in finding work far below their occupational abilities.

In the South the situation was even more hopeless. Charleston, South Carolina, is a case in point. In the summer of 1942, for example, Charleston had a severe shortage of manpower. Work-ers were moving into the city, but local Negroes, already housed, were walking the streets or doing non-essential jobs. There was no defense training for Negroes, and management and labor showed no inclination to relax the discriminatory practices. In addition to discrimination, there was a wave of physical intimida-tion and abuse. For example, in June, a Negro common laborer, Tom Weathers, was beaten by his white foreman who alleged that Weathers had been impolite to him. The foreman was quoted as saying, "That nigger talked back to me."

In September, 1942, plans were being made for the migration of 9,000 white workers into Charleston at a time when there were 4,000 Negro males registered with the local United States Employment Service. About 1,500 of these colored workers could have qualified for defense training, and, had there been job opportunities, the number of Negro applicants could have been increased by approximately 30 per cent.

The proportions of the situation on a national level were re-flected in a survey made in September, 1941, by the Bureau of Employment Security. At that time over half the openings ex-pected to occur in selected war plants during the period September, 1941, to February, 1942, were barred to Negroes as a matter of policy. The greater the skill involved, the higher the degree of exclusion. Even in industries traditionally open to Negroes, there was a definite policy of exclusion in the higher skills. And this was two months after President Roosevelt had issued an executive order barring discrimination in war plants!

The continuing exclusion of Negroes from defense training and war industries became the occasion of much public comment in all sections of the nation. During the fall of 1941 and the early part of 1942, many daily newspapers carried editorial comments on the subject. On May 7, 1941, the Committee on the American Negro in Defense Industries issued a carefully worded statement. It was signed by some sixty Americans from all sections of the nation, and it was reported in many of the leading daily papers. These events began to impress many communities with the folly of local industry's practices. Newspaper comments and editorials emphasized the responsibility of management for the existing situation, and many of them reported the discriminatory policies and practices of certain craft unions. They presented the cost of job discrimination to the local citizenry, showing how it complicated housing, transportation and recreational problems. By the summer of 1942, many people were asking how we could afford a racial occupational pattern which delayed war production and cost our cities millions of dollars of unnecessary expense.

Negroes as individuals and through their organizations petitioned employers and government to take corrective action. When results were not forthcoming and the proportion of Negroes among the unemployed increased appreciably, mass demonstrations occurred. Picket lines were used as a last resort. These developments had serious repercussions upon the majority of colored workers. Their discrimination-mindedness was strengthened. Again they were left out. Again they had to fight to achieve what was freely extended to other groups. Some became discouraged. Others became militant. Many individual job-seekers felt that here again there was the same old run-around. They concentrated upon getting the job which the white worker deserted.

Most Negro men—and a sizable proportion of Negro women

—who were potential war workers entered non-essential work. War production and labor shortages had meant more and better non-defense jobs for them. They re-entered service employment in hotels and restaurants; they received jobs as janitors; many of them went into lower-paid non-defense industries. They were not satisfied, but they often stopped looking for war work. Some of them were in jobs which paid decent wages and offered security, and they were most hesitant to leave such work. The majority of Negroes were not so well situated. Their employment had been short-lived; it offered no future and paid low wages. But it was a job and it afforded a livelihood. These Negro workers and their friends had tried to get better-paying defense work. They had been told "no openings" or "we are not hiring colored women yet." They were convinced that there was little chance for them in a war plant, and they were tired of being turned down. Negro workers were resentful, but as individuals they often stopped looking for defense work. They did, however, look to their organizations, press, and leadership to champion vigorously their right to participate in the war effort.

While white America was slowly waking up to the serious cost which the color line in war industries was extracting, another factor appeared. Additional areas had become real or potential tight labor markets, and many migrants to the earlier centers of labor demand learned that equally attractive jobs were available back home. These men and women often returned to the communities where they had roots. This movement was accelerated by the high cost of living in boom-towns and the inconveniences which resulted from the crowded conditions in such areas. Labor turnover increased to an alarming degree, absenteeism mounted, and production suffered. Management and government became alarmed lest the situation get out of hand and the labor market become disorganized. Neither was ready, however, to propose an all-out drive for full utilization of local labor resources.

The situation became progressively worse. Local restrictions upon the employment of minorities began to complicate the mobilization of manpower on a national scale. In many areas of labor shortages, it soon became clear that even if every worker available in the community were employed there would still be need for importing others. As the United States faced a national manpower shortage, it was difficult, and at times impossible, to prophesy from whence workers would be attracted. It was clear, however, that the task would be easier if local employment patterns permitted the greatest degree of flexibility in this regard. That is to say, if female, foreign-born, Negro, and older workers in the labor market had been fully utilized, thereby establishing a pattern of their employment, it would be possible to draw freely from these groups in areas of under-employment. And certain of these groups—Negroes in particular—were the most plentiful source of labor in such areas. Half of the surplus labor markets of January, 1943, were located in the South where the Negro population varied from 50 to 10 per cent. New York, the urban center with the largest Negro population in any city in the world, was also included.

Even if management and certain unions had not erected barriers to Negro employment, the use of colored labor in a war economy in which the majority of jobs required trained workers would have presented problems. This was an outgrowth of the fact that relatively few Negroes had been trained for production work in the past and that American industry had established general patterns of barring Negro women from industrial employment at the same time that colored men were for the most part restricted to unskilled and service jobs. The first step towards the absorption of Negroes was to train them. But training was not enough; there was need for acceptance of these workers in jobs for which they had been prepared. Unless such openings were immediately available, trained workers would seek and find other jobs in tight labor markets. Other potential trainees would not even bother to enroll in courses. This is what actually occurred in many industrial centers, and the disinclination of Negroes to take defense training was then cited as evidence of the Negro's lack of interest in the war effort.

In many areas, persons unfamiliar with the Negro community and the devices which minorities perfect to protect themselves from the frustrating effects of constant discrimination could not understand why, twenty-four hours after long-denied jobs or training opportunities were opened, thousands of Negroes did not flock to apply. The reasons were in part economic—some of the colored men were already working; and they were in part psychological, the reaction of the masses of Negroes created as a defense mechanism to deal with their status in the nation. In normal times patterns of segregation and discrimination extract a toll from the national welfare; after Pearl Harbor they were costly—too costly for a nation at war to afford. The War Manpower Commission expressed this fact in a statement quoted in a feature article appearing in Forbes': "We cannot afford the luxury of thinking in terms of white men's work. It isn't white men's work we have to do—it's war work, and there's more than enough of it."

CHAPTER III

THE COLOR BAR BENDS

WHEN the defense program was launched, there had been sufficient employment of Negroes by American industry to convince all but the most biased or the least informed that Negroes, as individuals and when subjected to the usual processes of training and selection, can do any and all types of production jobs. There were, in every industrial area, object lessons of the fact that white and Negro labor can work together on production and that management's policy has much to do with the white workers' attitude in the matter. At the same time, there was a large supply of Negroes with necessary aptitudes and education to fit them for defense training on the same basis as white youths. It seemed that our fight to defend democracy abroad would offer an opportunity to establish much greater economic democracy for our minority groups at home. Such results did not immediately follow, however, and until 1942 only the beginnings were being made in facing the problem of Negro integration into war industries.

The first major increase in employment incident to national defense occurred in the construction of army cantonments. Since many of the new and expanded camps were in the South, the acceptance of Negro workers on such projects was more than a matter of national policy; it was a necessary step if the manpower requirements of the region were to be promptly met. The issue was more sharply defined by the fact that, because of the nature of the construction, the most important single skill was carpentry. Indeed, the tent platforms and the barracks required but little masonry and practically no plastering work. They were made of wood and the processes used were mainly those which typified small-scale residential construction. Here was a demand for the type of skilled service the Negro carpenter was well qualified to perform. But at the same time most of the contractors were using union workers, and there were only small Negro locals or no Negro carpenters' unions in the areas from which labor would be first recruited for this construction.

More than 2,500 Negro carpenters had been employed by March, 1941, in cantonment and other army construction in the South. At Fort Jackson, near Columbia, South Carolina, at the peak of activity some 600 colored carpenters were employed. About fifty Negro painters and many Negro cement finishers were also used. There can be no doubt but that much of this employment resulted from the rather widespread participation of Negroes in the union movement in Columbia during the construction of public housing projects. The cantonment construction, however, led to a great increase in Negro participation in the union.

At Fort Croft, near Spartanburg, South Carolina, 300 Negro carpenters were employed. In addition, colored artisans constituted about 90 per cent of those used in the trowel trades on this project. At Camp Robinson, near Little Rock, Arkansas, there was some hesitancy on the part of the contractor, who was not using union labor, to employ Negroes. After local pressure and the influence of the federal government had been brought to bear upon him, he employed fifty Negro carpenters, fifteen cement finishers, several bricklayers and a plumber. His total Negro employment figure was as high as 3,331. Over 100 Negro union carpenters were employed at Fort Wheeler, outside of Macon, Georgia.

At Fort Forrest, Tennessee, fifty-four colored carpenters from Nashville and Chattanooga were used, and the Negro local in Chattanooga grew, in a few months, from less than a score of members to about fifty-eight. In the construction of Fort Knox, outside of Louisville, Kentucky, Negro carpenters, plasterers, and cement finishers were among the 1,000 colored workers employed. The skilled Negroes were members of the local A. F. of L. unions. Their affiliation with these unions began during the construction of public housing projects in the city.

At Camp Gordon, near Atlanta, there was much difficulty incident to the use of Negro carpenters. Federal agencies adjusted the matter, and at least forty colored carpenters were employed. These men belonged to the Negro local which had received its first charter during the construction of public housing projects in the city. Negro carpenters, cement finishers, bricklayers, plumbers, roofers, power-saw operators, gip-lap operators and other skilled workers were used on union jobs at Fort Benning, Georgia, and at Fort Blanding, near Stark, Florida. At Fort Bragg, in Fayetteville, North Carolina, hundreds of skilled Negroes were used in many crafts. The construction of this project was open shop.

Some 300 Negro carpenters—the largest number of colored carpenters ever employed on one project in the history of the city, according to the local Urban League—were employed on the construction of the Army Hospital in New Orleans. The Negro carpenters' local grew from about 125 members to approximately 700 in eight months. In March of 1942, approximately 90 per cent of its membership was employed. Of the 700 Negro union carpenters in the city, about 550 were engaged in construction of defense projects including the United States Naval Base Airport and the United States Army Hospital.

At Fort Meade, near Baltimore, about 165 Negro carpenters were employed. These men were chiefly from Washington and Baltimore, and they belonged to the Baltimore Negro local of the carpenters' union. This local received its charter during the construction of public housing projects in Baltimore and grew from a small local to a membership of over 170. When the construction at Fort Meade had been completed, over 120 Negro union carpenters were employed on six other defense contracts and in two USHA-aided housing developments.

A most significant development in the employment of Negro carpenters occurred in Kansas City, where the unions had long controlled the labor supply for all public and much private construction. Negroes had never participated in these local unions. When Fort Riley was being built with labor recruited principally from Kansas City, the question of Negro employment arose. The joint action of the government, the local Urban League, The Kansas City Call (a leading Negro weekly newspaper), and other groups in the city secured the first charter for Negro carpenters and soon some thirty colored carpenters were at work. When Camp Leonard Wood was started, there were difficulties incident to the use of Negro carpenters. The same forces united, and, as a result, job opportunities for several hundred Negro carpenters were created on that project.

But despite these gains for Negro carpenters—and they were real gains—there were other places where the situation was not so favorable. In the construction of Fort Eustis, in the Tidewater area of Virginia, and at Camp Lee near Petersburg, no colored carpenters were employed. In these cases, the contractors and the unions seem to have been in collusion, and, by the time an adjustment could be made, the peak of construction had passed. However, in the construction of Fort Monroe in the Tidewater area, Negro carpenters were used; and out of the Fort Eustis and Camp Lee situations and the problems incident to Negro employment in public housing projects in these two areas, arrangements were made for the acceptance of Negroes in the carpenters' organization. Work permits were issued to colored carpenters and new Negro locals were formed.

Although many colored carpenters and other skilled workers were employed on cantonment construction in areas outside the South, there was much discrimination. Perhaps the most unsatisfactory situation in this section was incident to employment on a large ordnance plant which was constructed in Illinois. In this case, Negro union skilled workers and laborers from Chicago were denied equitable employment opportunities, and the matter occasioned much negotiation between the government and unions. Finally an agreement for token Negro employment in certain skills was worked out.

The construction of a vast powder factory outside of St. Louis raised the whole question of Negro relationship with local craft unions. No Negroes had ever been admitted to any skilled craft union in the city except the painters, where colored workers had a separate local. Despite much negotiation and repeated pressures from Washington, no appreciable change was made in the St. Louis Negro's status as a union member or as a worker on large-scale projects. In this and other instances where Negro construction mechanics were barred from employment, stabilization agreements, negotiated by government and described below, were important in effecting the closed shop arrangements which facilitated discrimination.

Employment of Negroes in war industries has two principal aspects, the quantitative and the qualitative. The first relates to the number of jobs held by Negroes regardless of the occupational distribution involved. The second refers to the industries and the occupations in which these jobs are distributed. In a period when the nation was rapidly restricting the production of non-essentials and converting existing plants into war production, qualitative factors materially affected quantitative results. This was true because production for a highly mechanized war required new skills and the services of a larger proportion of trained workers than had been usual. Therefore, unless there were full opportunites for a given group of workers to enter diversified occupations in war production, their numerical employment would be materially limited.

In the case of the Negro, the matter of the kind of jobs was intimately associated with the question of how many jobs. This was amply illustrated in the automobile industry, which was converted to war production early. The converted industry opened many new machine, assembly, inspection and other types of production jobs; Negroes had been concentrated in foundries and generally excluded from assembly lines and skilled work. Management in the industry, despite the terms of the agreement which provided for transfer of workers on the basis of seniority and industry-wide experience, hesitated to assign colored workers to occupations for which they qualified but in which they had not been used in non-defense production. Many of the white workers took a similar position, and certain local CIO unions were hesitant to deal effectively with the problem. Such a policy limited the occupational advance and the numerical employment of colored labor since most Negroes with seniority were being assigned to the relatively few laboring and janitorial jobs, as were new Negro workers brought into defense activities of the converted industry. The potential Negro employment was therefore much less than would have existed had there been opportunities for the transfer and up-grading of Negroes into new jobs.

This occupational pattern was slowly changing by 1942. While the majority of new colored workers were entering unskilled and janitorial jobs, other Negroes were slowly finding jobs as welders, as riveters, and on other production operations in firms which previously did not so employ them. On the basis of the qualitative gains which had been made, the industry was in a position to tap the large reserve of Negro labor in Detroit. This was of more than theoretical importance in an area where there was to be great expansion in employment and need for much defense housing. As late as the summer of 1942, there were approximately a thousand Negro trainees in defense occupations available in the Detroit area. Their employment in war industries would have made a real contribution to production by easing the pressure upon housing, reducing future labor turnover, and eliminating the necessity for duplicating training.

The outstanding early advances in numerical employment of Negroes occurred in traditional occupations and industries. The number of Negro janitors grew steadily. In many sections, Negroes replaced white workers who formerly were employed as cooks, waiters, garage attendants, and house servants, and who had entered defense work. These gains, in most instances, represented only an indirect contribution to war production and often involved the use of skilled persons in non-essential work at occupations far below their training and abilities. They could not absorb the unemployed Negroes or facilitate the maximum use of this source of manpower. They did not contribute to the bolstering up of the morale of the colored citizen who saw white neighbors with no better or even poorer qualifications rapidly absorbed in better jobs in war industries.

In iron and steel production, Negro employment increased appreciably in the latter part of 1941 and the first half of 1942. Gains in this industry were concentrated in the larger firms which had traditionally used black workers. In most of these there were still serious occupational limitations preventing the up-grading of Negroes. Certain developments in this industry were, however, encouraging and illustrated the real contribution to war production which Negro workers could and did make.

At the Lackawanna plant of the Bethlehem Steel Corporation,

Negro labor has figured in production work since World War I, when colored workers were brought in by management during a labor dispute. The Negro workers remained, and by 1940 nearly all of them were integrated into the local CIO steelworkers' union. Two years later at least 150 shop stewards and a score of grievance adjusters were colored. The plant was engaged in war production, and the number of Negro employees increased materially in the eighteen months ending June, 1942, when about 20 per cent of the labor force was colored. Approximately 7 or 8 per cent of the Negro employees were skilled, and about 40 per cent were semi-skilled. Among the Negroes employed at the plant were crane operators, stampers, bricklayers, first-class machinists, engineers, switchmen, and a score or more other types of production workers.

The pattern of employment set by the Bethlehem Steel Corporation in its Lackawanna plant did much to facilitate the use of Negroes in other industries in the Buffalo area. It effectively repudiated the contention of local employers that Negroes and whites will not work together. It illustrated the fact that, even when colored workers are introduced during a labor dispute, labor has a stake in winning Negro members to its ranks and protecting their opportunity for employment.

In most of the older, established shipyards, Negro workers were employed prior to the war effort. In some of these yards their participation had greatly increased by 1942. This growth of employment, while significant, had been limited by occupational patterns which excluded Negroes from certain types of skilled and semi-skilled work. The most serious of these limitations, from the point of view of manpower, was the general disinclination to train and employ Negroes as welders. While in certain areas of small Negro populations, as in New England, a few colored welders were employed prior to the summer of 1942, this was by no means the general pattern. The traditional opposition to Negro machinists, machine-tool trainees, and electricians restricted the use of black labor in an industry which was admittedly behind schedule in production. At such large shipyards as the Newport News Shipbuilding and Drydock Company in Virginia, where over 5,000 Negroes were employed by the close of

1941, traditional attitudes toward the use of Negroes in certain important production jobs limited artificially the degree to which existing reserve of available Negro labor could be tapped. The United States navy yards were the first establishments in the industry to widen appreciably the occupations open to Negroes. Private yards slowly began to follow this lead; for example, the Sun Shipbuilding and Drydock Company in Chester, Pennsylvania, announced a program of training and employing thousands of Negroes in all occupations in 1942. Unfortunately, the company proposed to develop an all-Negro yard.

In the newer shipyards of the Southwest, only slight progress had been made in the employment of Negro production workers by the close of 1941, although most of the yards in this section used Negro common laborers. On the West Coast, however, hundreds of black workers had been added to the payrolls of the shipyards. The policies of craft unions had, however, limited the kinds of jobs and, consequently, the number of jobs open to Negroes. In the Southeast, Negroes employed in shipyards were generally restricted to unskilled and certain semi-skilled occupations. There were a few encouraging exceptions, but, throughout the area, management and unions had evaded facing the problem of utilizing Negro labor.

Labor supply considerations required government to bring the issue to a head. But government had previously complicated this problem. In order to prevent labor disputes and secure union cooperation, the Labor Division of OPM had sponsored stabilization agreements. These agreements were first effected in the construction industry and gave a closed shop to the Building Construction Trades Department of the A. F. of L. In certain of the stabilization pacts in the shipbuilding industry, the Metal Trades Councils of the A. F. of L. achieved similar closed-shop arrangements, and some of these metal trades unions secured a further monopoly over training for workers in shipyards. Many of the unions which were parties to these stabilization pacts either barred capable Negroes from membership, or created separate and auxiliary unions for Negroes and systematically discriminated against these Negro locals in referring men to jobs. In many instances the net result of stabilization pacts was to disqualify colored artisans and potential semi-skilled men from defense employment.

Specific cases will illustrate this point. During the construction of a vast ordnance plant at Milan, Tennessee, Negro carpenters, who were members of a colored local, were barred from employment. The all-white local had jurisdiction over the project and refused to grant clearance to any Negro union members. The business agent of the white union stated, "I don't care what card you hold; I don't recognize no Negro as a union member." He held to this position despite governmental pressure to modify his attitude.

Negro skilled mechanics were barred from construction work at St. Louis, Joliet, Mobile, and other places by actions of local A. F. of L. craft unions. But such situations were not limited to the construction industry. They occurred in aircraft and shipbuilding as well. In aircraft, the classic example was Boeing at Seattle. Many shipyards were affected. Under the stabilization agreement at the Bethlehem shipyards in the San Francisco bay area, for example, the Metal Trades Division of the A. F. of L. had a closed shop. When, in 1941, a Negro machinist attempted to secure employment in his trade at the shipyard, the International Association of Machinists successfully opposed his employment. The machinists were effective in this instance because of the strategic position they occupied in labor supply matters on the West Coast. This advantage was gained through the terms of the stabilization pact negotiated at the behest and with the concurrence of OPM.

In other shipyards, as the Todd Shipyards Corporation's unit in Richmond, California, the Tampa Shipbuilding Company in Florida, Gulf Shipbuilding Company in Mobile, and others, the Metal Trades Division of the A. F. of L., which had signed the stabilization agreements, effectively opposed the employment of skilled (and often semi-skilled) Negro workers. Government had secured recognition for unions which had always violated the spirit of non-discrimination in employment; at the same time government was committed to a non-discriminatory employment policy. As between the two inconsistent approaches, government decided to support the stronger and, consequently, took no aggressive steps to secure job opportunities for Negroes in skilled capacities at shipyards which had contracts with A. F. of L. unions. This decision was reflected in the concentration of Negroes in unskilled jobs in many yards on the West Coast and their similar distribution or complete exclusion in many yards of the South.

The recognition of discriminatory craft unions had an influence upon practices of certain local CIO unions. At Mobile, for example, there are two important shipyards, the Gulf Shipbuilding Company and the Alabama Shipbuilding and Drydock Company. The first had a contract with the metal trades unions of the A. F. of L., and the second had a contract with the CIO. In Gulf, only a handful of Negroes were used as unskilled laborers; no skilled Negroes were employed. At the Alabama yard about 20 per cent of the total payroll was Negro, and colored workers were used in many semi-skilled and a few skilled trades. When pressure was put on the CIO union to press for up-grading, it hesitated and failed to act. The principal reason was its fear of losing a forthcoming employee representation election to the A. F. of L. which was attempting to win over the yard. One of the appeals used by the metal trades unions of the A. F. of L. was an attack upon the "pro-Negro" policies of the CIO.

In the two-year period ending July, 1941, employment in aircraft increased over five-fold and reached 310,000; it, of course, continued to grow at a rapid rate. Since most of the workers in this industry have been trained for their new employment, tens of thousands of Negro Americans likewise could have been trained and employed in aircraft production. Such was not the case. In 1940 only a few colored men were employed by the industry; at the close of 1941, some 2,000 Negroes had entered aircraft; as of April, 1942, less than 5,300 colored workers were employed in forty-nine selected aircraft plants. Although a start in Negro employment had been made in this new and expanding industry by the spring of 1942, the numerical participation of Negroes in aircraft was still disappointing and woefully small in the light of the total employment figure for the industry. Only a few companies, such as the Lockheed Aircraft Company, the North American Aviation Company at Kansas City, the Curtiss-

Wright Corporation at Columbus, Ohio, and the Wright Aeronautical Corporation at Paterson, had laid solid foundations for really tapping the vital labor potential which existed in the Negro community.

The vast, expanding ordnance industry in the nation was affording Negroes a limited number of opportunities for employment by the spring of 1942. The Winchester Repeating Arms Company in New Haven, Connecticut, for example, had over 1,300 Negroes on its payroll. Colored men and women were on the production lines in many new ordnance plants, and plans for similar employment patterns had been developed in a score of other plants which were in various stages of construction and operation.

In many sections of the nation, these ordnance works were offering Negroes their first opportunity for industrial employment. In certain areas, notably in communities of the South and in northern areas with small Negro populations, there was opposition to the introduction of Negro men as production workers. This was even more pronounced in the case of Negro women. The bases for this opposition were the local beliefs that there were white workers still unemployed who should be absorbed before Negroes were used in any but unskilled and service capacities, and that the industrial employment of Negro women would upset local wage scales and "spoil" good domestic servants. The first of these considerations was usually a carry-over of depression thinking in the community, and management hesitated to consider Negro production workers until labor shortages forced the issue; the second was often championed by the middle-class housewives who did not want the cost of domestic service to rise. Early experience in ordnance illustrated two things: full mobilization of labor for war production in certain areas would involve occupational patterns which were new and would be opposed by certain community attitudes; and Negroes were satsifactory and efficient workers in what was largely a new industry to them.

In a production war, the machine-tool industry is vitally important. When the defense effort began, there were few Negro toolmakers and only a small number of Negro machinists. Labor organizations having jurisidiction over workers in these trades had generally either excluded colored workers or discouraged their entrance into the field, and vocational education officials often cited this opposition in justification of their failure to extend training to Negroes. With the advent of defense training, a few colored youth had their first real opportunity to learn the principles of machine-tool work. When the first Negroes completed defense training, however, they faced great difficulties in securing private employment because the old prejudices remained.

Gradually, war industries followed the lead of the federal establishments in accepting Negro machine-shop trainees. The initial steps in this direction occurred in New England, where labor shortages first appeared. By the summer of 1942, an increasing number of established firms such as Brown and Sharpe Manufacturing Company in Providence, Rhode Island; the Brewer Drydock Company on Staten Island, New York; the Morey Machinery Company in Queens, New York, had begun to accept Negro machine-shop trainees. Later the Taylor Chemical Company and Hartsook Machine Company of Cleveland and the Pressed Steel Car Company in Chicago followed suit. In most instances, however, only a limited number of Negro operators and trainees were used, and their employment was concentrated in the smaller firms. In Cleveland, where several of the larger establishments which hired a substantial number of trainees had manifested their willingness to employ colored machine-shop workers, the traditional attitude of white opposition continued. Much of this opposition was concentrated in the International Association of Machinists.

In the spring of 1942 the Negro Employment and Training Branch of the Labor Division of the War Production Board made a survey of 750 selected defense plants. These establishments were primarily large firms, and they were located in areas where there were available supplies of Negro labor. They were the firms which, if there had been no discrimination against colored workers, would have employed large numbers of them. The survey showed that, while most of the companies were employing some Negroes, in many cases this employment was either so small as to represent token compliance with governmental non-discrimination policies or was concentrated in unskilled and service occupations. There had been, however, two signficant gains. In hundreds of cases, Negroes were being inducted into production jobs in firms which formerly banned them from such employment. Although the numbers used were not significant, the occupational patterns being established offered a basis for fuller utilization of Negro labor. At the same time, encouraging gains in numerical employment and occupational diversification had occurred in government establishments, in firms which had long experience in employing Negroes, and in the majority of the newly constructed war production plants covered by the survey.

Since there were shortages of skilled Negroes in certain sections of the nation in occupations where skilled colored men had been employed in the past, Negroes needed training in these fields if they were to make the most of the forthcoming probable demand for their services. In those industries where Negroes had years of experience as helpers to mechanics, it was important that semi-skilled colored men refresh their aptitudes and knowledge so as to be able to rise in a period when industry was upgrading employees as a means of meeting shortages of skilled workers. In those occupations and industries where Negroes had not been employed in the past, they had to start from scratch. That meant that some—and preferably many—needed training for these types of work so that they would be available to pioneer the way to this important source of labor supply.

CHAPTER IV

AN OFFICIAL BOTTLENECK

ALTHOUGH much has been spoken and written about the importance of industrial education for Negroes, the truth is that colored Americans had received little worthwhile schooling for employment in modern industry. Many so-called Negro industrial schools in the South have been misnomers. They have either concentrated upon preparing women for service occupations, under the title of domestic science, or they have prepared some of the male students for hand trades. There was one compelling reason for this. It was the fact that modern industrial production has become increasingly mechanized, and a worker trained for employment in it must be taught on expensive and constantly modernized machinery. Practically none of the Negro institutions had the funds to provide such equipment. Most of those on the college level had become teacher training schools, with the best offering occasional good courses in a few occupations. The Negro industrial high schools in the South were even worse. They had little or no equipment, and their graduates were seldom prepared to earn a living in a skilled trade. At the same time, an increasing number of well-equipped and effective industrial high schools for whites had been built.

In the border states (between the North and the South), the situation was only slightly better. There were better buildings and more equipment, but, as in all segregated school systems, the least apt students were usually herded into the industrial school. The graduates were, with few exceptions, poorly prepared. Most of those who had learned a trade were working in construction, or shoe repairing, hairdressing, or dressmaking and cooking.

Most industrial northern cities had one or more well-equipped trade schools on the secondary level. The technical colleges of the North (as most of the white technical colleges of the South), were concerned with training architects, engineers, and other professional workers. The best trade schools in this section were often far removed from centers of Negro population. At the same time, Negroes were infrequently employed in skilled jobs. The net result was small Negro enrollment in these schools.

In both the North and the South, craft unions had developed an increasing influence and control over vocational education through a system of citizens' advisory committees. In many communities, the labor representatives on such committees came from unions which barred Negroes from membership. Others were drawn from unions which consistently discriminated against colored workers. Almost all of them had a vested interest in discouraging the training of Negroes, who, once they were prepared to enter a trade, would embarrass the local and international officials of their unions. Even when their own organizations were not involved, union representatives usually opposed the training of Negroes as a matter of principle and habit.

There was still another, significant feature of vocational education for Negroes. Almost half of the federal funds for education were allocated to vocational training. For more than two decades prior to World War II, the federal government had made substantial contribution towards the payment of salaries for vocational teachers. And the Office of Education had exercised considerable control over certain aspects of this training. During 1934-35, there were over 450,000 pupils enrolled in federally-aided vocational courses in eighteen states having separate schools for Negroes. Among whites, slightly over a third were in agriculture, a third were in home economics, and slightly less than a third were in trades and industry. Of the Negroes, over a half were in agriculture, slightly less than a third were in home economics, and only a sixth were in trades and industry. In these states Negroes constituted 24 per cent of the rural and 17 per cent of the urban population in 1930. They made up 22 per cent of the total enrollment in vocational agriculture, 14 per cent in home economics, and only about 10 per cent in trades and industry. But only 10 per cent of the federal funds for vocational education were spent for Negroes in these states. During the period under study over $8.00 of federal funds was expended per white pupil as contrasted with less than $4.75 per Negro pupil. The discrepancies in expenditure between Negroes and whites in state and local funds were even greater.

These developments in federally-aided vocational education had serious implications for the future. They had institutionalized inequalities between the races in the expenditure of federal funds for vocational education in areas where there were separate school systems. They had established situations in which the training of Negroes in trades and industries was neglected in all parts of the country. They had accustomed representatives of the United States Office of Education to accept such inequalities and neglect of industrial education for Negroes. They had conditioned state and local school officials in the South to expect the federal government to accept widespread racial discrimination in the distribution of federal funds for vocational education.

The inefficiency of vocational education as a method of preparation for Negro skilled workers was reflected in the findings of the survey of the training and employment of white-collar and skilled Negro workers conducted by the Department of the Interior in 1936. At that time, less than 2 per cent of the male Negro skilled mechanics in the nation had depended entirely upon formal trade school education as a means of preparation for skilled work; only 2.3 per cent had depended upon vocational education and apprenticeship, 7.0 per cent had been trained by a combination of vocational education and experience and 5 per cent had depended upon a combination of vocational education, apprenticeship and experience. In the Middle Atlantic states, 3.6 per cent of the skilled male Negroes listed trade schooling as their principal method of preparation. In the South Atlantic states, where vocational education for Negroes has been emphasized (in words), only 1.5 per cent of the skilled Negro men reported vocational education as the means of preparation for their occupation. As a matter of fact, over 91 per cent of the Negro male skilled workers in the South had not received any vocational training, a higher proportion than that for the nation as a whole, where 83.6 per cent had had no such training. In those regions where vocational education had been most helpful in preparing

Negro men for skilled work, it was centered in unsegregated school systems.

In order to train workers for war production, the federal government appropriated scores of millions of dollars. There was a multiplicity of training programs, the most important of which were pre-employment or refresher courses for those who wanted to brush up on an old skill or learn a new single- or semi-skilled occupation, supplementary courses for those already employed but anxious to secure up-grading into a higher skill, out-of-school youth defense training for rural areas, and NYA defense training. Both from the point of view of enrollment and expenditures, the Vocational Education National Defense (VEND) Training Program under the direction of the United States Office of Education was the largest. But it was in the pre-employment and supplementary training phases of this program where there was the greatest degree of racial discrimination.

This discrimination was in reality a projection of past practices. Most vocational education officials at the national, state, and local levels were not prepared to champion new policies relative to minority groups' training. There were many factors underlying the attitudes and actions of these officials. They had become accustomed to training a limited number of persons for an economy which offered only a few jobs to potential trainees. They were closely allied with management and union officials who opposed the training of Negroes for mechanical operations. They reflected community attitudes, and, in fact, often mirrored the most reactionary sentiments in their efforts to please the right people. Most of them accepted and championed the color occupational caste system.

Defense training was a vast program. It involved great expansion of operations, and pressures were exerted to get it started at once. Many vocational education officials were awed by the magnitude and immediacy of the need. They had ill-equipped schools serving Negroes, and they concentrated upon expanding those schools which were best equipped. There was still another factor. The early pre-employment defense training courses stressed refreshing skilled workers who had lost dexterity. Due to past economic and social situations, the proportion of Negroes among this group was small.

Prior to the war, NYA had operated youth training programs. As contrasted to the program of the vocational education division of the United States Office of Education, this was a directly federally-controlled activity. From the outset, NYA attempted to encourage full participation by minority groups. Although there was racial discrimination in NYA, the agency had policies prohibiting such practices and machinery for correcting abuses. It also had policies and personnel to encourage wider participation of Negroes in all parts of the country. It was natural, therefore, that its programs of defense training should afford widespread opportunities to Negroes.

Although official figures of Negro participation in the earlier phases of the program were not available at the United States Office of Education until 1945, data currently released by another source are available. The Bureau of Employment Security reported that of the 115,000 trainees in pre-employment and supplementary vocational courses, only 1,900 or 1.6 per cent were Negroes in December, 1940. By March of the following year, about 4,600 or 2.6 per cent were Negroes. At the end of June, 1941, only 20,800 Negroes had been enrolled in pre-employment defense courses; 5,750 had been in supplementary courses. NYA had trained 35,650 Negro youth for defense work, and 34,700 Negroes had enrolled in Out-of-School Youth Training. Negro trainees formed a small part of the total in certain important programs. As of June, 1941, for example, the 4,318 Negroes then enrolled in pre-employment courses constituted less than 6 per cent of the total enrollment; in supplementary training the figure was less than 2 per cent. Negroes made up 15.4 per cent of those in NYA defense training.

Hidden behind these over-all figures are two important aspects of early Negro participation—or lack of it—in Vocational Education National Defense Training. The vast majority of colored trainees were concentrated in northern areas where they had access to racially mixed schools, and only a small proportion of them were being trained in those occupations—welding, machine-shop and aircraft—in which there were the greatest existing and potential demands for labor. The first of these assertions has just recently had statistical support. According to figures released by the United States Office of Education in January, 1945, from the beginning of the defense training courses on July 1, 1940, through September 30, 1940, only 2,116 Negroes were enrolled in twelve southern states and the District of Columbia. This was 0.06 per cent of the total enrollment.

At the outset of the defense training program, Negroes were either discouraged or barred, or both, from many courses offered under the VEND training program in the North. This program was carried out in local vocational schools, and local vocational administrators and teachers directed it. In some cities, Negroes were discouraged when they sought to gain admission. More often, a few were accepted, and, when they could not get jobs for which they were trained, vocational education authorities recited their experience as an example of the futility of such training for other colored persons. Behind the scene was the influence of employers and labor officials. Many local school systems permitted employers to establish specifications for trainees. When such specifications eliminated minorities, they were usually accepted and followed. Labor union officials, too, opposed the admission of Negroes to these courses.

In the early months of defense training, there was violent local and national protest against these situations. In those cities where Negroes were numerically strong and politically powerful they were able to get a hearing and secured some relaxations in the barriers to their participation. In many instances, however, this was more of a gesture than a fundamental reform. As long as the most influential employers were opposed to hiring Negroes in skilled, single-skilled, and semi-skilled jobs, local vocational education officials did little to change their old practices. But pressures increased and the national government made some feeble efforts to break down discrimination. In many places these efforts resulted in an increase in the number of Negro trainees—often in occupations which were not extremely vital and in which there were not great demands for workers.

In the early part of 1942 there were many complaints of alleged discrimination against Negroes in the defense training program of Chicago. After some delay, defense courses were opened to Negroes, and thousands completed them. In January it was estimated that of the 8,000 trainees awaiting placement, 5,000 were colored. This situation reflected the fact that local war industries were still refusing to employ Negroes in large numbers and restricted them to unskilled and laboring jobs. The existence of a large backlog of colored trainees was advanced by certain officials, especially federal representatives, as a basis for opposing further training of Negroes. But this was superficial reasoning, for an examination of the local program indicated that a large number of colored men had been prepared for types of work not then in demand in the Chicago or any other area. Soon after the initiation of the defense effort, when there were insistent demands that Negroes participate, large numbers of Negro WPA workers were assigned to defense training in fields where facilities already existed without regard to aptitude or employability after training.

Late in 1941, Washington officials rightly ordered the elimination of training in fields which did not contribute directly to the war effort. Automatically, a large number of Negro trainees were eliminated because a disproportionately large number were in types of training which fell within the proscribed categories. By January, 1942, most of the unauthorized courses had been eliminated. The principal high school in the Black Belt had only aviation mechanics in the day and mechanical drawing in the evening school. Sheet metal and radio (essential war occupations) were two of the four courses eliminated. At the same time, the increasing emphasis upon and growth in supplementary training further retarded Negro participation; there were, for example, few Negro workers in the various branches of the metal trades who could qualify for such training.

Theoretically, Negroes had access without regard to color to all training opportunities in Chicago, defense or otherwise. And a few were scattered in schools outside the Black Belt, where facilities for training were infinitely better than in the schools serving Negro areas. Colored applicants stated that they were systematically excluded from these more adequately equipped defense centers. School officials insisted, however, that the only limitation upon Negro participation was the disinclination of colored men to exert the effort to apply, await their turn, and spend the extra money necessary to reach such schools. Doubtless there were bases for both positions. The important fact was that the absence of adequate facilities available to Negroes was reducing their participation in defense training. This, combined with the earlier sloppiness of much of the training readily available to Negroes, was definitely limiting the extent to which Negroes could prepare themselves for defense work.

Several agencies were involved in the Chicago situation. WPA, on whose rolls Negroes were constantly increasing, did not discriminate in referring colored workers for defense training. The local office of the State Employment Service certified applicants without question. Consequently, any discrimination against Negroes was due to the policies and practices of training officials. Local citizens reported that these officials had been unduly influenced by certain forces, notably the craft unions in the metal trades. No doubt many employers, who did not want to accept colored workers, maneuvered behind the scenes to effect their elimination from pre-employment courses. Management's discriminatory hiring practices were an automatic bar to Negroes' qualifying for supplementary training.

As late as the fall of 1941 it was impossible for a Negro to get into defense courses at the Vocational School in Paterson, New Jersey. This center was preparing workers for the local Wright Aeronautical plant, and the plant had devised tests which the school used in the selection of trainees. When a detailed investigation of the matter was made, it was discovered that the discrimination extended even beyond the Negro group and included other minorities as well. A sample study of three days' tests showed that fewer than 42 per cent of the applicants were successful; no Negroes passed; fewer than 18 per cent of the Italians were accepted; fewer than 24 per cent of the Jewish applicants passed; fewer than 50 per cent of other European nationalities extraction were successful; but approximately 68 per cent of the applicants of Anglo-American extraction were admitted to the courses. It is significant that in other New Jersey cities the rate of rejection for referrals of all nationalities and races varied from none to 12 per cent. This and subsequent investigations lent weight to the allegation that the vocational education authorities of Paterson and the Wright Company were in collusion to keep Negroes out of training for the Wright plant.

In Detroit, where defense training got an early and successful start, there were many instances of discrimination against Negroes in the earlier phases of the program. Due to the political power of the colored population and its militant leadership, local training officials soon took cognizance of the situation. An extremely capable Negro employee of the Board of Education was appointed as co-ordinator of defense training for Negroes. He, with the support of the Negro citizenry, was soon able to open many types of defense training to Negroes, and, by the summer of 1941, almost a quarter of the total enrollment in pre-employment training was Negro. The problem then was one of effecting placements, and it was complicated when the conversion of automobile production placed thousands of experienced, skilled workers on the labor market.

There are many other specific instances of discrimination against Negroes in defense training in the North. Citizens' groups complained loudly to local officials and finally to the federal government. As a result of these protests, the situation gradually improved, and by the summer of 1942 many northern cities had opened defense training to Negroes. Others followed suit in the succeeding six months. But by this time another development had complicated the picture. The labor market was constantly getting tighter, and the reserve of unemployed workers was rapidly depleting. This was reflected in the decline in enrollment in pre-employment courses which reached their peak in June, 1942, and the increasing importance of supplementary training. Even male (but not female) Negroes were finding jobs (most of which were non-essential). Defense training, in contrast to employment, offered no wages, and many Negroes joined white male workers in hesitating to take training. The job in the North soon became that of encouraging qualified Negroes to enter defense courses. The Negro community supported by federal agencies faced this responsibility and made great progress. Ultimate acceptance of colored workers by some war plants in skilled, single-skilled, and semi-skilled occupations created a favorable economic situation in which to carry on such activity.

Vocational Education National Defense Training for Negroes in the South was complicated by many factors. It had to be centered in separate Negro schools, and these schools had little equipment or facilities for offering first-class training. They had a long tradition of giving makeshift instruction in occupations which were totally unrelated to the war or the real needs of industry. This is amply illustrated by a recent statement of an official of the United States Office of Education that only ten of the twenty-two types of shop facilities reported for Negroes in southern states in 1939-40 were adaptable to the needs of war production. In addition, the direct administration of vocational education was in the hands of local officials who were generally opposed to widening the scope and extent of Negro industrial training. The United States Office of Education did not want to raise this controversial issue and thereby endanger its happy relationships with southern school officials. And the South was a region where there was an excess of population in relation to employment possibilities, where there was the strongest opposition to Negro participation in skilled industrial employment, save in heavy and dirty occupations. The South was an area where the bulk of vocational education for Negroes had been concentrated in agricultural courses.

Soon after the defense training program got under way two other factors complicated the picture. The National Association for the Advancement of Colored People was waging a successful battle for equalization of salaries, and state and local school officials were determined to fight the issue to the finish. Initially this fact caused even greater opposition to more defense training for Negroes. Ultimately, it gave impetus to federal pressures in that direction. By the time economic and administrative pressures had caused some relaxations in the opposition to Negro defense training in the South, the nation faced serious material shortages. They were most acute in the types of equipment needed by defense training, and such equipment could be secured only through priorities. Even when local officials really wanted to go ahead in establishing effective courses in Negro schools, there were long and tedious delays. Where local officials did not want to do anything, they were often able to hide behind the priority requirements as an excuse for inactivity. Of course, the absence of political power on the part of Negroes in the South was the principal factor in establishing peacetime discrimination; it became a terrific handicap in the Negro's fight for adequate defense training.

The state of Alabama offers an interesting example of resistance to Negro defense training. Birmingham, with its large reserves of Negro labor and its heavy industry, is a good place to start. In March, 1941, there were some 350 white men in twenty-six different pre-employment and supplementary courses. They received instruction in four well-equipped local high school shops and were being trained for occupations such as machine-shop practice, welding, drafting, and pattern making. On the same date, there was only one class for Negroes. It was in blueprint reading, and it was located at the so-called Negro industrial high school. Fourteen Negroes were enrolled, and the full equipment was one box of lead pencils and a few drawings.

The local director of defense training stated that the school board had neither money nor facilities for training Negroes. When pressed to apply for federal funds, he stated that it was impossible to get equipment because of the priority situation. When, later, it was pointed out that equipment might be borrowed from NYA, he countered with the declaration that the school board could not lease any quarters to house training for Negroes.

This local situation was symbolic of practices throughout Alabama. Vocational authorities on the state level were extremely pessimistic about the possibilities of training Negroes for defense jobs. They stated that industry would not use skilled Negroes and that the state was unalterably opposed to training workers for jobs which did not exist. Alabama was offering Negroes vocational training, but it was on the basis of the past, with emphasis upon agricultural trades and service occupations. The influence of organized labor (through the craft unions) was all-apparent in the state's insistence upon following patterns of training which had existed for seventy-five years. The State Council of Administrators (made up of representatives of federal agencies concerned with labor supply) was no more enthusiastic about establishing real defense training for Negroes. With the exception of a few sample classes like the one in aviation mechanics at Tuskegee Institute, there was no effective defense training for Negroes in Alabama. Even the courses at Tuskegee, because of the caliber of the trainees, were not preparing real skilled workers; they were producing potential helpers.

By December, pressures for defense training in the state were mounting. There was talk, but no evidence of action, about the establishment of a large defense training center for Negroes in Mobile. Existing facilities in Mobile were so inadequate, however, that all conceded that a new center would have to be constructed. There was no more than token training for Negroes in Alabama, and local training officials continued to exert themselves as little as possible where Negro defense training was concerned. State officials were toying with the idea of establishing a few centers in the state where some courses could be offered to colored citizens. The principal one was to be at Tuskegee. Already Tuskegee was being cited as an example of real progress, but its program was deficient in personnel and equipment, so that its contribution to national defense had been very small.

Another training center, often talked about by state officials, was located at the Negro land grant college, the Alabama Agricultural and Mechanical Institute. This was an Out-of-School Youth Training program and it offered instruction to less than a hundred farm youths seventeen to twenty-five years of age. Courses were given in woodwork, auto mechanics, electricity, and metal work. Less than $1,000 was available for equipment, and the result was that the courses had little more than hand tools with which to work. The trainees worked on farms during the day and were brought to the school (at government expense) for training from 7 to 10 P.M., five nights a week. The schooling represented in these classes averaged only fourth or fifth grade.

By January, the state had a proposed program for training Negroes of Mobile for employment in the local shipyards. It was to shift the training for that area to Tuskegee Institute! The plan had the approval of the United States Office of Education as well as the state educational authorities. It was obvious from the start that such a proposal would not work in view of the distance involved (about 200 miles), the lack of space and facilities at Tuskegee, and the cost of transportation and subsistance. Finally, the proposal to center defense training for Negroes at Tuskegee was abandoned, and the state turned its attention to setting up classes in Mobile, Birmingham, Montgomery, and a few other localities. This common sense decision, however, was not reached until the early part of 1942. Meanwhile much valuable time and much available equipment had been lost; training for whites had constantly expanded during the same period. After months of negotiation by certain federal agencies, the state agreed to establish defense training for Negroes in ten or more centers. As late as the summer of 1942, efforts were still under way to get the principal centers started; difficulties in securing equipment were now a principal impediment. Only at Tuskegee had any real progress been made. Outside of that center, and an effective training program in chemistry at the Huntsville Normal School, Negroes were generally barred from defense courses, relegated to rural youth programs, or concentrated in ill-equipped courses unrelated to the essential needs of national defense.

The situation in most of the other southern states was no better. In Tennessee, for example, the official in charge of defense training had opposed expansion of vocational education for Negroes long before the war began. Nowhere in the state was there anything approaching a decent program of defense training for Negroes as late as the summer of 1941. Knoxville, in many regards the most liberal city in the state in its treatment of Negroes, had perhaps the least satisfactory program. There were nine classes for the 205 white trainees. They were in drafting, machine shop practice, acetylene welding, arc welding, and sheet metal. Equipment had been requisitioned for additional classes in auto mechanics, electric motor maintenance, and radio communication. At the time the latter classes were scheduled to open, it was planned to establish two classes in auto servicing for Negroes. These supposed defense training classes for Negroes actually were no more than training in polishing cars, filling gasoline tanks and the like. They were to be located on a parking lot.

Local officials stated that the State Vocational Education Department was opposed to Negro defense training. The local proposals certainly represented the effective opposition of someone in authority. When the matter was pressed, these local officials suggested courses in concrete finishing, blacksmithing, and other occupations which were not essential to the war effort. An excuse for the neglect of defense training for Negroes was the fact that such a program was impossible because the white high school was equipped and the Negro high school was not. No reference was made to the fact that about five years earlier two of the most expensive pieces of equipment in the white high school had been taken away from the Negro school.

The discrimination against Negroes in defense training in Knoxville was typical of a state-wide picture. At the end of March, 1941, the United States Office of Education had given $230,000 for equipment for defense training in Tennessee. Of this, $2,000 had been used in Negro defense courses. And this was on a state-wide basis!

Charleston, South Carolina, was a center of shipbuilding activity. It was dominated by the local Navy Yard, where, by 1942, there were evidences of some relaxations in the occupational color bars. Private shipyards also operated in Charleston. Although there had been much migration of labor into the area, there still remained a large reserve of Negro labor—both male and female. Pre-employment training courses were training over 200 white males as shipfitters' helpers, twenty-two as spot welders, and sixty-five white women as bench machinists. Over 200 whites were in eleven different supplementary training courses. There were no comparable courses open to Negroes.

The local National Defense Training Council and the local board of education had continually put off taking any positive action relative to Negro defense training. By late summer of 1942 they had to do something and were about to open classes in sheet metal and bench machinists' work for Negro women. Thirty enrollees were expected. Although machinery (which was then at a premium and had been secured largely through action at the federal level) was available for training Negro men as welders, local officials claimed that there was no place to house such training. If this were not enough to delay further the establishment of significant training, the decision of local school officials to pay Negro instructors less than the rate for whites was sure to accomplish that result.

Similar examples could be cited from Florida, Mississippi, Louisiana, North Carolina, and Georgia. One instance from the latter state will suffice. Savannah was an important center of shipbuilding. Several representatives of the managements of these local shipyards had stated that they would use Negroes on production jobs. They may have been sincere or they may not, but the failure of local or state officials to establish a defense training program for Negroes designed to prepare them for such employment delayed any real test of management's intentions.

In light of the commitments of management, it was possible to get local and state officials to apply for equipment for Negro defense training. In the spring of 1942, some feeble action had been taken in this direction, but enough equipment for a really effective program had not been requested. A worse feature of the Savannah situation was the fact that all defense courses were centered at the Georgia State Industrial College in Thunderbolt. This was most unfortunate in that the college was removed from the center of Negro population in Savannah and could be reached only through automobile travel or by inadequate street railway facilities. If the latter mode of transportation was used, it cost twenty-five cents and required an hour a day.

There were five courses: automobile mechanics, boatbuilding, iron and forge work, sheet metal, and electric welding. The automobile mechanics course was non-defense and should have been cancelled according to the regulations of the United States Office of Education. Boatbuilding was limited to theory and nomenclature. The course in iron and forge work was, in fact, blacksmithing. There was no equipment in electrical welding. Although three welding machines had arrived, cable wire was not available and the machinery could not be set up for operation. Instead of welding, there was a course in "practical electricity." It was given from the blackboard, from drawings and from diagrams to students who had difficulty with simple reading. Sheet metal work was unsatisfactory because of lack of equipment.

The enrollees were recipients of WPA who considered this as any other assignment and were not particularly interested in defense training. They were useful, however, as the material out of which 125 Negro trainees could be recorded for Savannah and for Georgia. The hours were designed for WPA workers or millionaires. They were from 3 P.M. until 10 P.M. This was in contrast to the situation at the well-equipped, effective white training center where operations were on a twenty-four-hour basis, and more than 1,800 trainees were enrolled. Also in contrast was the fact that the college did not have buildings or shop space to accommodate the courses. And this situation existed in June, 1942!

No resumé of defense training for Negroes in the separate schools of the South would be complete without mention of Norfolk, Virginia. The Hampton Roads area, of which Norfolk is the largest urban center, was the first southern industrial region to offer Negroes significant up-grading opportunities in World War II. The Newport News Shipbuilding Company had long used colored workers in a limited number of skilled occupations and many semi-skilled ones. The Norfolk Navy Yard soon took effective measures to open new and higher jobs to Negroes. Yet local colored men in Norfolk could not get training in essential occupations. In this situation there were jobs open to them if they were trained. In fact, colored workers, trained in defense courses in other sections of the nation, were entering skilled, single-skilled, and semi-skilled jobs while Norfolk Negroes were unable to qualify.

The Negro community was aroused and discouraged. It did not fail to act, however. It called upon federal authorities to give assistance and then went to work itself. In order to refute the assertion that there were no available trainees, Negroes conducted a survey to give tangible evidence of a supply of eligibles who were interested and qualified. Soon there was a list of 900 adults and 350 high school graduates and pupils who indicated their availability. The Norfolk Navy Yard listed sixty-six trades open to Negroes—occupations in which defense training was accepted in lieu of six months' experience. But when the local United States Employment Service referred Negroes for such training they were advised to desist by the Norfolk vocational education director because there were no classes for colored workers in essential occupations. This same official discounted the value of the citizens' survey. He also discounted the importance of pre-employment training, despite the acceptance of it by the chief employer in the area. He was ready to offer supplementary training, but hesitated to initiate such courses because there was an insufficient number of Negro applicants.

Training for whites had, of course, been operating at full blast with complete equipment for some time. By the time that local defense training officials were committed to go forward with similar training for Negroes, shortages in equipment and priority requirements delayed their efforts. When the program finally really got under way (late summer, 1942), there was a scarcity of trainees. This was due to constant delays in setting up the program and the attractive job opportunities which were available in the Hampton Roads area. No doubt local officials misinterpreted this development and assumed it was a justification of their earlier fears in this direction.

The developments described above occurred in a program financed almost wholly by the federal government. They took place in spite of legislative and administrative provisions prohibiting discrimination. The agency responsible for the administration of this program was the United States Office of Education.

From the outset, the Office of Education resisted governmental and popular pressures to encourage its pressing for Negro participation in defense training. Despite recommendations and instructions to set forth federal policy in this regard in its regulations, the Office of Education failed to do so. Finally, it gave in half-heartedly, and on August 15, 1940, announced that "in the expenditure of Federal funds for vocational training for defense there should be no discrimination on account of race, creed or color." It had taken six weeks of constant conferences on the part of officials of the Advisory Commission to the Council of National Defense to get this statement—and, then, it was tucked away in a supplementary instruction. It was interpreted in the field as representing no departure from the existing practices of vocational education and had little practical value in widening Negro participation in defense training.

Resort was then made to legislation. The act appropriating funds for defense training in 1941 contained the following provision: "No trainee under the foregoing appropriations shall be discriminated against because of sex, race, or color; and where separate schools are required by law for separate population groups, to the extent needed for trainees of such groups, equitable provision shall be made for facilities and training of like quality." The phrase "to the extent needed for trainees of such groups" was inserted with the blessing, if not at the instigation, of the Office of Education. This same office issued separate regulations covering the Out-of-School Youth Training program provided for by the act referred to above. It did not, however, mention or include the non-discrimination provisions of the act. Again there were long negotiations, and finally the Office of Education issued a special letter. It was at least consistent; all early references to racial non-discrimination were in the form of supplementary statements issued after the regular instructions had been promulgated.

Not only were there resistances to regulations setting forth non-discriminatory policy at the top administrative levels in the Office of Education, but the very operating staff which had acquiesced and at times encouraged neglect of Negro trade schooling, was charged with the responsibility of carrying out policies which it and its superiors opposed. The results were what one would expect. A further evidence of the attitude of the educational authorities in Washington was the fact that it was late in 1941 before any current records indicating the degree of Negro participation in defense training were available. It was not until 1945 that the Office of Education released complete figures reflecting the degree of Negro participation in defense training. In light of the low percentages involved, it is clear why these data were "not available" years ago.

The Office of Education seemed to have no plan for the distribution of equipment (purchased entirely with federal funds) in a manner which would contribute toward equalizing the facilities available to racial groups in states with separate schools for such groups. Following practices under the state-aid program, it permitted the states to determine largely where the federally-financed equipment was to go.

As a result of these practices, during the first two years of defense training, Negroes were at no time more than 6 per cent of those in pre-employment courses. In some states there was no Negro participation in defense training. In other states there were only one or two courses in the whole state available to Negroes. Certain Negro institutions, eligible to participate in the program and having adequate equipment for instruction in critical occupations, had not been approved despite the fact that no Negroes were being trained anywhere in the state in these occupations. When prodded about these and similar situations, the Office of Education replied that it was working on the matter and expected results. Voluminous correspondence and small results followed. The Office of Education for two years resisted any and all changes in racial policy which would modify the states' traditional approaches to vocational education. And the existing patterns in the area with separate schools were such that much immediate change was required if the legal mandate and war necessity of non-discrimination were to be fulfilled. But the Office of Education administered the National Defense Training program in about the same way as it had handled its normal vocational education activities.

There were many criticisms of NYA training programs. Some of them were inspired by the objections of the vocational education authorities to a competitor in the field where they had maintained a monopoly. Other criticisms were more just. Some NYA training was superficial; some was in obsolete trades; some was poorly directed. But regardless of these circumstances, NYA made a signal contribution to the training of Negroes for defense. It offered courses to colored youth which they could not have secured anywhere else. It distributed its equipment and courses in a manner which approached equality. It observed the spirit, if not the letter, of non-discrimination in federal policies. In localities where there were resistances toward the training of Negroes for defense jobs, it took action to break these resistances down and establish training. It accepted Negro women trainees long before the vocational education authorities or industry would even consider them.

When, in 1942, relaxations in the occupational color-caste system occurred, it was usually Negro youth trained in NYA who were prepared to enter new types of work. Had it not been for that program, the utilization of Negro manpower and womanpower would have been delayed even longer than it was. In the training of minority groups' youth, NYA made a real contribution.

CHAPTER V

A PROBLEM IN CONVERSION

DURING the war Detroit became one of America's most important arsenals. Workers from all sections of the nation poured into the city as soon as the defense effort got under way. Some of them brought skills and aptitudes needed by the vast industrial plants of the area; others merely brought the hope for a job in this center of high wages. All of them complicated the problems of housing, transportation and health. In spite of this migration, Detroit soon had a grave problem of manpower. It was estimated in 1943 that its war activities would require about 200,000 additional workers. If full use had been made of all available local labor including Negroes and women, young workers, retired people, aliens and handicapped persons, it would have been possible to meet this need with a minimum migration of some 90,000. There should have been no ifs in this matter. For each unnecessary worker who moved into the city tended to disrupt the labor market and occasion wasteful allocation of critical materials for housing and transportation. He may well have come from an area where his services would soon be needed and to which he would probably return, thus adding to the general labor turnover.

In June, 1942, Secretary Knox of the Navy Department dispatched a telegram to the Hudson naval ordnance plant condemning the refusal of white employees to work with Negroes. The Secretary of the Navy added that such action was disloyalty to government and that those involved "are not only subject to immediate dismissal but may be prevented from obtaining employment in other establishments engaged in war production." This marked the climax of the initial skirmish in the battle of Negroes to participate in the war effort of the Michigan automobile industry. Although the battle had not been won, a funda-

mental principle had been established. Negro automobile workers were being transferred to war production in accordance with
their seniority and industry-wide experience as provided in the
six-point transfer agreement between government, management
and labor. This fact was significant because it opened to colored
workers many occupations which had been closed to them in the
past. It meant that occupational patterns were being established
which would facilitate fuller use of local Negro labor resources
in the area. The story behind the headline statement of the Secretary of the Navy was of long making. It is a chronicle of a community, of management policies, of union practices and of governmental activity. It is the saga of the participation of Negroes
in the automobile industry.

The Negro population of Detroit was fairly small until World
War I. As a result of the shortage of unskilled labor which occurred when the flow of migrants from Europe was stopped,
Negroes were induced to migrate there. In 1910 there were 5,741
Negroes in Detroit, by 1930 the number became 120,066, and
149,119 Negroes were reported in the city by the 1940 census.
Along with the shift of black labor, there came a similar shift of
white workers from the South, who brought along their racial
attitudes. The intense unemployment of the depression gave rise
to a spread of racial intolerance. Not the least influential among
organizations born of hatred were the Ku Klux Klan and the
Black Legion. These organizations flourished not only in Detroit
but also in other sections of the state, notably Flint.

Events during World War II indicated that these subversive
organizations have made race prejudice an important factor in
Michigan. This was brought to the public's notice in February,
1943, when white pickets stopped colored families from moving
into a federally financed defense housing project and precipitated a riot. The Sojourner Truth Homes (named after a famous
Negro woman) had been built for Negroes. When a small group
of white persons in Detroit objected to this occupancy, government housing agencies began to waver and reversed themselves;
then, Negroes protested, and these agencies returned to their
original position. At least three changes in policy were announced. The project was in an area where many Negroes lived,

but a small strip occupied by Polish families was located between it and the large bi-racial neighborhood of which the project and the Poles were a part. The underlying characteristics of this issue are illuminating since they had their counterparts in the local employment picture. Investigations at the time of the riot indicated that the average citizen of Detroit paid little attention to the controversy prior to the conflict. Had there been firm and decisive action on the part of responsible officials, it is extremely doubtful if a riot would have taken place. After its period of indecision during which the homes were vacant, government—federal and local—finally stood by its guns and Negroes moved in under the protection of troops. Shortly after occupancy was completed, the troops were quietly removed and all was well until the following summer when Detroit had a full-dress race riot.

Although many automobile plants hired colored skilled and semi-skilled production workers during the 1920's, the general pattern in the industry at the outbreak of the second World War was to restrict Negroes to foundry, general laboring and janitorial assignments. The one outstanding exception was the Ford Motor Company, where in 1941 the 11,000 Negro workers made up over 12 per cent of the total number of workers, and where there was the bitterest opposition to organized labor. At the Ford plants, while there were colored production and highly skilled workers, the majority of the Negroes were concentrated in the foundry, thus, to a degree, reflecting the general pattern in the industry. The Chrysler Corporation hired, in the spring of 1941, slightly over 1,850 Negroes who constituted about 2.5 per cent of the total labor supply in the corporation's Detroit plants. Approximately 1,400 of these were in the Dodge Motor Division where they were, as elsewhere in the corporation, employed as foundry workers and janitors. About 4 per cent of the 10,000 workers at the Packard Motor Car Company were Negroes, employed chiefly in the foundry. Only about 225 unskilled Negroes were employed among the estimated 12,200 at the Hudson Motor Car Company in 1941.

Throughout the various Michigan plants of the General Motors Corporation similar patterns existed. The Buick Division of

General Motors at Flint hired, in June, 1941, approximately 600 Negroes in its two foundry divisions. At the A. C. Spark Plug Company in the same city, there were twenty-three Negro janitors and janitresses out of a total of 3,500 workers. The Fisher Body Division of General Motors in Flint hired few Negroes— six janitors and car washers to be exact. Cadillac Motors in Detroit employed some 250 to 300 Negroes in the foundry and as truck drivers and janitors. At the Saginaw Steering Gear Division the usual pattern of Negro employment existed. At the Pontiac Division about 400 Negroes made up 4 per cent of the total workers in 1941; of the colored workers, 375 were concentrated in the foundry and the remainder were in non-production jobs. The Chevrolet Division plant in Flint employed over 300 Negroes as janitors, truck drivers, and machine cleaners. The Detroit Forge Plant of the same company employed some 200 colored workers.

In general the Detroit companies which supplied parts and accessories for automobile manufacturing had established similar patterns for Negro employment. In 1941, there were 350 Negroes at the Murray Corporation of America; they made up about 5 per cent of the total number of workers. Colored workers were used as production assemblers, welders, press operators, janitors and laborers. The Kelsey-Hayes Wheel Company employed about 350 Negroes. In accordance with the usual practices of the area, Negro workers were concentrated in the foundry. Colored employees constituted 7 per cent of the 22,000 workers employed by the Briggs Manufacturing Company in 1941 and were used as anodizers, paint sprayers, material handlers and laborers. Vickers, Incorporated, employed eighty to ninety Negro janitors and stock handlers among its 3,000 employees; Aeronautical Products, Incorporated, had one Negro machine cleaner in a labor force of 450 workers.

The conversion of the automobile industry involved a change in production which drastically affected Negroes and brought to a head the matter of new occupations for colored workers. The majority of the automobile companies were forced either to reduce materially or change the processes and materials used in their foundries. Since a large proportion of Negroes in the industry were employed in foundries, it became clear that under conversion colored automobile workers would either be absorbed in general production jobs along with other foundry workers or be assigned principally to new types of foundry and to lower-paying jobs which were traditionally Negro. These latter classifications were primarily laborers and janitors, and there were many workers competing for the relatively small number of openings in these classifications. With 75 per cent of defense jobs requiring trained workers, it was clear from a statistical point of view that if Negroes were to be used to the maximum degree, they must have skilled and semi-skilled employment outside of foundries. A further analysis of the labor demand indicated that the greatest needs for workers were concentrated in the very occupations in which colored men had not been used and where often there were the strongest resistances to their training and employment. Opening new types of jobs for Negroes was a prime necessity in any realistic program for the total utilization of this source of labor.

When the problem was first presented to management the reactions differed but the general pattern of response was negative. It was often contended that white workers would lay down their tools before they would accept colored men in new occupations. One of the larger automobile manufacturers' attitude was typical. As early as June, 1941, the company asserted that it did not then and did not intend to hire skilled Negroes. This attitude was supported by the statement that a stoppage of work had previously occurred when it was rumored that Negroes would be used on assembly lines. There were several companies which declared that, in accordance with government policy, there would be no discrimination in defense employment. Some of them gave lip-service to the pledge. Others were sincere at the outset but became timorous. A few really followed through on their statements of policy.

It was, however, in September, 1941, that the most dramatic development in the up-grading of Negroes occurred. When the Packard Motor Car Company transferred two Negro polishers to defense work, approximately 250 white workers staged a forty-minute sit-down strike which stopped operations in the unit. This development was followed in January, 1942, by a similar occurrence at the Hudson Motor Car Company. In order to understand these cases and the subsequent developments in other firms, it is necessary to analyze the status of the Negro in the UAW-CIO and the position of that union relative to its colored members.

As the United Automobile Workers was organized in the new Committee for Industrial Organization (which subsequently became the Congress of Industrial Organizations), Negroes were important in its development, and at the time of the defense program there were six colored international representatives. During the period that jobs in the industry were scarce, colored workers paid little attention to up-grading. Their principal concern, as that of their white prototypes, was job security. There was little general in-plant training, and Negroes did not press for admittance into apprenticeship schools. The official position of the UAW-CIO was equal seniority rights and promotion opportunities for all workers regardless of race, creed or color; but in the declining labor market which existed little was achieved in the direction of introducing colored workers on assembly lines. As a practical matter, as contrasted to constitutional provisions, the existing pattern of restricting Negroes to unskilled and foundry work was unchallenged by the union.

Not only did colored union members generally accept this situation but in certain instances they encouraged its development. At one of the large automobile factories in Flint, Negroes were employed as laborers, machine cleaners and truck drivers as well as janitors; however, contracts signed by the company and the local union classified all Negro employees as janitors. It had been the practice in the past that Negroes would have the janitor jobs exclusively, that they would be laid off and called back to work according to their seniority as janitors and that they would not be transferred out of the janitorial classification despite their actual work. Apparently Negro members of the union were generally satisfied because they had job security. However, curtailment of automobile production and the subsequent shifting to defense work tended to alter the picture. These once job-secure Negro workers found that, according to existing seniority agreements and the six-point transfer agreement between government, management and labor, they were eligible for a limited number of janitorial jobs only in war production, and they pressed for up-grading and a new interpretation of the union contract.

At an automobile parts manufacturing company the problem of transferring Negroes from non-defense to defense production revealed that some of the difficulties which arose in 1941 were due to Negro workers' lack of appreciation for and understanding of labor unions and seniority rights. The colored employees of this company had fought for and secured unit seniority. Since the foundry operated as a single unit and was built in 1935 (after the other plants had been opened), unit seniority had meant preservation of the status quo for the majority of colored workers, and it operated the same as departmental seniority in a plant where the foundry was a department rather than a separate unit. It had meant that white workers in other units of the company could not, during lay-offs, take the jobs in the foundry on the basis of seniority; at the same time it had limited both old and new Negro employees to foundry occupations. Here, as in the Flint factory mentioned above, the first step was to secure adjustments in union contracts or in the interpretation of contract provisions so as to permit plant-wide transfer of all workers.

Even in companies where unit or division seniority did not exist, the pattern of restricting Negroes to foundry and unskilled jobs had not been seriously challenged. When, however, curtailment and conversion of the automobile industry was undertaken, it was necessary either to up-grade Negro workers into new occupations or violate a basic principle of seniority since white men doing the same types of work as Negroes were being transferred to new defense jobs. Negro union members demanded the extension of their seniority rights to a plant-wide basis. The UAW-CIO officials were faced with a real issue, and in some cases local unions attempted to dodge it. Both unions and management were ready to place full responsibility upon government. Since, however, there was no indication that the UAW-CIO locals were in a position to control their membership and enforce their announced non-discrimination policy, and since white union workers—a minority it must be remembered—threatened to walk out if Negroes were introduced into certain types of work, it seemed clear that the most effective approach to the problem was to secure commitments from management and effectuate them through the co-operation of local unions. The traditional approach of passing general resolutions condemning discrimination would not suffice. A program of action and a swift campaign of education were needed. Events in the Detroit area forced such an approach.

In August, 1941, a group of Negroes in the Dodge foundry stopped work for a short time on two occasions as a protest because management was arranging the transfer of some white foundry workers to production jobs at the Chrysler tank arsenal and would not transfer Negroes. A group of workers took the matter to company officials and were informed that management alone determined who should be transferred. When the union established an official committee to handle the matter, management reiterated its position. The matter was then referred to the OPM for settlement and work continued in the foundry.

Later some white janitors at the Dodge plant were transferred to bench work at the arsenal, while colored men with longer seniority and wider occupational experience were barred from such employment. Negro employees again met and considered staying off the job in protest. A few white workers were ready to join them, but there was a sufficient number of workers willing to stay on the job to keep the plant going. Again the local and international officers invited OPM to come into the picture. Early in October the matter was presented by government to labor and management in a joint meeting. The company admitted that Negro workers had not been transferred as had whites, but it denied total responsibility for the situation and placed most of it at the door of the local union. The international representatives of the union accepted partial responsibility and admitted the need for firmer control over locals which did not exhaust established grievance machinery set up for such a purpose. The Corporation then agreed to negotiate these and similar grievances through the established union machinery and refer unsettled issues to the international. Final appeal would be made to government agencies. Already the International executive board had, at the behest of its Negro staff members, taken cognizance of the problem and established an international interracial committee.

In the meantime, the Packard Motor Car Company had acted. In accordance with its earlier commitments to OPM, the company transferred two Negro metal polishers from civilian to defense production. When the colored workers began their new assignment, approximately 250 white polishers started a sit-down strike which stopped the operations of the unit. The shop committee requested the Negro workers to return to civilian production until the local union could make a decision. Although the local union voted on the matter, its officers delayed taking action. Negro union members then attempted unsuccessfully to get the international representative to intervene, and the local interracial committee made continued excuses but declined to refer the matter to the international interracial committee established by the executive board. A month after the transfer, at the insistence of OPM, the case was referred to this committee. The international president of UAW-CIO addressed a letter to the Packard local re-emphasizing the position of the international executive board in setting up the interracial committee and stating that he would stand by the committee and the executive board in seeing that there was no discrimination in the transfer of employees. Despite this communication, the local again failed to act and its officers were called into conference with leaders of the international. The latter were adamant in stating the policy of the international union. Later the shop committee of the Packard local informed management that it was the will of the local and the international union that the Negro metal polishers be transferred to defense production. The representatives of the company's personnel department warned the two colored workers involved that if they accepted the transfers there would probably be bloodshed. Shop stewards, on the other hand, advised them to accept, and the men decided to do so. Management then refused to grant the transfers on the ground that such action would cause racial disturbances and retard production. The international president of UAW-CIO stated in a letter to the company that he believed there would be no such disturbances and that the UAW-CIO would assume every responsibility in connection with such transfers.

Further action on the Chrysler and Packard cases was temporarily delayed on account of the UAW-CIO convention in Buffalo. In the meantime the Hudson Motor Car Company requested a conference between government, labor and management to lay the groundwork for the transfer of colored workers. At Hudson a situation similar to that at the Packard Motor Car Company was developing. Management had opened up-grading training to all workers, and twelve Negroes entered the course. There had already been anonymous threats of alleged Klansmen in the plant; and while management was hesitant, it was ready to discuss the problem with OPM and the union. By this time the Packard situation had become further complicated by the report that there were several hundred Klansmen in the defense polishing division.

While these three important cases were pending, Briggs Manufacturing Company, Kelsey-Hayes Wheel Company and Consolidated Brass Company initiated programs of up-grading Negro workers on defense employment. In none of these plants was there serious trouble, and evidence was at hand that when both management and labor took a firm stand such transfers could be accomplished without work stoppage. In addition, Negroes were gradually being employed at the Chrysler tank arsenal as janitors, truck drivers, material handlers and washing machine operators.

In January, 1942, two Negroes were transferred to milling machine operations at the Hudson naval ordnance plant, and approximately 200 white employees stopped their work. Management then returned the Negroes to janitorial jobs. The company stated that it was willing to transfer the men again but did not wish to delay production; at the same time, the president of the local union stated that he was not able to control his men. When the matter was presented to the local union, that body proposed segregated employment for Negroes on machines. This the rank and file of Negro membership refused to accept. There was a general membership meeting but no action resulted, and a few days later, the plant manager hired a colored typist in his office in answer to those union officials who accused him of race discrimination.

In the latter part of January, the Chrysler Corporation stated that it had issued an order to the effect that all loaders and boxers in Department 501 at Dodge main plant would be transferred to defense work as loaders and boxers at the Chrysler Highland Park plant in accordance with seniority regulations. Although the company had heard that some white workers threatened to stop work, management stated that the transfers would take place. Upon being apprised of the threats, the international union assigned a strong representative to be in Detroit on the date of the transfers. When, in February, the Negro workers were transferred, a stoppage took place. The international and local union representatives advised management to fire all workers who refused to return to their jobs. By 1 A.M. the following day, colored and white men were working together without friction although there had been a five-minute stoppage at midnight. On the day after the transfer, management stated that all was well at the Highland Park plant and that one Negro had been promoted to a crane operator. Other promotions of colored workers took place at the Dodge main plant.

Meanwhile, events in Detroit and the growing consciousness of management and labor of the necessity for up-grading Negroes had their influence in other parts of the state. The Negro international officers and the interracial committee were effective in this field. At the Oldsmobile Division of General Motors in Lansing, Negroes were working for the first time as production line assemblers, precision machine operators and in other skilled and semi-skilled capacities. In the Buick Motor Company at Flint, General Motors Forge of Lansing, and Pontiac Motors at Pontiac, colored men were working or being trained for jobs in which they had never before been used. This had been made possible in every instance because organized labor supported, but sometimes not without a struggle, the rights of colored union members to participate in training, up-grading, and promotion on the basis of seniority and ability.

Early in February the local at the Chrysler tank arsenal was informed by union officials that the UAW-CIO international union and the Chrysler Corporation now insisted that Negroes be employed on defense for any job to which they were entitled and for which they could qualify. It was further agreed that if any worker did not wish to work with Negroes so transferred, that worker would be dismissed. Management stated the same thing to foremen at a staff meeting. Later in the day the word spread throughout the plant, and many white workers were reported to have said to Negro union members that they would assist them in every possible way.

Despite these gains, there was no solution of the Hudson and Packard cases. The riot at the Sojourner Truth housing project frightened those in labor and management who had been hesitant to act on these matters and gave comfort to the subversive elements within the union. Government continued throughout February and March to press for the re-transfer of the Negro metal polishers at the Packard Motor Company. In the latter part of the month, management stated that it would effect the transfers if the shop committee would request, in writing, that this be done. The bargaining committee of the local issued such a letter, and management and the union completed plans for the transfer. On the first of April, the Negro grinders reported for work. There was a slight disturbance but it soon passed over and all was well at the plant.

In the February election two Negroes were named to the executive board of the Hudson local. These new officers planned a program of education and action to deal with the Hudson naval ordnance plant transfer problem. At its April meeting the executive board of the local went on record for the first time as favoring the up-grading of the Negro employees and appointed a committee of five to negotiate with management on the matter. The meeting took place in May. It was jointly agreed that a notice stating positively the position of management and labor would be posted throughout the plant. The poster prepared by the union stated that the Hudson local had been requested by WPB to "take appropriate action to facilitate equitable employment of Negro workers at the Hudson Motor Car Company . . ." and that "Hudson Motor Car Company management has assured your local union representatives that it will co-operate

to the limit in carrying out the principle of no discrimination."
There was also this notice to violators:

. . . Hudson Local 154, UAW-CIO, solemnly warns any members who feel disposed to violate the principles of no discrimination, that the local is prepared to support President Roosevelt, the War and Navy Departments, the WPB, and of course the UAW-CIO Constitution and the International Executive Board in every possible way. Violators cannot expect to get the support of Hudson Local 154, UAW-CIO, in any discipline they may suffer as a result of defying the President of the United States, their own Union Constitution, International and local officers.

While the final plans were being developed to settle the Hudson case, another situation arose at one of the Chrysler plants. At the insistence of the WPB, some twenty Negroes were transferred from the Dodge main plant to the Dodge truck plant. There they were employed as material handlers, strippers, boxers, and shippers. A small group of white workers stated they would march to where the Negroes were and throw them out of the plant. The march started, and others joined the small group so that about 300 were involved. They stopped en route to hold a demonstration and a total of 600 gathered—most of them out of curiosity. This, of course, stopped production. Management then closed the plant. The international representative of the UAW-CIO stated publicly that he would see that all union members abided by the body's non-discrimination policy and that if the protesting workers did not report to work on the following day, he would insist that they be discharged from the union. The company was no less adamant in its stand that Negro workers should remain in their new jobs. The day after the stoppage, both union and management marked the incident closed. Subsequently, two white workers were fired by the company because they were leaders of the demonstration.

On June 17, when the Hudson Motor Car Company was planning for the immediate transfer of Negro workers, management, local union officials and the resident naval officer anticipated strike action on the part of some of the white workers. They were prepared, however, to insist that qualified and eligible

Negro workers remain on their jobs. On the morning of June 18 work stoppages occurred and occasioned a complete shut-down of certain units. The international president of the UAW-CIO immediately issued a strong statement. At one o'clock the Secretary of the Navy sent the following telegram to his representative at the plant:

Following is for your guidance and transmission by you to Hudson Motor Company and local union of Hudson employees at your plant.

The Navy Department is informed that production employees in your plant have refused this morning to continue work following introduction of a few Negro employees, who, I am informed, are union members, as machine tool operators at the plant.

Such action is clearly in violation of the President's Executive Order No. 8802 and is known to be without sanction of national and local union officers.

This plant is engaged solely in vital war production, is entirely owned by the government, which bears all operating costs, and has been designated as a military reservation.

Under such circumstances, the refusal to continue normal work warrants assumption the men are disloyal to the government and not only are subject to immediate dismissal, but may be prevented from obtaining employment in other industrial establishments engaged in war production.

At 1:45 most of the striking workers who were still in the plant returned to work. When Negroes were added to the afternoon and midnight shifts, there were some slight stoppages. After the first days of the transfer, a few workers attempted to disrupt production by calling white workers from their machines, whereupon, at the request of the Navy Department, the agitators were apprehended and fired. Throughout the difficulty several representatives of the international co-operated with management and government in effecting the transfers.

The problems incident to the transfer of Negro men from non-defense to defense work in automobile industry were not entirely settled with these developments. These events indicated, however, that labor, management and government were prepared to deal promptly and realistically with situations which might arise in the future. There were also problems of Negro participation in union affairs. Many of these were inherited from the occupational patterns which existed in the industry when it was in civilian production. The correction of such situations became a joint responsibility of the union and its colored members. It was also a responsibility of the Negro community which conditioned the attitudes of Negro workers.

At Buick in Flint, where many Negroes had been up-graded, a situation of this type developed. The principal elements in this difficulty were the general misunderstanding on the part of both white and Negro workers of what was going on and the failure of colored workers to join and participate in the affairs of the union. Rumors were being spread in the plant by both colored and white workers that Negroes with little seniority were to replace white workers with much seniority. Some of the foremen, unsympathetic with the up-grading of Negroes, were said to have participated in spreading such false information. Union leaders recognized the need for an effective job of education and stressed the point that Negro employees should join the union if they expected to enjoy the full benefits of agreements which the organization had secured. During civilian production from 500 to 600 Negroes had been employed, and all but a dozen were foundry workers. In the summer of 1942 all Negro workers with seniority had been rehired, and the majority were in other than the foundry division of the plant. The fifty still in the foundry had sufficient seniority to retain some of the better jobs they held during automobile production. The 550 Negroes who had been integrated throughout the entire plant were working in fourteen occupations; included among these were drill press operators, bench workers, heat treaters, grinders, milling machine operators, lathe operators and welders. In spite of this advancement which was secured through the co-operation of the union, it was reported in July that less than 50 per cent of the Negro workers at Buick were union members while, in contrast, almost 90 per cent of the white workers were affiliated with the organization.

While the events described above occurred, other automobile plants were making progress in widening the occupational patterns open to Negroes. The work of the international officers and executive board had done much to bring to local unions a realization of their responsibility to get their own houses in order. Government, through OPM, WPB and WMC, as these agencies successively operated in the field, had impressed management and labor with their responsibilities in the matter. The issuance of Executive Order 8802 and the creation of the President's Committee on Fair Employment Practice bolstered up government's policy of non-discrimination, and the forthright action of the contracting agencies, the War and Navy Departments, indicated that the policy was more than words.

The Aeronautical Products, Incorporated, which is located two blocks from the Sojourner Truth Homes, had slowly increased its Negro employees. Finally in June of 1942 a colored worker was up-graded from an unskilled job to a semi-skilled position as a grinder. At first some white workers objected and molested the Negro as he worked at his machine. This minor disturbance subsided and the colored worker performed his new job without difficulty. The local union co-operated in this matter.

In June, 1942, the Fisher Body Division of General Motors announced that persons would be employed regardless of race, creed or color. Nine Negroes were immediately hired as panel burrers, and colored machine-tool operators were also being interviewed for employment. Other General Motors divisions had already established similar policies. At the Saginaw Steering Gear Company, it was reported in June that 170 colored workers had been up-graded. Up-grading programs were initiated at the A. C. Spark Plug Company in Flint and the General Motors Forge Plant in Lansing; the Chevrolet Motors Division in its gear and axle plant in Detroit and in its Flint plant up-graded colored men to production operations on assembly lines in plants where they had never before been so employed.

The Murray Corporation of America was among the first Detroit firms to accept Negro production workers on war contracts. The firm transferred its non-defense production workers to comparable jobs in defense and then began to recruit aircraft assemblers from the outside. The Briggs Manufacturing Company was slower in initiating such a program, but by December of 1941 it had employed colored aero-riveters and was training and employing colored men in all types of assembly work for aircraft production.

These and other similar developments in Michigan were but a first step toward the ultimate goal of full use of Negro man- and womanpower. Labor supply surveys indicated that a labor shortage in the area was inevitable. Government policy, the need for conserving critical materials and the requirements for maintaining an orderly labor market dictated that full use be made of all sources of local labor supply. This meant complete absorption of available, qualified and trainable Negroes. The opening of new and wider occupational classifications for colored workers was an important step in achieving such results. Progress had been made in dealing with the qualitative aspects of the problem. There was pressing need for stressing the quantitative side in the future.

Detroit had, by the summer of 1942, begun to modify the color-caste occupational pattern in its industries. The UAW-CIO had become convinced that it had to face honestly and aggressively the problem of opening new and better jobs for its Negro members. A pattern for effecting changes had been made; great changes were to take place in the months which followed the Hudson strike. The most difficult problem in this area was to be that of achieving employment opportunities for Negro women.

CHAPTER VI

WARTIME EMPLOYMENT

BETWEEN 1940 and 1944 significant changes occurred among Negro workers. Over a million Negroes entered civilian jobs. They moved from the farm to the factory. The number of Negroes employed at skilled jobs doubled, as did the number of single-skilled and semi-skilled colored workers. There was a sharp decline in the proportion of Negro women employed as domestic servants. But the most significant development was the employment of Negroes in new industries and plants, where they entered occupations which few had followed before the war. Although even in 1944, as in 1940, one out of every five Negro men was working at an unskilled job, several hundred thousand were in production work. The static proportion in unskilled work was due to the replacement of up-graded colored men by over twice as many new recruits to industrial work, most of whom started in lower job classifications. At the same time, Negroes had been on the move again, and they had gone principally to those communities where there had been the greatest demand for workers.

These changes in a period of four years represented more industrial and occupational diversification for Negroes than had occurred in the seventy-five preceding years. Only in World War I, when colored workers made their first real entrance into the labor market of industrial centers, had anything approaching them taken place. But in the earlier period, the changes were in conformity with the occupational color-caste system. Much of what happened between 1940 and 1945 was contrary to the accepted pattern of Negro employment and is significant, largely, because of this departure from older practices. For the war gave many Negroes their first opportunity to demonstrate ability to perform basic factory operations of skilled, single-skilled, and semi-skilled types in a wide range of industries and plants. It also permitted some Negroes to work alongside white workers in many individual establishments on the basis of industrial equality.

The expansion of employment opportunities for Negroes in war industries has been even more concentrated in time than the consideration of the four years as a single period might suggest. Most of the gains occurred after 1942. In the summer of that year, for example, it was estimated that only 3 per cent of those in war industries were colored; by September, 1944, the proportion was over 8 per cent. Up-grading was, of course, a necessary, concurrent development in an economy where so many jobs required trained workers; and, with expansion of Negro employment, there came participation in higher types of work. As a matter of fact, the entrance of a few Negroes into semi-skilled jobs was a preliminary step to greater numerical participation in most plants.

The figures in Table 1 indicate the relative incidence of Negro workers in principal war industries. As one would expect, the largest participation of colored labor has been in heavy industry. It was in such industry, also, that Negroes got their initial job opportunities in defense work. But after 1942, labor shortages and governmental pressures occasioned the entrance of many colored workers into other, less traditional types of work. This was reflected in the gradually increasing proportion of non-whites (of whom about 95 per cent were Negroes) in aircraft, communication equipment, explosives, general industrial machinery, guns, plastics, and similar munitions industries.

There are no accurate figures for the occupational distribution of Negroes in war plants. Careful analysis in the field indicates significant changes which are supported by current census data. In 1940, for example, only 4.4 per cent of all male Negro workers were in skilled industrial jobs; in 1944, the figure was 7.3 per cent. In 1940, about 13 per cent of the same group was in semi-skilled industrial work; by 1940, the figure was 22.4 per cent. An even better indication of the developments during the four-year period is afforded by comparing the incidence of Negroes among the total employed workers in specific occupational groups. In 1940, male Negroes constituted 2.6 per cent of the skilled workers and craftsmen in the nation; by 1944 they were 3.6 per cent. Negro women made up 2.2 per cent of this female occupational group in 1940; by 1944, they were 5.2 per cent of the total. But the really significant gains occurred in single-skilled and semi-skilled

TABLE 1

PER CENT OF NON-WHITE WORKERS EMPLOYED IN SELECTED WAR INDUSTRIES
1942-1945

Industry	Year						
	1942		1943		1944		1945
	July	Nov.	Mar.	Nov.	July	Sept.	Jan.
All War Industries [1]	5.8	6.2	6.7	6.8	7.7	8.1	8.2
Agricultural Machinery and Tractors	1.9	2.4	3.6	4.5	4.0	4.3	6.0
Aircraft	2.9	3.3	4.0	4.8	6.0	6.2	5.8
Aluminum and Magnesium Products	7.1	7.1	8.0	12.5	13.2	13.5	13.5
Blast Furnaces, Steel Works, and Rolling Mills	9.8	11.1	12.2	11.6	11.6	12.0	11.8
Communication Equipment and Related Products	0.7	1.6	2.9	4.5	4.9	4.8	4.9
Electrical Equipment for Industrial Use	1.0	1.3	1.7	2.3	2.7	2.9	2.7
Engines and Turbines	1.9	2.4	2.3	3.2	2.6	3.5	2.3
Explosives	3.3	4.5	4.9	5.3	6.3	6.8	7.1
Firearms (caliber .60 and under)	[2]	2.7	3.2	4.4	3.7	3.4	4.8
General Industrial Machinery	1.6	2.2	3.1	3.9	4.4	4.7	4.9
Guns	3.4	4.2	4.5	5.8	6.2	8.5	8.4
Iron and Steel Foundry Products	18.6	22.3	23.1	24.9	24.5	24.6	25.4
Metal Working Machinery	1.0	1.3	1.6	1.5	1.7	2.0	2.0
Ordnance Accessories, not elsewhere classified	1.4	2.0	2.6	6.0	6.3	6.3	5.8
Plastic Materials	[2]	4.9	4.6	6.7	8.2	7.8	7.7
Primary Smelting and Refining of Nonferrous Metals and Alloys	8.7	9.0	8.8	11.9	9.8	9.3	9.2
Rolling, Drawing and Alloying of Nonferrous Metals (except Aluminum)	4.6	5.3	6.3	9.2	9.4	9.0	9.9
Scientific Instruments	0.9	1.5	1.9	2.2	2.3	2.4	2.4
Shipbuilding	5.7	7.0	8.7	10.0	11.3	12.2	11.7
Small Arms Ammunition	7.2	4.2	7.5	6.7	7.4	7.9	8.9
Tanks	2.2	3.6	4.8	5.9	7.0	7.6	13.0
Tires and Inner Tubes	3.3	4.4	5.2	7.4	8.8	9.6	9.5

[1] Including Mining, Construction, Manufacturing, Transportation, Communication, other public utilities, and Government Service.
[2] Figure not available.

occupations. In 1940, for example, Negro males were 5.9 per cent of all male operatives; four years later, they were 10.1 per cent. Negro women constituted 4.7 per cent of all female operatives in 1940; in 1944, they were 8.3 per cent of the total.

While these gains were being made, there were other occupations in which the status quo in racial employment patterns was giving little if at all. Even after four years of war, over 98 per cent of the clerical and sales force in the country remained white; about 95 per cent of the professional, proprietary, and managerial jobs were held by whites also. While the proportion of Negro women in domestic service jobs decreased from almost 60 per cent of all Negro women gainfully employed in 1940 to slightly less than 45 per cent in 1944, the proportion of Negro women in the total number of domestic servants increased from 46.6 per cent to 60.9. A large segment of the Negro women who left domestic work went into other service employment where they found jobs as waitresses, cooks, hairdressers, and the like. Some went into factories, although the acceptance of Negro women by war plants was delayed until most other available labor had been absorbed, and the number of colored women who entered domestic service was slightly larger than the number which left servants' jobs. The employment of Negro males, however, was not dissociated from the use of women. A review of those industries which delayed longest the employment of Negroes discloses that they were usually light and clean manufacturing. They were the industries in which women (white) were used in the largest proportions. In some of them, and in many individual plants, Negro males were not considered for employment until great progress had been made in tapping the reserve of available white women. And Negro women were not considered seriously as a source of labor supply until there was a shortage of colored men.

In industry after industry, a few plants took the lead in tapping the reserve of Negro labor. Early in the defense program, one or two establishments began to employ colored workers in new occupations. Even in the spring of 1943, when slightly over 6.5 per cent of war workers were non-white, it was not unusual for the vast majority of Negro workers in an industry to be concentrated in one or two plants. This is illustrated by a few specific cases. In March, 1943, only two or three of the major twenty-eight firms producing machine-guns employed more than a few non-white workers. The rapid introduction of Negroes into machine-gun production was delayed and complicated by management's preference for women. As late as the spring of 1943, women comprised almost a fourth of the workers in the industry; non-whites were less than 3 per cent of those working on machine-guns. Women made up over a third of the labor force in the principal carbide producing plants; non-whites were but 6 per cent of the total, and over four-fifths of them were in one firm.

Data on over-all employment are composite figures, derived from a series of data from the local level. In order to appreciate what has happened to the Negro worker, it is necessary to look beneath these over-all figures and inquire into the racial employment patterns of local labor markets. It is impossible to present a detailed account for each such area, but a few selected centers of industrial activity and large Negro populations will give a rough indication of typical situations in various sections of the country.

A survey of 113 important firms engaged in war production in Pennsylvania, New Jersey, and Delaware revealed some interesting developments. In January, 1942, these establishments employed 358,000 workers of whom 4 per cent were Negroes. By October, 1942, they hired 421,700 workers of whom 7 per cent were colored. In the period of nine months, the total labor force in these selected firms increased 17.7 per cent, while their Negro labor force increased 120 per cent. Eighty-five of these establishments used Negroes as production workers and forty employed colored women. By March, 1943, significant increases in Negro employment had been made. One shipyard in Pennsylvania employed over 10,000 colored workers in many types of occupations, and a large aircraft engine plant in New Jersey had 1,400 Negroes in various levels of skills. In the last six months of 1942, there had been 12,400 Negroes entering pre-employment and supplementary defense courses in Pennsylvania, New Jersey, and Delaware.

The participation of Negroes in war industries was concentrated in the tight labor markets of the area. Labor shortages were real or potential in Trenton, Newark, Perth Amboy, and Paterson, New Jersey, in Philadelphia and Pittsburgh, Pennsylvania, and in Wilmington, Delaware, in November, 1943. At that date Negroes made up 7.2 per cent of the war workers in Trenton, 8.8 per cent in Newark, 8.3 per cent in Perth Amboy, 4.6 per cent in Paterson, 13 per cent in Philadelphia, 7.2 per cent in Pittsburgh, and 11.4 per cent in Wilmington.

From May to December, 1942, non-white employment in important war industries (outside of shipbuilding) in the Los Angeles area increased almost four-fold, while the total labor supply grew about 50 per cent. In May, non-whites made up 1.1 per cent of the workers in these war plants; by December, they were 2.6 per cent of the total. The higher-wage shipbuilding industry was more attractive to male workers, and in December over 2,500 Negroes were employed in the yards of the area. For the state as a whole, 3,693 Negroes had entered pre-employment and 1,535 had entered supplementary courses during the last six months of 1943.

Los Angeles was an area of extreme labor shortage by November, 1943. At that time there were some 18,000 non-white workers in the principal war plants of the area; the vast majority were Negroes. They constituted over 4.5 per cent of all war workers. A year later, the labor market was still tight, and the number and proportion of non-white war workers increased. At the latter date, some 25,000 non-whites were in the larger war plants, and they made up about 6.5 per cent of the war workers in the area.

In the bay area around San Francisco, it was estimated that over 8,000 Negroes were in the shipyards by the close of 1942. In March of the following year, private shipyards in the area hired over 20,000 Negroes. The largest shipyard in the bay area hired 8,000 Negroes, of whom 900 were women. Over two-thirds of the colored workers in this yard were in skilled and semi-skilled occupations. In November, 1943, some 30,000 non-white war workers were in the larger war plants of the bay area; they constituted about 8.5 per cent of those in these plants. A year later, the total non-white figure had declined slightly, but the proportion was about 11 per cent.

In the Kansas City area, a tight labor market seemed imminent at the opening of 1943 and orders were standing at the United States Employment Service for Negro operators at an aircraft factory and an ordnance plant. Colored men and women were being paid while in training for war production work; in the state of Missouri, 1,542 Negroes entered pre-employment and 319 entered supplementary courses during the last six months of 1942. Negroes constituted 5 per cent of the war workers and about a third of the defense trainees in Kansas City in the spring of 1943. The number of colored registrants at the United States Employment Service was 50 per cent less than in January, 1942. There was far from full utilization of Negro labor but the numerical gains had been large in 1942. The widening of occupational classifications had been significant, and a decided trend toward using Negroes in keeping with their training and ability was observed.

By November, 1943, the Kansas City area had a slight surplus of labor. Despite this fact, the relaxations in the color-caste system continued, once they had been initiated. About 10,000 Negroes were in war plants, and they made up over 8.5 per cent of all war workers. A year later, when there was a real surplus of labor in the area, the number of Negro war workers remained substantially the same; their proportion of the total, however, had increased to slightly over 10.5 per cent.

During 1942, the participation of Negroes in the continuing tight labor market of Baltimore increased. A survey of 92 important defense plants of the area in May, 1942, revealed 11,580 Negroes who constituted 7.1 per cent of the total. By January, 1943, some 140-odd defense firms had hired 25,564 Negroes, or 10.8 per cent. Thirty-two of the largest of these establishments employed 25,458 Negroes, who made up 13.2 per cent of the total employees in March, 1943. Twenty-four of them used 2,250 Negro women; the remainder employed few. Four large establishments employed over half of the colored workers, and in these four, 8.2 per cent of the Negroes were skilled, and 17.8 per cent were semi-skilled.

Widening opportunities for colored workers were reflected in the increasing participation of Negroes in local defense training. As of February, 1943, there were 845 Negroes in pre-employment training courses who constituted 63.1 per cent of the total enrollment. Colored enrollees made up 8.6 per cent of those in supplementary courses. In November, 1943, over 36,000 Negroes were in Baltimore war plants; they were 15 per cent of the total. A year later, the Negro employment figure had declined slightly, but the proportion of Negro war workers had increased to over 16.5 per cent.

From the inception of the defense program, Negro labor found employment in the Hampton Roads area of Virginia. In February, 1943, four government establishments and the largest private shipbuilder employed 17,000 Negroes. Of these 2,000 were skilled, 7,000 semi-skilled, and 8,000 unskilled. Sixteen other essential war industries in this extremely tight labor market reported a total of 15,000 employees of whom 5,350 were colored. The local United States Employment Service was placing Negro men and women in clerical, skilled, semi-skilled and unskilled jobs.

In addition to Hampton Roads, there were several critical labor shortage areas in the South at the beginning of 1943. Six of these were engaged principally in shipbuilding. In none was there a trend toward employing Negroes in new occupations. Negro workers were finding new jobs and receiving higher weekly earnings than ever before, but they were almost exclusively in unskilled or helper assignments. With rare exceptions, the few Negroes who did find skilled employment were concentrated in those building trades, foundry, and mining operations which had traditionally been Negro jobs. Colored women had not found industrial employment except in a few places. The past paucity of defense training in the separate Negro vocational schools and the concentration of areas of excessive labor supply in the region reinforced the status quo. But even where there were tight labor markets, little relaxations had occurred by 1943.

Mobile, an early area of critical labor shortage, offered a striking illustration of the situation in the South. The three largest private war firms, the leading government establishment, and the construction industry employed 12,000 Negroes in the spring of 1943. Only 1.1 per cent were in skilled jobs, divided equally between the construction industry and the government establishment. Fifteen and eight-tenths per cent were in semi-skilled jobs, and 82.8 per cent were in unskilled work. Although the principal need in the area was for welders, no Negroes were used in that capacity. By November, 1943, the numerical picture was slightly better. About 11,000 Negroes were in war plants; they made up 17 per cent of the area's war workers. A year later, the number of Negro workers had increased slightly, and their proportion of the total labor supply was slightly less than 20 per cent. Occupational relaxations had occurred, and Negroes were being trained and employed as welders and as other types of production workers in shipbuilding. In considering these figures, it must be remembered that in 1940 Negroes made up 37 per cent of those who lived in Mobile.

The racial occupational pattern of Houston was typical of the Southwest. By November, 1943, this was an area with a slight labor surplus; a year later, it was still in that category. In March, 1943, the principal industries of the city hired 6,500 Negroes; only seventy-nine were skilled, and 317 were semi-skilled. Defense training was given to Negroes in welding, burning, and blacksmithing; upon completion of defense courses, colored trainees were sent across the continent to jobs on the Pacific Coast. This was done despite the fact that local shipyards needed welders, burners, and blacksmiths. In November, 1943, about 9,500 Negroes were in the local war industries, and they constituted about 10.5 per cent of the total. A year later, Negroes constituted about 11.5 per cent of the total war workers.

A few subsequent developments indicated a slow and painful relaxation of occupational limitations for Negroes in the South. At Atlanta and Dallas, Negroes were being trained for aircraft production jobs in local plants in 1944. Negro welders were being employed at a shipyard in Brunswick, Georgia, and some ordnance plants in the South were using Negro men and women on production lines. These developments were delayed, and most of them occurred so late that there was little chance of their occasioning widespread acceptance of Negroes in new types of employment.

In September, 1944, there were about a million and a half Negroes in war industries. Almost a half of them were concentrated in areas of acute labor stringency. Nor was this all—nine large industrial centers of labor shortages accounted for 35 per cent of all Negro war workers. They were Newark, Philadelphia, Baltimore, Hampton Roads, Cleveland, Detroit, Chicago, Los Angeles, and the San Francisco bay area. Four other cities—Pittsburgh, Birmingham, New York, and St. Louis—accounted for another 9 per cent of the Negro war workers. Thus, nine industrial centers in tight labor markets and the four other areas jointly accounted for almost 45 per cent of the colored workers in war plants.

War workers as a whole were not so concentrated. Only 38 per cent of them were in areas of acute labor shortage (as contrasted with 48 per cent of the Negroes). About 28 per cent of the total and 20 per cent of the Negro war workers were in areas of labor stringency. In labor markets of slight surplus, many of which had a·large proportion of Negro residents, 10.6 per cent of the total and 10.8 per cent of the Negro war workers were found. In areas of substantial labor surplus 10.2 per cent of the total and 9.7 per cent of the Negro war workers were located. In no large southern labor market area, except Hampton Roads and Birmingham, was the proportion of Negro war workers more than 60 per cent of the proportion of Negroes in the population in 1940. The majority of colored war workers were concentrated in cities where there had been appreciable migration of workers. Many of these centers will experience great labor turnover in the post-war period. Many of them are centers of shipbuilding and aircraft. Negroes were often concentrated in these industries, and they, as all workers so engaged, will face local post-war labor markets in which there will probably be a limited demand for workers.

Early impediments to Negro participation in defense training have been noted above. By 1942, most northern areas where labor shortages existed had relaxed the color bars in training courses. When white women were first accepted, there was usually hesitancy in enrolling Negro women. Gradually this discrimination gave way as the combined force of labor shortage and governmental pressure became stronger.

In the South, resistances to Negro training were more pronounced and persistent. A part of this was due to the difficulties

which the separate school systems presented. A part was due to
the attitudes and practices of local and state vocational education
officials and the inefficacy of federal agencies directing defense
training. By 1942, however, the federal government had taken a
more aggressive stand, and over-all labor supply agencies were
putting pressure on the United States Office of Education. As a
result, more courses were opened to Negroes and statistical information on the situation was made available. Despite these developments, the training of Negroes for war employment lagged
in the South. This is illustrated in the figures for the period July-
December, 1942. Eight states, California, Illinois, Indiana, Maryland, Michigan, New York, Ohio, and Pennsylvania, accounted
for over 70 per cent of the Negroes entering pre-employment
and supplementary courses during the six-month period. Eighty
per cent of all Negro trainees were in states outside the South.

At the beginnig of 1943, there were over twenty-five areas of
acute labor shortage where war training was making a contribution to meeting the pressing need for trained workers. Seven of
these were in the South; three were in border states, where there
are separate schools for Negroes; the rest were in the North.
Five of the southern cities had no defense training for Negroes.
The two remaining southern cities had such courses, as did the
border cities and all of the northern areas where there were appreciable Negro populations.

The training picture outside the South was more encouraging.
The registration rate of Negro pre-employment trainees in the
nation tripled during the eighteen months from July, 1941, to
December, 1942, and the proportion of Negroes among all pre-
employment trainees doubled, growing from 5 to 10 per cent.
The majority of the colored trainees were being prepared for
shipbuilding, machine shop, and aircraft—occupations from which
they had been almost entirely excluded in the earlier phases of
the defense effort. In 1943, over 112,000 Negroes enrolled and
completed war production training and related courses. By October, 1944, a total of 323,496 Negroes had received pre-employment and supplementary defense training; of this number 203,660
had been in pre-employment courses and 119,836 in supplementary. Colored trainees made up 7.8 per cent of all who had taken

pre-employment training and 2.8 per cent of those in supplementary. Whereas in 1942-43 two-thirds of the colored pre-employment trainees were outside the South, in 1943-44 only two-fifths were outside the South. This is a reflection of three developments: the increasing acceptance of Negro trainees in industry, the reduction of pre-employment trainees outside the South from 698,258 to 136,418 as compared to a decline from 286,459 to 72,538 in the South, and the increasing and more effective pressures of WMC and FEPC upon the Office of Education. These same forces combined to increase the proportion of Negro pre-employment trainees in shipbuilding courses from 18 per cent of all colored enrollees in 1942-43 to 35 per cent in 1943-44 and the proportion in aircraft from 18 to 29 per cent.

Defense and war training are not the only avenues through which colored workers have acquired new skills. There was up-grading and training on the job as well as the training programs of the armed forces. No estimate can be made of the extent of up-grading or training on the job. The growth in the volume of Negro participation in skilled, single-skilled, and semi-skilled occupations, however, indicates that formal training courses have not done the whole job. And employment of Negroes in production jobs is evidence of the fact that colored workers have received training in new types of occupations from many sources. For Negroes, however, pre-employment vocational education and NYA defense training have been the two most important modes of preparation. It was these two types of training which prepared the bulk of workers who entered new occupations. A group which had little occupational status was largely dependent upon training as a requisite for being considered for employment in production work. Had NYA not offered its training and had Negroes not insisted upon entering pre-employment courses early in the defense effort, their limited acceptance in new types of work would have been delayed on the traditional basis that there were no qualified colored applicants.

Preparation for armed services in a mechanized war involves much training. For Negroes, to a greater degree than for whites, this training has represented the exposure of inductees to mechanical pursuits for the first time. Although Negroes have been concentrated in service units in the army, many of them have been trained in skilled, semi-skilled, and technical pursuits. New fields of activity, such as radio and electrical work, radar, the maintenance and operation of motorized units, and even clerical work, have been opened to a sizable number of colored men in the United States Army. Some idea of the magnitude of this training can be supplied by a few illustrations. There were 73,-686 Negroes in the air corps by September, 1944; although the majority were in ground work, many had received thorough training in various aspects of aviation maintenance. Five hundred colored men had been trained as pilots. Over 133,000 Negroes were in the engineers. Here again, an appreciable number have learned new methods of road construction and have acquired new skills. The thousands of colored troops in transportation have learned how to dispatch, drive and maintain trucks of various sizes and types, and many of the 36,000 Negroes in the coast and field artillery have been trained in technical work.

In the Navy, the scope of training has been even more significant in changing the nature of the Negro labor supply. It can safely be said that the most extensive and the best program of industrial education ever made available to Negroes in one installation has been centered at the Great Lakes Naval Training Center. By the end of 1944, between five and six thousand Negroes had graduated from the various schools at that center. They had been trained in machine shop, radar, radio, marine motor repair and maintenance, refrigeration, turbine work, electricity, molding, sheet metal and carpentry. Similar but less extensive training had been offered Negro sailors at Hampton, at other training centers, and aboard ships.

The concentration of Negro war workers in industrial centers of the North and West has resulted from and occasioned a great migration. As has been noted above, the Negro moved away from farms to factories. He also moved from farms to other types of urban employment. And the earlier trend of movement from the South to the North was again set into motion at a rapid rate.

From the outset of the war effort, large numbers of white workers moved into industrial centers. Negroes participated little in this initial migration, but after 1942, when the color bars began to relax, Negroes entered tight labor markets. Since 1940, a million Negroes have gone to urban centers. A large proportion entered the cities where there developed the greatest concentrations of war workers. Chicago's Negro population grew from 270,000 to about 350,000. Detroit's Negro population increased from 150,000 to about 230,000. But the really significant change occurred on the West Coast. In that region, Negro populations not only grew by the tens of thousands, but in some cities the new migrants outnumbered the original Negro dwellers eight to one.

More than a half million persons from all parts of the United States poured into the San Francisco bay area between 1940 and 1944. With this movement there was a decided rise in the number and proportion of Negroes; in 1940 the area had slightly less than 20,000 Negroes, by 1944 there were almost 65,000, an increase of over 225 per cent. The Negro population in the Portland, Oregon-Vancouver, Washington, area grew from 2,000 to over 15,000 between 1940 and 1944. While the absolute numbers involved were fewer than in the bay area, the rate of growth was decidedly larger. During the same period, the total population of the Los Angeles area increased about 15.1 per cent; Negro population grew from 75,000 to 134,000, or 78.2 per cent.

The number of Negro residents in many southern and border cities increased materially during the first four years of the war. This was most pronounced in shipbuilding centers such as Hampton Roads, Mobile, Savannah, and Charleston. Border cities such as Baltimore, Washington, and Wilmington received tens of thousands of new Negro residents. In every section, the over-all effect of this population movement was to concentrate further the Negro in urban areas and in the large industrial cities.

Five years of war occasioned many changes in the economic status of Negroes. Not only were they in a more diversified pattern of employment, but they were much more widely distributed geographically. These changes created new situations. Many Negroes faced difficult problems of urban adjustment; they faced extreme housing shortages in most urban communities. But most important, the Negro, along with his white prototype, faced an industrial future which was full of unknowns.

After much delay the Negro entered war industries. This was the result of many factors, but by far the most important was economic necessity. Once it was decided to utilize colored workers, it was necessary to employ them in new types of work. They had to be prepared for such work, and consequently, they began to participate in defense training. But these developments were uneven. Since they were occasioned principally by economic necessity, they were most pronounced in those areas where there were the tightest labor markets. In the South, the occupational color-caste system was so firmly entrenched that even in the majority of tight labor markets, there were but slight relaxations.

Analysis of employment data indicates two important characteristics of Negro participation in war industries. Most Negro war workers were in the larger industrial centers where tight labor markets first appeared. They were concentrated in certain industries, although the degree of such concentration declined somewhat after 1943. Negroes were also concentrated in certain large plants in most industries. Consequently, even in those areas where most Negroes were employed and a growing proportion were in war work, there were numerous individual plants which refused to hire Negroes or relegated them to unskilled and service jobs as late as V-E Day.

New training opportunities for Negroes changed the nature of the colored labor supply. Not only were there vastly greater opportunities for training, but for the first time much of this training was of high quality. In the North, public schools accepted large numbers of colored persons in trade courses; in the South, more equipment has been installed in Negro schools than had accumulated in them over a period of two generations. In the North, it will be difficult to keep the Negroes out of trade courses after the war; at the same time, there will be much pressure to use effectively the training equipment which separate Negro schools now have.

The Negro has moved again. More Negroes are now in areas where they have political rights and where organized labor is most effective. No doubt, the colored worker will use the ballot and the union as instruments of expression and pressure.

At the close of World War I, the Negro emerged with a foothold in unskilled jobs in heavy industry. During World War II, he acquired a foothold in single-skilled and semi-skilled jobs in many industries and a place as a worker in a wide variety of industries and plants. In order to understand what the chances of his retaining some or many of these gains will be, it is necessary to analyze the way in which the color occupational system operates and to describe the forces which have played important roles in effecting wartime changes. On the basis of such information, it will be possible to evaluate current trends and project future developments in the framework of over-all economic developments in the nation. This much we can say now, the Negro has improved his economic status during the war emergency. On V-E Day he was still far from the ultimate goal of equality of opportunity, and the gains which he had made had come as a result of wartime necessity.

PART II

INTERPRETATION

CHAPTER VII

RACE AND JOBS

RACIAL occupational patterns in America have been determined by traditions, economic fluctuations, and changes in methods of production. Once Negroes enter a type of work, they, as a group, tend to remain in it. Conversely, if it is traditional to exclude Negroes from certain jobs, these occupations become accepted as white men's work. Any move to substitute black labor or to introduce that labor in the occupation is opposed as a departure from the color occupational pattern. There is less opposition to Negroes' doing hot, heavy, dirty and lower-paid work than clean, light and higher-paid work. This, too, is in accordance with the concept of a color-caste system since the former type of employment is obviously more in keeping with the status of a people stigmatized as inferior.

Negroes' acceptance in all types of employment is endangered in periods of depression. In periods of economic expansion, when there is great need for labor, Negroes often enter new types of work. This, however, is usually delayed if the employment involves a departure from established color occupational patterns. The intensity of resistance against Negroes' initial entrance into light manufacturing occupations became apparent early in the second World War. Soon after the defense program got under way, shortages of workers developed in aircraft, machine-tool production, and electrical machinery, but available colored workers were not trained or employed in these essential jobs. Even in a period of national emergency and economic need, the color line gave way slowly and only after great resistance.

Radical changes in methods of production are most decisive forces in influencing the occupational status of minorities. We have already indicated how the increasing importance of large-scale construction in the South accelerated the displacement of

Negro carpenters. In this instance, the new emphasis upon large operations and fireproof buildings brought a change in employer-employee relationships and the introduction of new materials and methods. In such a setting the white carpenter was able to use separate Negro locals, political power, and racial appeals to displace Negroes. Traditional color occupational patterns and racial employment practices combined to keep Negroes out of training for new types of work. And the rapid elimination of black carpenters followed in the favorable setting of the technological changes we have described.

Negroes had long been engaged in the construction of ships. Most of them were in unskilled and helper capacities and they made up a sizeable proportion of the carpenters in the shipyards of the South. It was in World War I, however, that the black worker became outstanding as a shipbuilder. His numerical concentration in the industry and his feats of production were greatly publicized, and it was claimed that Negroes made up a significant part of the skilled workers in shipyards. Detailed analysis of the occupational distribution of colored shipyard production workers in the first World War, however, indicates that they were concentrated in three occupations: carpentry, calking, and fastening.

In the immediate post-World War I period the number of Negro ship carpenters declined from about 1,500 to less than seventy-five; the number of colored calkers and fasteners declined 75 per cent. On the other hand, there was a slight increase in the number of Negro riveters, and Negro bolters grew from fewer than 400 to over 1,100. These changes in the occupational distribution of Negroes in the industry reflected the influence of two forces: the decline in shipbuilding after the war and the shift from wood to steel ships. The first of these reduced the total number of workers in the industry; the second occasioned a marked decline in the number and proportion of carpenters employed at the same time that it stimulated a rapid rise in the proportion and number of bolters, riveters, and others needed in the construction of steel ships.

Since there was little activity in shipbuilding in the 1920's, payrolls fell appreciably, and the number of Negroes attached to the industry decreased at an even more rapid rate. By 1930, slightly less than 8.5 per cent of all shipyard workers were colored; subsequently, there were greater declines so that by 1940 the 9,000 Negroes made up only about 6.5 per cent of the workers in the industry.

This steady decline in the proportion of Negro workers in shipbuilding was due primarily to the fall in the total volume of employment in the industry. A similar decline in the proportion of skilled Negro workers was occasioned by several additional factors. First, the substitution of steel for wood as the principal material displaced the Negro carpenter. Later, another technological change was to occasion a rapid decline in the demand for workers in the few types of production jobs in which most Negroes were concentrated. This latest radical change in the direction of the demand for labor resulted from the successful introduction of welding, a process of assembly which, by 1940, had been substituted generally for bolting and riveting.

Welding became important in shipbuilding during the depression. At a leading southern shipyard where Negroes had long been used in many levels of skill, the following events took place. Most of the riveting, bolting, and fastening was done by colored labor, and Negroes in these heavy and dirty occupations constituted a large proportion of the trained colored workers. When welding was first introduced, management decided to train electricians for such work since there was a sizable number of them seasonally unemployed. In that shipyard, as in most of the industry, Negroes were excluded from electrical work; they were likewise excluded from training in welding. Once this pattern was established, it became self-perpetuating, and when additional workers were trained for welding, Negroes continued to be barred.

Apparently, similar patterns of Negro exclusion from training and employment in welding developed in other shipyards, including government establishments. At the outbreak of World War II, colored workers, who constituted 10 per cent of all employees at the Sun Shipbuilding Company in Chester, were employed in unskilled and service jobs and as blacksmiths, foundry workers, bolters, reamers, and riveters. A few were in the pipe fitting department. At the Federal Shipbuilding and Drydock Company in Kearny, New Jersey, Negro workers, who were 5 per cent of the total, were employed as carpenters, red-leaders, fabricators, riveters, bolters, reamers, and drillers. Even in the United States navy yards, where there was a somewhat more favorable racial occupational pattern, few Negro welders were employed. Detailed figures are available for the Norfolk Navy Yard. Although this establishment increased its Negro employees from 2,211 to 5,426 in the period from September, 1940, to September, 1941, at the latter date the occupational distribution was essentially similar to that in the private shipyards. The vast majority of trained colored workers were classified as drillers, foundry chippers, and riggers. There were eight electricians, fourteen joiners, twenty-three machinists, seventeen shipfitters, twenty shipwrights, and only four electric welders. In addition, there were 640 Negro shipfitters' helpers and 208 machinists' helpers.

The delayed acceptance of colored workers in shipyards during World War II was closely associated with a technological change. This change came during the depression, and it gave rise to the new occupation of welding. Colored workers were, from the start, excluded from training for this new occupation. Even when other occupations (some more highly skilled) were opened to them, they faced extreme opposition in breaking through the color bar in welding. Largely because of their exclusion from welding, they were not able to participate proportionately in the rapidly expanding employment of the industry.

The United Mine Workers of America had done one of the most outstanding jobs of organizing Negro and white workers in the South prior to the second World War, and it was upon their successful experience that many of the newer CIO unions leaned as they attempted to resolve racial questions. It is significant, therefore, to look into the developments in coal mining incident to the introduction of machinery as we attempt to interpret the contribution which organized labor can make in influencing color occupational patterns. Herbert R. Northrup, in his recent book, "Organized Labor and the Negro," has described the developments in this industry, and the events in Negro employment in coal mining presented below are taken from that source.

Negroes entered coal mining in the bituminous fields of the South, and they are still concentrated in that region. Their participation in the coal fields involved racial conflict, bloodshed, and strife. And it was into such a situation that the UMW entered to organize both white and Negro workers. The number and proportion of Negro miners increased greatly between 1910 and 1920. In the succeeding ten-year period, when there was a 14 per cent decrease in total employment in the industry, the number of Negro miners increased by 5 per cent. In the following decade, this gain was more than wiped out. In light of the relatively friendly and fair policies of the UMW toward Negroes, the story of the decline in the proportion of colored coal miners has some interesting implications for the post-war period—a period when several hundred thousand Negroes in CIO will face adjustments to a changing and perhaps declining economy.

Segregation by occupations or physical working conditions has generally been absent in coal mines; at the same time Negroes in the southern mines had been concentrated in hand loading operations. Although some of the hand loaders were white, manual loading was predominantly a Negro occupation in the South. And it was this occupational concentration which made Negroes especially vulnerable to technological displacement. Prior to 1933, mechanization of loading operations was not important in the southern fields (including West Virginia). When, in the wake of union recognition under NRA, the southern mines were thoroughly organized and wages were increased, mechanical loading came into the coal fields of the areas; in its wake Negro displacement occurred. As in the case of the substitution of welding for bolting and riveting in shipbuilding, this development of a new technical process did not involve a compensating increase in the number or proportion of Negroes in the new operation.

In the southern coalfields the operation of a machine has traditionally been a white man's job. This had been established before the advent of the UMW and it still continues. In this respect the situation is essentially similar to that which arose in a southern shipyard when those engaged in electrical work—a white man's

job—were selected for training in welding. The fact that white
men had been operating machinery in southern coal mines prior
to the introduction of mechanical loaders placed them in a better
position to learn how to operate loading machines. It also meant
that employers did not consider placing colored labor on the new
mechanical devices. In both shipbuilding and coal mining, the
new occupation was lighter or cleaner or both lighter and cleaner
than the old; it soon became associated with white men's work
and remained in that category. The new types of operations
which evolved reduced the importance of occupations in which
most of the semi-skilled Negroes had long been concentrated.

It is important to note that the relative decline in Negro participation in coal mining occurred as the result of a technological
change which was introduced at a period of general depression
and loose labor market. That the technological factor was important, if not all-controlling, is indicated by the fact that in an
earlier decade, 1920-1930, the proportion of Negro miners increased while the total number of miners declined. In coal mining, a reduction in the proportion of colored workers did not
automatically accompany a reduction in the working force. It
was effected only when such a development was simultaneous
with the extension of a technological change, and it progressed
despite the official policy and general practice of non-discrimination on the part of the United Mine Workers of America.

Since the latter part of the nineteenth century, the Brotherhood of Locomotive Firemen and Enginemen has been dedicated
to eliminating Negro firemen in the South. The details of this
campaign were presented by Northrup at the railroad hearings
of FEPC and later recounted in his book on "Organized Labor
and the Negro." Events concerning Negro firemen presented
here have been taken from Northrup's account. In 1899, the issue
was presented at the organization's convention, when the four
railroad brotherhoods, which controlled the operating personnel
of the industry, called upon their membership to "give their support toward clearing our lines of this class of workmen." Despite
the all-out efforts of the brotherhoods, and the Locomotive Firemen in particular, the Negro has persisted. By 1941, however,
agreements had been effected which would eliminate all Negro

firemen in less than two decades. It is instructive to see how the Brotherhood of Locomotive Firemen and Enginemen was able, in a period when there was a great demand for firemen, to effect a program for complete elimination of the black worker, while in preceding periods of slack employment in the industry, the brotherhood had never been so successful in this objective.

At the outset, it should be observed that management had institutionalized the employment of Negroes as firemen and trainmen. At the same time, it had generally barred colored men from working as locomotive engineers and conductors. Thus the Brotherhood of Locomotive Engineers had been able, through its tactics of Negro exclusion, to keep the black worker out of jobs as conductors and engineers. Although the brotherhood having jurisdiction over the firemen had also maintained bars to Negro membership, it has not been able to eliminate Negroes entirely from the craft. Management had an economic incentive to retain colored firemen since the industry had maintained a racial wage differential until 1918; this wage policy had also been an important factor in conditioning the white worker in his anti-Negro bias.

When World War I occasioned the movement of Negroes out of the South into the higher-wage industrial centers, for a time it appeared that the Negro would eliminate himself from railroad firemen's work. Then in June, 1918, Secretary of War McAdoo removed the racial wage differential. This had two effects: it stayed the Negro's movement away from the railroads, and it disproved the brotherhood's prediction that if there were no racial differential, the Negro would disappear from skilled work in the industry. Because of the scarcity of trained and reliable workers, it also changed management's attitudes; Negroes were described as efficient and desirable railroad workers, despite the fact that the railroads had justified a racial wage differential in the past on the basis of the lower efficiency of colored firemen.

In the post-World War I period the drive to eliminate the Negro fireman was renewed with unprecedented intensity. Strikes and murder were employed. But the really effective work was not the campaign of terror but the persistent, peaceful campaign against Negroes by the Brotherhood of Locomotive Fire-

men and Enginemen. The campaign for the black fireman's elimination during the 1920's was executed under economic conditions
favorable to its success. There was a decline in the total railroad
employment, and the wage differential based on race had been
removed. These conditions automatically eliminated two of the
strongest inducements for the use of Negro labor. Their absence
and the continuing pressure of the unions succeeded in reducing
the number and proportion of Negroes.

The displacement of the Negro fireman continued into the
1930's, but at a rate in the South somewhat lower than in the preceding decade. Despite the fact that the tempo of the Negro firemen's displacement slackened, his doom was sealed in the plans
for his complete elimination which the brotherhood began to
formulate during this same period. Again, violence was used.
Again, despite the known killing of ten Negro trainmen and
firemen and the wounding of twenty-one others in the Mississippi
Valley in the early '30's, violence failed to effect the elimination
of the Negro. What violence could not do, what union exclusion
and unfair contracts could do only gradually, technological
changes seemed sure to facilitate.

When, in 1937, the Interstate Commerce Commission ruled
that by July, 1943, most engines for use in fast passenger or
freight service must have mechanical stokers, the brotherhood
began to angle for agreements with management. The purpose
of these agreements was to secure the use only of union members
on mechanical stokers. Since Negroes were not admitted to the
union, this was, in effect, a very drastic extension of the earlier
action to limit the area in which colored firemen could be employed.

The Diesel engine is a comparatively new innovation. It has
reduced the need for firemen, and its advent was seized upon by
the brotherhood as a means of restricting further the employment of colored men. An agreement was finally proposed by the
brotherhood which provided for the use of a fireman (in fact a
helper) on all Diesel engines and restricted such appointments
to men who were in line for promotion. Because of the industry's
racial occupational patterns and the attitude of the other brotherhoods, this in effect limited the assignment of firemen on the new

engines to whites. The proposition was made to twenty-six southern railroads, and all but five agreed to it. Finally the matter
reached the National Mediation Board, and on February 18, 1941,
the board approved an agreement between the carriers and the
Brotherhood of Locomotive Firemen and Enginemen providing
that Negroes shall not exceed 50 per cent of those on nonsteam-
powered engines. The Mediation Board further stated that it was
"expressly understood" that this agreement in no way interfered
with the right of the union and carriers to negotiate other agreements "which will restrict the employment of helpers on other
than steam power to promotable men."

When in the railroad industry there were two important technological changes, the Brotherhood of Locomotive Firemen and
Enginemen was able to achieve an objective it had been seeking
for over fifty years—namely, the perfection of a plan to eliminate Negro firemen. The fate of the Negro fireman illustrates
graphically the importance of technological change upon the
black worker's occupational status. The Diesel engine has, in
effect, done away with the operation which the locomotive fireman performed, and the union has created a new job on this
engine for its members. This new job is not that of a fireman but
rather an operation specially created for those who have served
in that capacity on steam engines. And a powerful union, backed
by government mediation machinery, was able to devise a means
of keeping Negroes out of this new job. This it could do in a
relatively short time, while it had not been able to eliminate the
black fireman in fifty years as long as the nature of the job did
not change fundamentally. Fortunately, the action of the FEPC
and recent litigation in the Supreme Court have challenged the
plans of the brotherhood. The Supreme Court ruled, in a unanimous decision in 1945, that the Brotherhood of Locomotive Firemen and Enginemen must represent non-member Negro firemen
without discrimination. This decision may wreck the elaborate
plans of the brotherhood to eliminate colored firemen by agreements between the union and management under the Railway
Labor Act.

Although the color occupational system in America has generally relegated the Negro to unskilled work, there have been

exceptions to this rule. Colored men have been used in certain
heavy and dirty industries, but even in such cases, they have
generally been kept out of the higher paid occupations. In the
building trades and in certain phases of railroad operation, Negroes have long had a position as skilled workers in certain lines.
The occupations involved have been those which were first
learned during slavery and in which the Negro inherited a place
and generally received a lower wage rate. When the operations
associated with these occupations changed, the Negro was excluded from the newer expressions of the trade.

The color occupational system is most firmly entrenched in
the South where it is an economic expression of a well established
color-caste system. The late arrival of the Negro to northern
and western industry occasioned his concentration in unskilled
and heavy work, and the color occupational system seemed to be
extending geographically. In the industrial expansion which followed World War I there were occasional variations which indicated that the system was less firmly entrenched. Yet race prejudice was growing in areas outside the South, and the northern
and western Negro did not rise occupationally to any appreciable
degree; nor had he inherited a place in a small number of skilled
occupations. He was the late comer to all types of jobs. When
a few Negroes did get into higher types of work, they often
went into occupations which were inconsistent with the southern
occupational color system. These slight gains were largely wiped
out by the depression and the unemployment which came in its
wake.

The large volume of Negro unemployment in the North during the depression emphasized the marginal position of the black
worker. He was not accepted as an integral part of the labor
force, and, at the same time, he was not the traditional worker in
certain occupations. The result was that, in a period of slack demand for workers, he suffered extreme displacement, and his
economic opportunities in the North were less than in the South.
On the other hand, when war production created a great increase in the demand for labor, the Negro in the North received
defense training and better jobs earlier than the black worker in
the South. For the more firmly the color-caste system is en-

trenched, the more protection from white competition the Negro has in certain traditional types of jobs and the more difficulty he faces in securing training and employment in new and better types of employment in periods of economic expansion.

The greatest impetus to the Negro's elimination from traditional types of work has been technological change. This is due to several factors. Such change often comes in periods of declining labor markets. In these periods there are many and varied economic and emotional forces opposing the introduction of minority groups into new operations. The most important of these is the fact that in periods of general unemployment white male workers are extremely conscious of Negroes, women, or any other minority groups as potential competitors and aggressively oppose the training and employment of such groups.*

The color occupational system is an expression of the tradition of white men's jobs and black men's jobs. In the first World War, the introduction of Negroes into certain branches of northern and western industry was accomplished without great resistance. This was possible because the Negro was used primarily as an unskilled worker in certain heavy industries. But in the second World War, there was much greater opposition to the integration of Negroes in new areas of work since, in World War II, much of the Negro's employment was not consistent with the color occupational system.

The black worker has become a symbol of a potential threat to the white worker, and the Negro's occupational advancement is consciously or unconsciously feared. This fear has been bred in the economic realities of America. Its origins lie in the unfavorable position of the "poor white" in the slave era and under the intense competition for employment in the South during Reconstruction. The repeated introduction of the Negro as a strike-

---

* This is not a racial matter. In any nation and for any group or groups, "one man's work is another man's unemployment" in periods of slack labor demand. Consequently, the entrance of married women, the pensioner, or the refugee into the labor market is resented. (See William H. Beveridge, "Full Employment in a Free Society," p. 121.) Due to the existence of a color line in the United States, the most violent expression of this fear of competition for too few jobs is directed toward the color minorities.

breaker, particularly in the industrial North and West, was instrumental in spreading the fear geographically and infecting organized labor with its germ. It has grown out of the American worker's experience with an economy which has seldom had enough jobs to absorb the labor supply. In such an economy, its development was an inevitable consequence of a caste system which perpetrates the concept of white men's jobs and black men's jobs; while, at the same time, it was used to secure the support of the white worker for such a system.

Resistance to advances in the economic and occupational status of the Negro persists even in periods of full employment, such as during World War II, because better jobs for him represent a direct challenge to the accepted color-caste system. To some, the changes represent a loss of Negro servants and laborers; by others they are interpreted as a threat to the white man's job in the post-war economy. Also, the higher earnings of the Negro make him an effective competitor for limited available supplies of housing, transportation, food, clothing, and other goods and services.

In light of these facts, it is clear that the industrial employment of Negroes in World War II has been much more fundamental and significant than that in the first World War. It is also apparent that the greater resistance to the use of Negro labor in World War II was not the expression of a new form of prejudice. It was an inevitable development in an economy where white workers had acquired a vested interest in most desirable types of work. When the war required the entrance of Negroes into these areas of employment, white workers saw in the development a threat to what they considered their exclusive preserve. The occupational color line—like all expressions of the color-caste system—was wasteful and inflexible. When a total war required its modification, there were strong forces prepared to resist any change.

CHAPTER VIII

AIRCRAFT—A PHASE OF LABOR UTILIZATION

Nowhere are the resistances to the entrance of Negroes into a new industry or new types of occupations better illustrated than in aircraft. It was a young industry; it was destined to expand at an unprecedented rate; it was dependent, for the most part, upon young and inexperienced workers; it planned to train its own labor supply. One large reservoir of potential labor was the Negro; yet, at the start of the defense program, the industry did not even consider employing colored workers. This was due in part to the fact that Negroes had never been used in the past (in 1940 there were only 240 Negro employees). It was also due to the fact that aircraft was a clean and light industry in which a large proportion of the workers were engaged in single-skilled and semi-skilled occupations, just the sort of employment from which it had been traditional to exclude Negroes. Of no less importance was the industry's effort to capitalize upon the glamour of all things associated with the airplane in order to attract the cream of the labor crop. And the Negro was not only considered no part of the cream, but his employment was believed to be an impediment to securing the most desirable "native, white labor."

When, in 1940, there was pressure from the Negro community for employment in aircraft, management did not attempt to hide its anti-Negro bias. The most outspoken opposition to the employment of Negroes was centered in the West Coast plants where payrolls were rapidly expanding. For example, W. Gerald Tuttle, director of industrial relations at the Vultee Aircraft Company in Southern California, addressed a letter to a Negro organization stating, "I regret to say that it is not the policy of this company to employ people other than of the Caucasian race, consequently, we are not in a position to offer your people employment at this time."

This attitude, while less vocal in other sections of the country, was none the less widely accepted in practice. Various government agencies concerned with labor supply attempted to secure relaxations, but they had made little progress until 1942. In June of the preceding year President Roosevelt had created the Committee on Fair Employment Practice to enforce the non-discriminatory policy established in Executive Order 8802. Despite this action, there was only slight relaxation of the color bar in aircraft in the months immediately following. On the basis of a very exhaustive survey, the Bureau of Employment Security announced that as of September, 1941, only 5.9 per cent of the establishments which anticipated hiring unskilled workers for aircraft production employed Negroes; 24.3 per cent did not then employ colored workers but expressed a willingness to do so in the future; 69.8 per cent of the firms did not then and did not intend to employ Negroes. But these figures do not give the whole picture. The majority of aircraft workers are trained persons in production jobs, thus the real problem was that of opening single-skilled and semi-skilled jobs to Negroes. This was made clear when pressures were put upon the industry to use Negroes and it attempted to respond by offering colored people a limited number of maintenance and unskilled jobs. An example of this attitude is reflected in the early statement of the president of the North American Aviation Company to the effect that Negroes would be employed only as janitors in the company's new Kansas City plant.

Many circumstances and devices prevented the early entrance of Negro workers into production jobs in aircraft plants. The most important, of course, was the announced policy of management to bar them. In addition, some of the new plants of the industry were committed to the use of local labor only, and in many instances there were few colored workers in these restricted labor markets. As governmental and community pressure increased, management made promises, delayed action, and sometimes resorted to subterfuges. Among the most important techniques employed to delay the use of Negroes were the elimination of Negro trainees from vocational training courses, postponement of consideration of Negroes until there were tem-

porary layoffs or cessations in employment due to material shortages, refusal to consider Negro applicants until the local labor
market had absorbed the cream of the crop and then asserting
that colored applicants were not of high caliber; refusal to employ Negro trainees until there were local labor shortages, thus
discouraging the development of a supply of qualified colored
workers; dependence upon a single individual to recruit Negro
workers, thus limiting the number of colored persons considered
for employment, acceptance of untrained white workers for production jobs while requiring Negroes to finish training courses
before assigning them to similar work. In a few plants where
there were closed shop agreements, craft unions effectively opposed the employment of colored workers.

Developments in specific aircraft plants indicate how management's early policies of excluding Negroes and training officials'
disinclination to admit them to defense courses complicated and
limited the full utilization of this source of labor. These events
also illustrate the influence of developments elsewhere in the
labor market upon the availability of colored workers for aircraft. They indicate the manner in which labor union restrictions
combined with other factors in delaying the employment and
up-grading of colored workers.

The situation in Buffalo was somewhat unique in that the defense courses in the vocational schools were open to colored applicants, and there was a backlog of about a hundred trained
Negro youth available for placement early in 1941. In the summer of that year after OPM had urged employment of minorities
in a direct appeal to management, the local Curtiss-Wright Corporation plant hired its first Negro production workers at a time
when there were about 9,500 employees in the plant. From the
start, the company arranged for a local Negro dentist to select
colored trainees and thus restricted artificially the field from
which colored applicants could be drawn.

While Curtiss-Wright was making this slow start, Bell Aircraft Corporation was even more hesitant. In the latter firm's
main plant there were no Negro workers in the summer of 1941;
at the new plant in Niagara Falls, there were about twenty colored sweepers. By the fall of the year Bell had four Negro pro-

duction workers and seemed reluctant to put on more, although
several scores of trained colored youth in the community were
anxious to enter the industry. The Aviation Division of the
UAW-CIO offered its co-operation in effecting the employment
and integration of colored workers, but it was not until April,
1942, that Bell hired its first skilled Negro.

By the time Bell had opened up and Curtiss-Wright was ready
to go ahead with a real non-discriminatory employment policy,
certain developments had occurred in the Buffalo labor market.
There was a labor shortage, and Negro men were finding well-
paying jobs in other industries. Unskilled laborers in iron and
steel plants and automobile factories earned more than production workers in aircraft. Skilled workers were better paid in other
industries, and the neighboring Lackawanna plant of the Bethlehem Steel Corporation had taken the lead in opening new and
better jobs to Negroes.

Although similar delays were encountered incident to the
training and employment of Negro women, there was not as
long a time lag between the introduction of white women and
the acceptance of Negro women in the Buffalo aircraft plants
as in the case of men. By the latter part of the summer of 1942
Curtiss-Wright was training and hiring on the average of thirty
colored women a month. At the same time, colored women were
being accepted from the Employment Service and at the gate,
as well as through the Negro dentist. At Bell there were still two
evidences of discrimination: all Negro applicants were required
to take blood tests, while whites were not; and colored men and
women could get semi-skilled and single-skilled jobs only after
completing training courses, while many whites were hired and
trained on the job because they "seemed to be the right type."
In spite of these difficulties, Negro men and women could get
into the aviation industry in Buffalo by late summer of 1942 if
they took vocational education, NYA or Curtiss-Wright training
courses—all of which were open to them. Since, however, trainees
were not paid and most colored males in the labor market were
employed, this late relaxation did not result in the entrance of a
large number of male Negro workers into the Buffalo branch of
the industry. Because Negro women entered the plants with less

delay than Negro men, they were absorbed at a more rapid rate. This was reflected in the wider participation of colored women in defense training for aircraft in the vocational schools. By November, 1942, there were 145 Negro women in this training.

Most of the Long Island aircraft plants limited their employment to bona fide residents of Nassau and Suffolk counties; consequently the bulk of aircraft training was centered in the schools of these counties, and only local residents were accepted. It was generally known that Negroes were not hired for production work, and few applied for defense training. Those who did attempt to enter the courses were weeded out by aptitude tests. Although it is difficult to be sure about such tests, a spot check in the summer of 1941 indicated that these particular tests seemed to be fair. This is a tentative conclusion, however, since more detailed analyses of aptitude tests in other localities indicated that they were often used as justification for eliminating certain groups which management considered undesirable in a loose labor market.

By the fall of 1941 so much pressure had been put upon the State Employment Service to refer Negro trainees that all who had ever applied were suddenly told to come in for referral, and tests were eliminated. At the same time trainees from Queens were accepted. This opened a larger field from which to select Negro applicants, since the colored populations of Jamaica and Flushing could be tapped; it did not, however, reach the centers of Negro concentration in Manhattan. By November, 1941, there were about twenty Negroes in the Long Island training schools for Grumman and Republic, and they included about all the colored male youths in Nassau and Suffolk counties who were interested in aircraft training. These trainees and a few other local male Negro workers were ultimately hired.

In accordance with the usual pattern, Negro women were not accepted for employment in the Long Island aircraft factories until after white women had been used for some time. In October, 1942, however, Brewster, Republic and Grumman began to employ a few colored women on production work. At this point, the problems of the colored female aircraft worker were complicated by a muddle in defense training. The NYA operated two training centers on Long Island—one at Oyster Bay and the other at Glen Cove. Slightly less than a hundred colored women were enrolled in these courses, some of which were in aircraft. A much smaller number of Negro women were in the Long Island vocational schools. There seemed to be competition between the two sources of training since the total number of available trainees was less than the capacity of the facilities. NYA began to train women in anticipation of the needs of the labor market; the vocational schools, in accordance with their pre-war habits, refused to admit women until the plants were definitely committed to their employment. And equally in accordance with tradition, the vocational schools were reluctant at first to accept Negro women; NYA, on the other hand, welcomed Negro women. But the aircraft plants did not welcome NYA trainees. Thus, white women trainees of the vocational education courses were being readily employed in late summer, 1942, while many Negro women trainees of NYA could not get jobs.

Gradually the situation began to clear up. In the process there were several significant developments. Ranger (a subsidiary of Fairchild) hired three colored NYA girls on production work—its first Negroes in this capacity. But many of the NYA girls had been trained in woodwork, an occupation wholly unrelated to aircraft, and they were quite discouraged when they could not get jobs. At Oyster Bay, NYA offered three courses; one of these was in machine-shop, and there was no demand for its trainees. Most of the Negro girls were in this course, which, in addition to being least productive of placements, required the longest period of training. Those colored girls who finished the vocational education courses for Grumman and Republic, on the other hand, were virtually assured of employment. By October most of the women who had been at the two NYA centers were transferred to the vocational education defense schools and were going from the schools into plants without much difficulty. Meanwhile, colored men were continuing to find a limited number of jobs in the larger Long Island Aircraft plants; they were admitted to any training school, and they were hired by Grumman, Republic, or Ranger as fast as they finished.

The Allison Division of General Motors was the largest aircraft plant in Indianapolis, Indiana. From the start management took the position that Negroes should be introduced into production capacities slowly, if at all. This policy was defended on the ground that white workers might object to the use of Negroes in higher type jobs. Apparently this, in turn, was based upon the experience in General Motors and other automobile plants in connection with up-grading colored workers. Such a position confused the issue; the situation in the automobile industry was quite different from that at the Allison plant. In the first instance, there was a long tradition of restricting Negroes to unskilled and heavy, dirty jobs, and white workers had come to expect colored workers only in such capacities. Thus the existing color occupational pattern had created an attitude of opposition to the up-grading of Negroes. But the Allison plant was new, it had no traditional racial occupational pattern, and management could, as it did, establish a pattern which would gain acceptance by the majority of workers.

From the time of its opening and until at least the fall of 1943, Allison restricted Negro workers to unskilled and service jobs. Although a few were classified as semi-skilled, none was on the production line. As in many other plants, the initial assignment of colored workers to certain lower levels of employment became a justification for failure to up-grade them. In time, the early occupational pattern established by management became the chief element in white worker's opposition to Negro upgrading. It also had repercussions for the growth of Negro employment. The concentration of Negroes in occupations such as custodial workers, parts washers, sub-foremen, and crew leaders resulted in a ceiling upon the total Negro employment in the plant and ultimately complicated management's problems of labor recruitment. Since certain occupations became "Negro jobs," available white workers would not accept them at the time when colored workers were no longer available.

A particularly flagrant situation existed at the Consolidated-Vultee plant in Fort Worth, where Negroes were excluded from training given by the company until a few months before the end of hostilities in Europe. Although colored trainees were finally accepted and employed on production jobs, they were quickly released because of cutbacks.

Boeing Aircraft at Seattle was one of the few aircraft plants which established early relationships with organized labor. It had an agreement with the International Association of Machinists, A. F. of L., making membership in the union a condition of employment. This union has had restrictions barring Negroes since its inception, and it still has a ritual provision limiting membership to white persons. Although the company stated that it would hire any qualified American, regardless of racial identity, provided the union would clear him, as a matter of fact, all the blame for Negro exclusion cannot be placed on the union since the company failed to employ Negroes prior to 1935, when it had no union agreements.

The issuance of the President's executive order barring discrimination in defense plants on account of race, creed or color placed Boeing in something of a dilemma: it had contracts with the government requiring non-discrimination, and, at the same time, it had a union-shop agreement with a labor organization which officially practiced discrimination. The union, however, was ready and willing to take the pressure off management and defend the status quo on the grounds that it was protecting the machinists' established racial policy and the sanctity of collective bargaining agreements.

But this was not all of the picture. On July 11, 1941, Bernard Squires, executive secretary of the Seattle Urban League, appeared before a meeting of the local union where more than 1,300 members were present. Mr. Squires reported that after he had presented the problem, the group unanimously passed a motion to allow Negroes to work in the plant; the action was subsequently rescinded by the union's executive board on the ground that the meeting was dominated by Communists.

When the handful of Negro trainees who had completed defense courses in the local schools applied for employment at the Boeing plant, management did not flatly refuse to hire them; rather, it informed them of the company's agreement with the union and said that it would be impossible for them to work more than a few days before the union would request their discharge.

At the same time, the supply of potential Negro production workers was kept to a minimum by the actions of instructors and advisory defense training committees. Both groups, which were drawn from union officials, plant employees and management representatives, repeatedly discouraged Orientals and Negroes from entering aircraft training in the Seattle schools.

No final solution of this problem was achieved until the President's Committee on Fair Employment Practice referred the policies and practices of machinists' local No. 751 at Boeing to President Roosevelt. As a result of this action, arrangements were made for the issuance of work permits to Negroes. Even when the international officers were ready to co-operate in this arrangement, the local union officials opposed it. Here again, constant delays in opening job opportunities limited the number of Negro workers employed. At the time of the first placements (1942) there were no Negroes in defense training aircraft classes, no Negro registrants either at the local employment service or at the Urban League, and few prospects of finding local colored applicants for employment. Other types of employment, particularly at a local shipyard and at a quartermaster's depot, had absorbed the available manpower. As late as the spring of 1942 the officials of the Boeing machinists' local were still objecting to Negro employment on the ground that the use of Negroes represented a change in the agreement between the union and the company and would adversely affect production efficiency.

In the summer of 1942, Boeing Aircraft was open to Negroes. Many of the past difficulties had been removed: management seemed ready to fulfill its obligation incident to the employment of Negroes; the hostile attitude of aircraft training instructors had greatly abated. The union was ready to clear colored workers, and had but one reservation—that the colored workers be local persons. In time, this restriction gave way, and the Negro employment at the plant grew.

The position of the machinists' local No. 1125 at the Consolidated Aircraft Company in San Diego, California, is difficult to determine. Management asserted that the union had not been in favor of the up-grading of Negroes when that problem had been presented to it. Indeed, the subsequent approach of management to this matter was alleged to have been based upon the union's suggestion that colored workers be accepted in clerical capacities in the administration offices before they were considered for employment in production jobs. On the other hand, officials of the local stated that they had not objected to the up-grading of Negroes, provided the influx of colored workers was not over-stimulated. These allegations have some support in the fact that the local had accepted Negro members despite the international's ritual bar to them. This much can be said: the machinists did not have a closed shop or a membership maintenance agreement; they did have bargaining rights. In this situation, the selection and assignment of workers was exclusively in the hands of management.

Perhaps the most significant, and certainly the earliest example of a sound approach to the integration of Negroes in aircraft production occurred at the Lockheed-Vega plants in Southern California. The details of this development will be described in Chapter XI. Suffice it to say here, in the spring of 1941 management decided to hire Negro production workers. It explained its program, interpreted the reasons for the new policy, and took steps to secure the whole-hearted support of supervisory personnel. From the start non-segregated patterns were established, and Negroes were used on production jobs.

Although the North American plant at Kansas City is outstanding because of the early statements issued by officials to the effect that Negroes would be used only as janitors, the effective work which it, the local community, and the government did to integrate colored men and women is less generally known. When the discriminatory employment policy was announced, national publicity was given to the incident. The local Negro community united in loud and effective protest, and government, through the Labor Division of OPM and FEPC, began to press the company to change its policy. Although no new decisions had been determined at the home office, the local management at the Kansas City plant adopted a temporary policy of no discrimination in hiring workers. The problem of translating this attitude into reality was difficult, and it offers one of the few instances in aircraft where the use of Negroes on production jobs was at least considered, if not effected, from the time operations began.

In response to management's request, school officials began to train Negroes for aircraft before the plant was completed. Repeated shortages of materials delayed the assignment of Negroes to production jobs, and this increased the suspicions in the Negro public. While these delays were occurring, the matter of employing Negro women was discussed, and management stated that colored women would be considered and hired when, and if, female labor in general was introduced. It was expected that all available men would be used before women were hired. By February, 1942, a beginning had been made in assigning Negro trainees to production jobs, but management was still thinking in terms of having certain sections manned entirely by Negroes.

In March, the idea of separate sections was abandoned and a few Negro trainees had been placed on instrument assembly and sheet metal fabrication. Since most of the Negro trainees were subject to the draft, only a part of the 100 available could be called to work. But there was a sizable backlog of eligibles. As the total Negro employment increased, some of the colored trainees were hired. Soon management reported that Negroes were opening new jobs for themselves; that is to say, they were doing their work so well that foremen were asking for colored workers in various departments. Negro women enrolled for sheet metal training courses for North American; meanwhile colored men continued to enter new departments. By the first of June there were about 175 Negro employees. Then there were shortages of material and a delay in the employment of colored women. This situation prevailed for two months, but the company indicated that it intended to use colored women.

In the fall of 1942, management had arranged for the training and up-grading of Negro janitors in response to a just complaint that colored service workers could not get a chance to improve their status. This move and a concurrent one to recruit trained Negro sheet metal workers attached to other industries were stymied due to the wage rate structure; workers in aircraft sheet metal received sixty cents an hour as a beginning rate, whereas janitors earned seventy-five cents an hour and construction workers much more. By October colored women were entering production jobs in a steady, if small, stream. There were sixty-two so employed. In November, there were 500 colored male and female workers in eighteen departments.

The Wright Aeronautical Corporation at Cincinnati, Ohio, has hired more Negroes than any other aircraft plant in America. This factory was engaged in the production of airplane motors, and its early acceptance of Negroes was closely associated with the traditional use of colored labor in the foundries of automobile engine plants. Similarly, in the later developments at the Cincinnati plant, the UAW-CIO played an important role.

By the winter of 1941, the Wright plant employed 500 Negroes out of its 5,000 workers, but Negroes were limited to foundry and unskilled work. Management continued to assert that Negroes and whites could not work together, and it hesitated to integrate black workers into new sections or departments for fear that its "finely balanced" production program would be upset. It defended its racially restrictive policy by citing the undeniable fact that Wright hired more and a larger percentage of Negroes than any other defense plant in the area.

There were repeated protests from Negroes in the local labor market; FEPC and OPM received many specific complaints, and the UAW-CIO entered the area in an attempt to organize the plant. While management insisted that the "time was not ripe" for abolition of segregation and racial occupational limitations, the UAW-CIO promised equal job opportunities and no segregation and pointed to the contribution which the UAW had made to the up-grading of colored workers at the Curtiss-Wright plant in Columbus, Ohio.

At the beginning of 1942 the situation was substantially unchanged; there were some 600 Negro workers, but the occupational pattern was the same. The UAW, however, had begun to concentrate upon the foundry because of its strategic importance in supplying parts for the rest of the factory. It was clear that if the union could control the initial stages of production, it would be in a powerful bargaining position; because of the concentration of Negroes in the foundry, where these stages were centered, it was most important to organize them.

During the period that the organizational campaign was going on, Negroes participated freely in the affairs of the local No. 607 of the Aircraft Division of the UAW-CIO. Colored organizers were used, and constant appeals were made to Negroes. The continuing concentration of Negro men in certain departments, their exclusion from the machine shop and more highly skilled jobs, and the stubborn refusal of the company to use Negro women offered fertile material out of which to make an effective campaign. Meanwhile the plant employed an able and experienced Negro personnel man; it also continued to hire large numbers of colored workers although no great changes were made in the racial occupational pattern.

The combined force of the federal government, the local UAW union and the inside pressure of the Negro personnel official secured more relaxations. New departments and better jobs were opened to Negroes, but on a segregated basis. Wright was the first large plant in the Cincinnati industrial area to offer jobs to Negro women. At first they were greatly limited occupationally, but gradually their employment possibilities expanded. By the latter part of 1943, the union was well established and Negroes played an important part in its administration. In the early 1944 union election, there were many Negro candidates for office, and there was an appreciable amount of intra-union racial tension. After the election, additional progress was made in Negro employment, and Negroes continued to participate in the affairs of the union. When, for example, a Negro chief steward was suspended on a charge of sabotage, he was completely exonerated and restored to his former job. This was accomplished largely through the activities of the UAW-CIO local.

In 1940 Negroes constituted only 0.2 per cent of the workers in aircraft. By the summer of 1944, there were about 100,000 Negroes in aircraft, and they were about 6 per cent of the total. Some 33,000 Negroes were producing airframes; over 45,000 were in aircraft engine parts plants; about 1,500 were in aircraft propellers and propeller parts factories, and 20,000 were engaged in making miscellaneous aircraft parts. This growth in participation had been uneven and was, for the most part, of recent origin. It resulted, as all increases in Negro employment in war production, principally from the tightness of the labor market and the

TABLE 2

Proportion of Non-whites in Selected Industrial Centers, 1940; Proportion of Non-whites in War Industries, 1943 and 1944; and Proportion of Non-whites in Aircraft Plants, Summer, 1944

Industrial Area (Areas of current acute labor shortage)	Per cent non-white population, 1940	Per cent Negro population, 1940	Per cent non-white war workers			Per cent non-white workers in aircraft	
			Nov., 1943	May, 1944	July, 1944	Name of plant	Per cent Summer, 1944
Hartford, Conn.	4.3	4.3	2.5	2.2	2.2	Pratt & Whitney	small
Buffalo, N. Y.	3.2	3.1	5.9	5.9	8.2	Bell Curtiss-Wright	2.2 3.1
Baltimore, Md.	19.4	19.3	15.0	15.2	16.1	Martin	5.8
Chicago, Ill.	8.3	8.2	8.8	10.0	10.3	Buick Studebaker Dodge Douglas	16.0 10.0 11.0 4.8
Los Angeles, Cal.	6.5	4.2	4.6	5.1	5.3	Lockheed-Vega Douglas North American Vultee	5.0 4.5 7.2 3.2
San Diego, Cal.	3.1	2.0	3.3	4.0	4.0	Consolidated	2.7
Seattle, Wash.	2.9	1.0	2.5	3.4	4.3	Boeing	2.9

	Company					
(Areas of labor stringency)						
Paterson, N. J.	3.1	3.1	4.6	5.2	5.3	Wright — 8.9
Columbus, O.	11.7	11.7	11.3	12.2	14.2	Curtiss-Wright — 9.4
Indianapolis, Ind.	13.2	13.2	9.0	9.2	10.5	Curtiss-Wright — 8.3
Wichita, Kans.	5.0	4.9	2.2	2.5	2.6	Boeing — 2.6 / Beech — 0.4 / Cessna — 3.6
Oklahoma City, Okla.	9.6	9.5	6.5	6.5	6.3	Douglas — 4.0
(Areas of slight labor surplus)						
Cincinnati, O.	12.2	12.2	9.3	9.5	10.8	Wright — 18.1
Kansas City, Mo. / Kansas City, Kans.	10.5 / 17.3	10.4 / 17.3	8.7	10.1	10.2	Pratt & Whitney — 8.5 / North American — 8.3
Nashville, Tenn.	28.3	28.3	8.8	9.4	9.4	Vultee — 4.9
Atlanta, Ga.	34.6	34.6	13.2	13.3	12.8	Bell — 6.3
Dallas, Tex.	17.1	17.1	6.6	8.1	8.0	North American — 6.5
Fort Worth, Tex.	14.3	14.2	5.5	7.5	7.7	Consolidated — 3.2
(Areas of substantial labor surplus)						
New York, N. Y.	6.4	6.1	5.6	5.9	5.7	Grumman — 3.2 / Republic — 3.1
St. Louis, Mo.	13.4	13.3	10.0	11.0	10.8	Curtiss-Wright — 3.5

attempts to enforce the executive orders banning discrimination in defense employment.

With a few notable exceptions, such as Vultee at Nashville and Beach at Wichita, the plants included in Table 2 employed Negroes in production capacities. There were a few technical and professional Negroes in the industry, and colored men and women were in some skilled occupations. Few supervisory jobs were held by Negroes. In the border states (between the North and South) and in southern plants, Negro production workers were usually assigned to separate factories or units. Elsewhere they were generally integrated on production lines.

It is difficult to measure accurately the extent to which all elements in the local labor market have been absorbed by any given industry; there are, however, certain interesting leads. By comparing the proportion of Negroes in our cities in 1940, the proportion of non-whites in war industries and the percentage of non-white workers in selected aircraft plants, we may draw some rough conclusions relative to labor utilization. For example, if a given plant hired a larger proportion of non-whites than all war industries in the area and in excess of the 1940 percentage of Negroes in the population, it is safe to say that it has done a good quantitative job of utilizing minority groups. The more detailed account of racial occupational patterns offers a key to the qualitative aspects of this question.

With the exception of those establishments which draw their principal Negro labor supply from New York City, all of the aircraft plants in the East, included in Table 2, were in areas of acute labor shortage or labor stringency in the summer of 1944. All of the West Coast plants were in areas of acute labor shortage. Thus, in these areas, economic factors were operating to accelerate the employment of local Negroes and encourage the in-migration of others. In contrast, only one of the southern plants was in an area of labor stringency; the rest were in areas with labor surpluses. One of the centers of aircraft production in the Middle West, Chicago, was an area of acute labor shortage; three were areas of labor shortage; two were areas with slight labor surpluses and one was an area of substantial labor surplus.

On the basis of the criteria of labor utilization outlined above, it is possible to arrive at some tentative conclusions. The Pratt and Whitney Aircraft Corporation, like most defense plants in the Hartford, Connecticut, area, did not achieve anything approaching full utilization of Negroes. The Bell and Curtiss-Wright plants in Buffalo, New York, did better; but, because they were late in accepting colored production workers and other local industries offered these workers earlier and better paying job opportunities, the degree to which they used Negro labor was far less than that for all war plants in the area. During the war New York City was constantly an area of labor surplus, and the Long Island aircraft plants did not use as high a proportion of Negroes as other local war industries. This is due to several factors: the early patterns of exclusion discouraged the entrance of Negroes; the distance of the plants from the centers of Negro populations also contributed to this result, and the failure of these aircraft plants to expand greatly after they had begun to employ Negroes freely established an automatic ceiling upon total non-white employment. The one exception among the Eastern aircraft plants covered in this survey was the Wright Aeronautical plant in Paterson. This was probably due to two or three factors: this plant manufactured airplane engines and hired a large proportion of workers in occupations which had become traditionally Negro jobs; the Wright Corporation generally assumed responsibility for securing wide utilization of Negroes; the Paterson plant, as that in Cincinnati, hired an able Negro personnel man to assist in recruiting and up-grading colored workers.

Because of their late introduction and the relegation of Negro production workers to a sub-assembly factory, a much smaller percentage of Negroes were in the Glenn L. Martin aircraft plant than in other Baltimore war industries. In contrast to the Baltimore plant, the Omaha, Nebraska, Martin factory hired a significant percentage of Negroes. Although the proportion of Negroes in Omaha is much smaller than that in Baltimore, the proportion of Negro workers in the local plant was almost as high as the figure for Baltimore. In the summer of 1944 about 5.5 per cent of the Omaha employees of Martin were Negroes.

The aircraft plants on the West Coast included in Table 2 generally did a fair job of Negro labor utilization. It varied in degree from company to company, with North American doing the best quantitative job and Lockheed-Vega and Douglas doing the best qualitative job. All three of these plants hired a large proportion of females among their Negro workers.

The most favorable numerical situation in the Middle West was that in the Wright plant at Cincinnati where management and the union had alternated in taking the lead in encouraging Negro employment. In the summer of 1944, over 6,000 Negroes were employed at this plant. Almost a half were in the foundry division. Although there was a general pattern of segregation in job assignment, Negroes were employed in almost all occupations and major divisions of the plant. Chicago, which was the tightest labor market in the area and which specializes in aircraft engines, presented a favorable picture. It was not as favorable as the percentages might suggest since only the largest plants were covered and the in-migration of Negroes had been greater than that of whites, so that Negroes constituted about 10 per cent of the total population in 1944. Although Negroes were concentrated in traditional occupations, some colored workers were in highly skilled work and up-grading into more desirable single- and semi-skilled jobs had been slowly progressing in 1944 and early 1945. Curtiss-Wright at Columbus had given employment to several thousand Negroes. The qualitative picture was good; a large proportion of the Negro workers were female and many of the colored workers were in new types of jobs. The somewhat favorable picture at Kansas City was due, in part, to the fact that aircraft engines were produced in the Pratt and Whitney plant where over 1,500 Negroes were employed in the summer of 1944 in many occupations. Progress in the utilization of Negro labor in the North American plant in Kansas City was more significant because it, like the situation at Curtiss-Wright in Columbus, represented the establishment of entirely new racial occupational patterns. In Wichita, one plant, Boeing, had established a favorable picture. The worst situation in the region existed at the Curtiss-Wright plant in St. Louis, where Negroes were concentrated in a separate production factory. It affords another example of the fact that segregation spells fewer job opportunities and discrimination. The Curtiss-Wright plant at Indianapolis had made only slight progress in up-grading, but it had done a better job in the numerical employment of Negroes than the St. Louis factory.

The picture in southern aircraft plants was uniformly bad, the least undesirable situations occurring at the Douglas plant in Oklahoma City, the North American plant at Dallas, and the Bell plant at Atlanta. With the exception of Oklahoma City, all of the southern establishments surveyed were located in areas of slight labor surpluses. In addition, these plants had segregated units or sections for Negroes, and the number and kinds of production jobs open to colored workers were definitely limited. Aircraft, as a clean, light industry, hired a lesser proportion of Negro workers than all war industries in these southern cities; but even in the case of heavy industries, the proportion of Negroes was much less than their percentage in the total population. As in aircraft, this was due chiefly to occupational limitations, continuing discrimination against Negro women, and the practice of segregated work arrangements.

In order to appreciate the role of labor unions in influencing racial patterns of employment in aircraft, it is necessary to understand their position in the industry. With a few notable exceptions, such as Boeing at Seattle, employment was well advanced before the unions had bargaining rights; few aircraft factories, even by V-E Day, had closed-shop agreements. This meant that management usually established patterns of Negro exclusion and that where management was successful in introducing or encouraging Negro employment and up-grading, it did so in the face of worker opposition which was inevitable once white labor had come to have a vested interest in certain types of employment. It was inevitable also that in a situation such as this, labor unions were much more important in encouraging or impeding up-grading than in securing or preventing initial employment opportunities for minority groups. At the same time that management bears the main part of the responsibility for the early exclusion of Negroes, so it deserves most of the credit for the initial relaxations of the color bar.

In a situation of this sort, it is misleading to divide aircraft factories on the basis of their union affiliation. Factors which pre-

ceded organizational success often determined the extent of
Negro employment; this latter development contributed greatly
to the degree of enthusiasm with which the union approached
the matter of Negro employment and up-grading. Despite the
presence of the machinists, Lockheed-Vega initiated the employment of Negro production workers on the West Coast. At the
California North American plant, the UAW-CIO, which was
probably in a stronger position than the machinists at Lockheed,
did little more than give lip service to its non-discrimination
pledge in the summer of 1941. Once Lockheed had introduced
Negroes, the machinists' local went along and actually took some
colored workers into its membership (later it stopped doing so
because of the international's ritual). Once management at North
American had introduced Negro workers, the union went into
action on the matter, but it did not take the initiative. That was
supplied by government and applied to management; results were
obtained when there was a change in the personnel department.

The machinists' unions have actively opposed the employment
or up-grading of Negroes, *where they felt that management was
prepared to go along with such a policy*. In several areas the machinists have bowed to the inevitable, and in most instances, they
have issued work permits, cleared, or attempted to organize Negroes in auxiliaries. Examples of this are found at Pratt and Whitney in Kansas City, Boeing at Wichita, and Curtiss-Wright at
St. Louis. In each of these plants the machinists had bargaining
rights and Negroes were relegated to auxiliary locals. The fact
that two of the plants which hired large numbers of Negroes in
a variety of occupations, Pratt and Whitney in Kansas City and
Lockheed-Vega in Southern California, had bargaining agreements with the machinists indicates that where management has
been firm, the union has gone along. In some instances the machinists have pressed for segregated eating or rest facilities.
When they insisted upon such a pattern in the cafeteria at the
Pratt and Whitney plant, the Negro workers boycotted the segregated facilities and organized to push for full membership in
the union. As contrasted to the UAW-CIO, there are no evidences of the machinists' locals ever taking the initiative, or
actively pressing management to expand employment opportuni-

ties for Negroes, or working to abolish patterns of segregation. In one case, at the Boeing plant in Wichita, a local readily agreed to a non-discrimination clause proposed by management in a contract negotiated in 1944.

As far as can be discovered UAW-CIO local unions in aircraft never fronted for management's discriminatory practices or openly proposed any of their own. At Brewster on Long Island, at Wright in Cincinnati, at Curtiss-Wright in Columbus, and in some other plants, the UAW pressed for the up-grading of colored workers, and in most areas where it had a contract, the UAW contributed toward the advancement of Negro workers and breaking down patterns of segregation. Because of the delayed negotiation of membership maintenance agreements and the general absence of closed-shop contracts, the union has not been in a position to do much more in aircraft plants. As contrasted to the machinists, the UAW-CIO unions have always been open to Negroes who were accepted as first-class members, and, even in some of the southern plants, participated fully and often actively in the affairs of the union.

The history of aircraft illustrates clearly that when economic necessity and governmental pressures require the introduction of minorities into new types of work, it can be achieved. Aircraft illustrates the strategic position of management in effecting relaxations in the color-caste system in employment. At the same time, variations in the degree of Negro utilization from area to area and from establishment to establishment show that the most important single factor occasioning the employment and up-grading of minorities was the degree of tightness in the labor market.

The industry also illustrates that, given economic necessity, relaxations in traditional bars to Negro employment are most easily and extensively achieved in industrial centers where the color-caste system is least firmly entrenched. An early evidence of this fact was afforded by the lesser amount of resistance to opening defense training in aircraft to Negroes in areas where there were non-segregated schools. The development of Negro employment in the industry, with the final result that the largest proportion of colored workers were in the engine branch, sup-

plies another evidence of the importance of the color occupational system. For processes in aircraft engine production are
similar to those in the engine branch of the automobile industry,
and it had been traditional to employ Negroes in this phase of the
latter industry; it had not been traditional to use colored workers
in sheet metal, machine-shop or kindred work.

The experience of the aircraft industry clearly shows that
segregated work arrangements are wasteful of labor resources.
There had not been anything like full utilization of Negro labor
in a single aircraft assembly plant where Negroes worked in separate shifts, buildings, or units. Nor had it been possible in tight
labor markets to secure a steady flow of manpower in any plants
where certain jobs had been assigned exclusively to Negroes.

The aircraft industry did not afford Negroes full and equal job
opportunities during the war; it did, however, break down earlier
exclusionist patterns in many individual plants. In the process of
doing this it established racial occupational patterns which its
leaders once said were impossible. It successfully used tens of
thousands of Negroes in new types of production jobs.

CHAPTER IX

GOVERNMENTAL APPROACHES

The Negro was considered, if not included, from the outset of the defense effort. When the National Defense Advisory Commission was set up as the first over-all defense agency in World War II early in 1940, an administrative assistant was appointed in the Labor Division of the commission to facilitate the employment and training of Negroes. Shortly thereafter, the United States Office of Education announced that there *should be no* discrimination on account of race, creed, or color in the expenditure of federal funds for vocational training. This was followed by a statement that workers in defense industries *should not* be discriminated against because of age, sex, race, or color. And Congress inserted an ambiguous non-discrimination clause in the appropriation for defense training passed in October, 1940.

These statements of policy were significant as pronouncements of official intent. Earlier chapters have indicated how little influence they had upon employers and how they were ignored by school officials. As a matter of fact, management paid only slight attention to any of the federal policies for labor supply; it paid even less attention to statements that minorities *should not* be discriminated against on defense work. Earlier experience with federally financed public construction programs illustrated graphically that non-discrimination statements mean little unless they are implemented. And, with the exception of some construction projects, there were few instances where the commission's policies were translated into action.

Out of the experience with craft organizations in the building trades, it became clear that certain unions were often serious impediments to the utilization of Negro artisans. Accordingly, the National Defense Advisory Commission began to discuss the matter with leaders of labor. Out of these discussions came an agreement that the American Federation of Labor and the Congress of Industrial Organizations would assume responsibility for removing barriers against Negro workers in defense industries. This helped some, but it did not come to grips with the problem of union discrimination. It was ineffective chiefly because the agency which negotiated it had no powers of enforcement.

In recognition of the general inadequacies of the commission, a new agency, the Office of Production Management, was created in 1941, and its Labor Division assumed responsibility for labor supply. In response to great pressure from Negroes and the liberal press, Sidney Hillman, as co-director and head of the Labor Division of OPM, issued a letter to all holders of defense contracts urging them to "examine their employment and training policies at once to determine whether or not these policies make ample provision for full utilization of available and competent Negro workers." At the same time that this letter was issued, the Negro Employment and Training and Minority Groups Branches were created in the Labor Division of OPM. These new offices had small field staffs operating out of Washington, and they were assigned responsibility for encouraging and facilitating greater participation of minorities in war production.

As a result of these steps, a few defense contractors indicated their willingness to co-operate with government policy; some of them began to expand their Negro employment. It is interesting to observe, however, that up to this point the labor member of the directorate of OPM had taken all steps for the agency in dealing with minority groups' employment on defense contracts; the management representative had never given an official endorsement to the program. And the growing corps of business representatives, temporarily in government service with OPM, had almost universally taken a hands-off attitude. Small wonder that industrialists outside the government paid little attention to the appeals of OPM for full utilization of minorities.

Continuing discrimination in a federally financed program of defense training was most embarrassing to defense agencies. Negroes and others constantly pointed out the inefficacy of the federal government in translating its policies of non-discrimination into reality even in a program which it directed. As a result of these and other pressures, OPM urged more direct action. In June, 1941, the director of defense training in the Federal Security Agency set forth an official policy calling for the training of Negroes even where there were no immediate employment opportunities, but where there was a probability that their services would be used at a later date. This was the first official statement which clearly indicated that the traditional approach of vocational education to train workers for immediate job opportunities only was not to be followed in defense training. It accelerated the opening of such training to Negroes in some cities with mixed schools, but it had little immediate effect in the South.

As slight improvements in Negro training and employment were taking place, the total volume of defense employment grew appreciably. In many areas, all local white male labor had been absorbed and white women were entering defense plants. White workers from elsewhere were moving into tight labor markets, while local Negroes were still finding few jobs and most of those which they secured were in non-defense work. The proportion of Negroes among the unemployed steadily increased, and the degree of minorities' participation in defense industries showed no signs of expanding appreciably; in face of these developments the Negro community became aroused. OPM responded feebly to the new demands of Negroes. The staff of the Negro Employment and Training Branch was slightly expanded, and other branches of the Labor Division of OPM expressed concern about the situation. For the most part, however, the majority of those in the Labor Division was content to rely upon persuasion (to be applied by the numerically small staffs of the Minority Groups and the Negro Employment and Training Branches) and looked to economic necessity as the source of needed pressure to enforce official pronouncements of non-discriminatory hiring policies. The Management Division of OPM remained apathetic and continued to evade the issue. Meanwhile, the Labor Division had sponsored stabilization agreements which assured closed shops in certain shipyards, in aircraft plants, and on construction projects. As has been indicated in Chapter III, many of these agreements involved craft unions which either barred or discriminated

against Negroes. Where, in such instances, there was a conflict
between the operation of these agreements and the announced
policy of non-discrimination in defense employment, OPM supported the stabilization pacts.

With this minimum support, the Negro Employment and
Training Branch was able to get a few things done. By negotiation and persuasion, it facilitated the employment of Negro
craftsmen on war construction projects, opened some new plants,
secured greater participation in training, and laid the groundwork for the use of Negroes in new types of jobs in aircraft,
electrical machinery, ordnance, shipbuilding, and machine-tools.
In a score of cities, particularly in New England and New York,
it secured the acceptance of Negroes in new industries and establishments. But the problem was not one of a score of cities or a
few hundred plants in selected industries. It was a national issue,
and it involved thousands of defense contractors. It could not be
met by the Labor Division of OPM alone; certainly, it could not
be handled effectively by a staff of about ten field representatives.

Negroes and their friends protested in all parts of the country.
Conferences seemed to produce but small results, and a plan was
developed for more drastic action. Representative Negro leaders
met and devised strategy. Under the inspiration of A. Philip Ran-
dolph, president of the Brotherhood of Sleeping Car Porters, they
finally decided upon a March on Washington as a means of
dramatizing the plight of Negroes in war industries. A date was
set for 50,000 colored men and women from all sections of the
nation to march down Pennsylvania Avenue in protest. To many
government officials, the prospect of 50,000 Negroes in a mass
demonstration was most frightening. Representatives of the administration tried to get the march called off, but the leaders
would not budge.

In the midst of these developments, President Roosevelt spoke.
On June 12, 1941, in a memorandum addressed to Messrs. Knud-
sen and Hillman, he placed the full support of his office behind
the Hillman letter to defense contractors. The President declared,
in part, "Our government cannot countenance continued discrimination against American citizens in defense production. Industry must take the initiative in opening the doors of employ-

ment to all loyal and qualified workers regardless of race, creed, color, or national origin. American workers, both organized and unorganized, must be prepared to welcome the general and much-needed employment of fellow workers of all racial and nationality groups in defense industries."

This statement, the most forthright in the defense effort to that date, was too late. Negroes were suspicious of words, and their leaders insisted upon machinery for direct action. On June 25, 1941, President Roosevelt issued Executive Order 8802 reaffirming a policy of full participation in the defense program by all persons, regardless of race, creed, color, or national origin. By July, the Labor Division of OPM had established regional offices to deal with matters of labor supply. On the national level and in the regions, there were labor supply committees to coordinate the work of federal agencies in this field. The chiefs of the Negro Employment and Training and the Minority Groups Branches were among the twelve officials on the federal Labor Supply Committee, and field representatives of the branches served in a similar capacity on the regional Labor Supply Committees.

During the period from July, 1941, until January, 1942, FEPC functioned within the Labor Division of OPM. When, on January 26, 1942, OPM was abolished, the committee was transferred to WPB where it remained until the War Manpower Commission was set up in the summer of 1942. During this one-year period, the Negro Employment and Training Branch of the Labor Division of OPM and later of WPB continued to operate in close co-operation with the committee. The branch conducted systematic visits to industrial employers in order to promote the utilization of Negro workers, conducted preliminary investigations of individual complaints for the committee, reviewed the training programs in various communities, encouraged compliance with federal policy on defense training, and worked with the United States Employment Service in order to secure placement of Negroes. During the period it was within OPM, the Committee on Fair Employment Practice served as a board of appeal for the Negro Employment and Training Branch and the Minority Groups Branch, dealt with discrimination in federal agencies, urged the contracting agencies of the federal government to enforce the non-discrimination clauses in defense contracts, and maintained contacts with state and local agencies in order to combat discrimination. The committee received individual complaints and held formal hearings.

With the advent of Executive Order 8802, federal offices concerned with combatting discrimination were strengthened. In the first place, the executive order directed vocational training officials to take special measures to assure the administration of their programs without discrimination. Secondly, and more important, it stipulated that all future defense contracts should include non-discrimination clauses. Finally, it established a Committee on Fair Employment Practice (subsequently known as the President's Committee on Fair Employment Practice, or FEPC) to receive and investigate complaints, take appropriate steps to redress grievances, and recommend to the various federal agencies and the President such measures as the committee deemed necessary to carry out the provisions of the order. A supplementary communication to the committee and a letter to the heads of all federal departments and independent establishments indicated that the order covered government employment and that federal agencies were expected to put into effect the policy of non-discrimination.

With Executive Order 8802 and with the needs for labor in war industries mounting steadily, there were gains in Negro training and employment. It is impossible to discover how much influence each of these developments had on the final results, but both were extremely important. The experience and contacts of the field representatives of the Negro Employment and Training Branch permitted them to use the new executive order as a pressure to accelerate their work with management and training officials as well as with labor unions. Plants which had given them the run-around in the past were less unconcerned after Executive Order 8802 had been issued. Some began to employ and up-grade Negroes; others resorted to tactics of delay and evasion. FEPC, however, selected certain cities, Los Angeles, Chicago, and New York, where there were outstanding instances of racial discrimination and conducted public hearings. These hearings were fully reported in local newspapers, and they made the news wire services. As a result there was widespread publicity about firms and unions which discriminated against minorities in war employment.

Since large and powerful corporations, such as Vultee Aircraft in California, Buick Aircraft in Chicago, and Wright Aeronautical in Paterson, New Jersey, were cited, it was firmly established that the committee was prepared to focus the searchlight of public censure upon malpractices regardless of the economic power of the corporation involved. The exposure and pressure upon the International Association of Machinists at the Los Angeles hearings and the mechanical building craft unions at the Chicago hearings served a similar purpose in regard to labor unions. Plants and unions which persisted in barring Negroes from employment were constantly needled and faced the threat that they might be brought before the whole committee in a public hearing. All of these efforts led to greater employment of minorities.

There was one phase of the committee's work which could soon be measured; it was employment in the federal agencies. By the fall of 1942, there were dramatic evidences that Executive Order 8802 was effective in increasing the participation of Negroes in government service. In agency after agency, the old barriers to Negro clerical workers were giving way, and colored women, in particular, were entering the government in increasing numbers. This was especially true in Washington where, in 1938, less than 8.5 per cent of the federal employees were colored and 90 per cent of the Negroes were in subclerical capacities. By November, 1942, about 17 per cent of the federal workers in Washington were Negroes, and almost half of the colored employees were in clerical and professional capacities. (These figures must be considered in light of the fact that over 20 per cent of Washington's population is Negro.) In the field and regional offices of government agencies, however, progress was much slower and, in most areas, imperceptible.

FEPC, as a creature of pressure, had to present tangible evidences of achievement or lose its backing. And from the very start there was constant sniping at the committee from those who did not like an aggressive campaign for securing fair employment practices. Faced with the pressure to produce immediate, dramatic results and constantly harassed by powerful economic and political forces opposed to its existence, the committee concentrated upon those activities which would corral support for it. This resulted in neglect of long-run planning and programming. The most conspicuous example of such neglect was the failure of the committee to pursue fully the possibilities of getting the contracting agencies of the government to enforce the non-discrimination clauses in their contracts. Closely associated was the tendency of the committee to take over all governmental operations relative to the development of employment opportunities for minorities in war industries. This action succeeded in developing widespread support for FEPC among minorities and their friends, but it did not lead to the most effective and aggressive enforcement of Executive Order 8802.

As we have noted, the Negro Employment and Training Branch and the Minority Groups Branch of OPM and WPB had limited staffs. As long, however, as the committee remained within the same agencies as these branches, it faced difficulties in securing appropriations for regional offices. At the same time, because these branches, and the Negro Employment and Training Branch in particular, had direct contacts with a large number of employers, they were often associated in the mind of the public with employment gains. This, in turn, weakened the committees' appeal for the popular support of Negroes.

As a first step to meet this situation, the committee began to do more and more of its own field work. Because of its limited staff, however, it could not handle quickly and adequately the cases which came to it. There had to be a choice: either the cases would be carefully investigated, or they would be quickly and partially investigated. The latter alternative was decided upon in many instances. As a result, many employers received formal letters from FEPC, charging them with violation of Executive Order 8802 and directing them to cease and desist from such action in the future; some of these communications were issued without any prior detailed investigation. This was, perhaps, the most serious administrative error that the committee made, and it occasioned much loss of prestige for FEPC both inside and outside of government.

The War Manpower Commission (which took over the functions of the Labor Division of WPB in the summer of 1942) was charged with responsibility for supplying the labor needs of the war effort. It was clear, long before 1942, that if this was to be accomplished, two things had to be done: the labor market had to remain an orderly one, and maximum effective use of available sources of manpower had to be made. Both of these requirements demanded full use of labor resources and the establishment of flexible racial employment patterns so that minorities might be used freely. As far as minority groups' employment was concerned, the War Manpower Commission had two principal responsibilities: the direction of existing labor supply and training agencies of the government so as to assure full utilization of local labor resources, and the establishment of practices by war industries and labor which would assure this result.

Effective over-all action on the utilization of all local labor supplies was at first delayed by constant administrative changes within the commission. In a few localities such as New York City, the War Manpower Commission was effective in integrating the Negro and other minorities in its approach to labor supply problems. But often the commission ignored, delayed, or evaded this phase of labor utilization. In general, where minority group employment could be achieved without upsetting other phases of the program and endangering relations with management groups (as in New England) and where the labor market was tight, the commission was able to secure consideration for minorities. The regional offices of WMC co-operated in such efforts to a greater degree than had those of preceding agencies. The most significant aspect of the commission's early work in this phase of its over-all job was in the realm of public relations. Repeatedly, Chairman Paul V. McNutt and other top officials indicated the necessity for using all elements in the population. Many radio programs and feature articles dealing with the problem were inspired by WMC. The commission prepared and widely distributed an illustrated booklet on Negro manpower, but still few operating programs treated the employment of minorities as an integral part of the approach to manpower.

The possibilities of what the War Manpower Commission could have done on a large scale are reflected in its program in Baltimore. In that city, the commission conducted an intensive program for securing full utilization of local labor resources and an orderly labor market. The commission established its first voluntary job control program in Baltimore during the summer of 1942. Stabilization agreements covering referral of workers through the United States Employment Service, provisions for cessation of labor pirating, further utilization of women, and acceptance of Negro production workers were developed. At the same time, WMC officials in Baltimore and at Washington secured increased training facilities for Negroes, and contacts were made with the Negro community. As a result of these and previous activities, Negro workers began to move into defense plants in large numbers. The program did not solve the problem of upgrading, but it did break down many barriers and provide more and better war jobs for Baltimore's Negroes and for the thousands of other colored workers who moved into the city.

As the War Manpower Commission was announcing and adopting fine statements of policy relative to full utilization of Negroes without establishing adequate machinery to translate these pronouncements into fact, the Negro Manpower Service, which had taken over the staff of the Negro Employment and Training Branch, was operating in the field. In some areas, as in Region V in Ohio, Michigan, and Kentucky, in Region II in New York State, and in Region VI in Illinois, Wisconsin, and, to a lesser degree, in Indiana, it secured the support of regional WMC offices. In most other regions, it worked alone. (This was particularly true in the South and, to a large degree, on the West Coast.) In most areas, the Negro Manpower Service was slowly securing new work opportunities for Negroes as its field workers became integrated into the regional offices where they were known as Minority Groups representatives. But still WMC had developed no over-all, effective, and consistent program for assuring minority groups' equal and full employment.

Meanwhile, FEPC was increasing its activities. Its administration setup had been changed and its techniques were improved. Hearings were being developed with greater care, and the committee had succeeded in establishing a few regional branch offices. In July of 1942, the committee was transferred "as an organizational entity" to the War Manpower Commission under the supervision of the later body's chairman. When hearings on discrimination against Negro railroad firemen were announced in the fall of the year, there were many pressures exerted to prevent their being held. Finally, the chairman of the WMC called them off. This precipitated a storm of protest from Negroes and liberals, and finally resulted in the issuance of a new executive order (9346) and the transfer of FEPC to the Office of Emergency Management in May, 1943.

Following these events, the committee was again reorganized, and it established regional offices in all parts of the country. The War Manpower Commission had become completely decentralized by this time, and operating agreements between WMC and FEPC were negotiated. These agreements outlined the responsibilities for each agency in carrying out the non-discrimination executive order. Because of the autonomy of certain WMC regions and many area offices within the regions, these agreements were difficult to translate into operation in the field. They did, however, represent a new and improved approach on the part of the committee, for they were but one of a series of operating agreements with federal agencies. Such agreements with contracting agencies were most important because they gave these agencies direct responsibility for enforcing the non-discrimination clauses in their contracts, and they provided the committee with more direct administrative lines for following up on the work of contracting agencies. They meant that the resources of many federal agencies were, in varying degrees, being used to supplement and support the work of the committee in enforcing Executive Order 9346.

No better key to the weaknesses of the approach of the War Manpower Commission to full utilization of Negro labor can be found than in the commission's operating instructions relating to its responsibility for facilitating the enforcement of the President's executive order. This document was issued in September,

1943, as a result of the previously negotiated operating agreement between FEPC and the commission. Even at that late date, it was necessary for the commission to urge regional, state, area, and local offices to take specific action to insure the inclusion of Negroes and other minority groups in all recruitment programs.

Since WMC had often certified housing needs for an area where resident Negroes were unemployed or under-employed, the instructions stated that in any future certification of such needs the availability of resident minority groups' labor and the needs of such groups for housing should be considered. In addition, the instructions specified that each voluntary agreement between WMC, management, and labor for the stabilization of the labor market should contain a specific provision for full utilization of all sources of labor. This provision was in recognition of the fact that some of the stabilization agreements had either evaded or watered down references to Negro workers' utilization. The ultimate responsibility for determining the adequacy of adjustments made in cases of alleged discrimination was vested in FEPC, although WMC assumed an initial responsibility for eliminating discrimination. The instructions provided for adequate liaison to co-ordinate the activities of the committee and the commission and stipulated that there should be personnel designated to perform this function in each regional office of WMC.

The operation of federal agencies was important in opening new job opportunities for Negroes. Their efficacy was due largely to Executive Orders 8802 and 9346. Prior to 1942, the over-all labor supply agencies through their Minorities Groups and Negro Training and Employment Branches established the framework in which future gains were achieved. Subsequently, FEPC established its own field staff and assumed many of the functions which the service branches of OPM and WPB had originally performed. Fortunately, however, by the time that the committee had largely displaced the branches, it had begun to call upon the operating agencies of the government to assume responsibility for enforcing non-discrimination clauses in their contracts.

Early in its development, FEPC established a procedure of basing its operations upon the receipt of specific complaints alleging discriminatory employment practices. Later, it authorized staff members to act upon information pertaining to discriminatory advertisements, placement orders, or application forms. Despite these modifications, the committee's basis of operation remained principally the individual complaint.

This administrative practice created difficulties from the start; after 1944, it limited the effectiveness of the committee. In light of the Negro's long experience with color discrimination, he was ready to expect barriers in his quest for employment. As we have noted above, early in the war effort individual colored workers often assumed that they would not be employed by most war plants. When a few establishments were open to them, the majority of Negroes flocked to the gates of these "sure" plants. This meant that few applied at the establishments which continued to discriminate against black workers; it also meant that many applied at plants which had the most favorable racial employment policies. At the same time, the Negro Employment and Training Branch and the Minority Groups Branch of OPM and WPB had concentrated upon a few of the larger plants. And the individual complaints which came to the committee were often from plants which had done the most to open their doors to minorities; few came from the large number of smaller establishments which continued to bar non-white workers.

When, therefore, the committee conducted its early hearings, it often had no basis for citing plants which had the worst records of violating Executive Order 8802. On the other hand, it often had complaints against firms which had made relative progress in utilizing minorities. Many of these complaints were valid, but because of their volume, some were not. Consequently, at the committee's earlier hearings, firms which had opened new occupations to Negroes were often cited along with establishments which had done little or nothing in this direction; other establishments, which retained inflexible color bars, were not even questioned because no individual had filed a complaint. This situation often occasioned intense employer resentment against FEPC.

An example of the type of problems which arose can be taken

from the Los Angeles hearings. Among the companies included was the Lockheed-Vega Aircraft Corporation. This was the first aircraft plant on the West Coast to open production jobs to Negroes. At the time of the hearings, it employed more Negro production workers than any other aircraft plant on the Coast, and it was constantly adding others. Yet there were many individual complaints against it, and the committee cited Lockheed-Vega for violations of Executive Order 8802. Doubtless, Lockheed-Vega did continue to discriminate against minorities, but there were other plants in Southern California which clearly barred Negroes from production jobs or totally excluded them from employment and which were not so charged at the Los Angeles hearing. Those employers who were opposed to FEPC cited Lockheed-Vega's experience in support of an allegation that firms which initiated action to integrate minorities might well find themselves embarrassed by FEPC as a consequence.

This latter observation was not entirely accurate but there was some truth in it. Had FEPC been more concerned (and better informed) in its earlier existence about the over-all aspects of minority groups' utilization, it could have avoided this unnecessary administrative defect. The issue was one of deciding upon an economic as contrasted to a legalistic approach. Yet, had FEPC decided to concentrate upon firms which had the least satisfactory over-all records of fair employment practices, some modification of the use of individual complaints would have had to be made. Subsequent hearings seem to indicate that the committee was able to reconcile the dependence upon individual complaints with a consideration of the relative practices of different plants; it did not, however, succeed in bringing pressure upon establishments which continued to discriminate, but against which there were no specific complaints.

In many labor markets where there was full employment of Negroes in 1944 and subsequently, a large number of plants, many of which will be important in the post-war period, continued to discriminate against minorities. But few individual complaints against these firms were filed with FEPC. Since the committee was still basing its operations upon specific complaints, it was still not in a position to question the racial employment practices of these establishments. This was a serious limitation, and, unless modified, it is sure to handicap minorities in their post-war employment experience.

No account of government activity in minority or any other groups' employment would be complete without some consideration of the United States Employment Service. It is difficult to present a short and, at the same time, accurate account of this agency. Like the United States Office of Education, it had been operating before the war, and its personnel was conditioned to certain procedures and attitudes. The most important of these was the desire to comply fully with employers' specifications.

There were other serious carry-overs too. The defense program was initiated after a long period of depression. During that depression, the Employment Service had become extremely conscious of soliciting employers' business, and it never dared alienate its customers. It had, in addition, developed a fetish for reporting a large volume of placements, and its budget requests were often evaluated on the basis of its placement figures. Most of its Negro placements were in common laboring work and in domestic service. Seldom did it place a skilled Negro, save in a few building trades; as a result, few skilled Negroes registered with it. It was natural, though unfortunate, that USES would continue in wartime to seek the favor of employers. This attitude was re-enforced by the fact that during the earlier phases of the war effort, management was free to seek its workers on the labor market, and most of the larger plants called on the Employment Service only for workers in occupation in which there was a scarcity of labor.

At the outbreak of World War II, and during the first years of the war, the United States Employment Service was, in fact, a series of state employment offices. The people who actually made placements were not federal employees but were responsible to a state organization. The United States Employment Service Division of the Bureau of Employment Security of the Social Security Board had an over-all supervisory position. Its most effective service, prior to the war, had been the development of good practices and the collection of accurate statistics.

Policies issued from Washington were in the form of regulations which were issued to state offices.

The Washington officials of the United States Employment Service were conscious of the deficiencies of local employment offices from the start. As contrasted to the United States Office of Education, they collected and released current data indicating the condition of the labor market and the need to utilize minorities in war industries. After much urging, they issued specific regulations which set forth official policy, but they did not pursue them forcefully. In some states, local officials completely ignored the Washington bulletins dealing with minority groups. In other states, they were read and forgotten.

At the outset of the defense effort, there were four general practices of the United States Employment Service which delayed the acceptance of Negro workers in war plants. In many areas of the country, skilled Negro workers were encouraged to register in unskilled capacities on the theory that they could more easily be placed in such work. Statements of policy from Washington urging proper classification for all workers were ignored; and as a matter of fact regulations, even if followed, would have been inadequate since, from bitter past experience, many skilled Negroes had ceased seeking work through the USES.

When an employer requested a worker, many local employment offices in the North and South alike would ask him what racial type he preferred. Faced with such an abstract question, the average employer made an abstract answer to the effect that he desired white workers. The Employment Service justified this practice by saying that it did not want to embarrass colored workers or send them on a wild goose chase. As a matter of fact, such a procedure protected the employer from charges of discrimination and denied the individual Negro worker a chance to sell himself and his qualifications to the employer.

In southern and border cities there were separate Negro USES offices. Most of them received calls for unskilled and domestic workers only. In few instances were these offices exposed to the over-all demands for workers which came to the local Employment Service. Nor did the personnel of the Negro office have a chance to participate in discussions about job specifications, and most of the specifications for desirable openings were drawn up in terms of the white labor supply. The directors of the Negro offices usually were not afforded an opportunity to have direct contacts with employers. Consequently, most employers knew nothing about the qualifications of the available Negro registrants and did not consider employing them.

Few Employment Services exerted any effort to sell Negro labor to employers. Even in instances where tight labor markets developed early in the defense program, Employment Service offices accepted "white" specifications and imported white workers without calling employers' attention to the fact that qualified local Negroes were available.

Although the Washington office sent out statements suggesting reforms, no significant changes were made until after Executive Order 8802 was issued. And even then, improvements were slow and spotty. As late as October, 1941, four months after Executive Order 8802 had been issued, the Chief of the United States Employment Service Division of the Bureau of Employment Security was not prepared to take a forthright stand on non-discrimination in referrals. His thinking was in accord with the traditions and the then current position of the Employment Service.

When, for example, it was suggested that the United States Employment Service refuse to accept discriminatory orders (which were in effect evidences of violation of Executive Order 8802), the chief of the USES was quick to observe that it was not the Employment Service that was discriminating but rather the employer. And he added, despite the President's statement, that this discrimination on the part of the employer was not illegal. In his opinion, it was an undesirable social and economic practice and, as such, could not be eliminated by the Employment Service. If the USES refused to accept discriminatory orders, he observed, the Service would lose the employer's business, the employer would get workers elsewhere (applying the same discriminatory criteria), and the USES would become a less vital factor in the labor market.

There was much validity in this last argument. It is another illustration of the crucial influence of the general inefficacy of government's controls over the labor market upon its programs for full utilization of all sources of labor supply. As long as employers were free to secure their workers on the open labor market, it was futile to expect a labor exchange which was constantly selling itself to employers to attempt aggressively to modify its customers' specifications. In only two states did the Employment Service take effective steps in this direction. In New York, where a state law prohibited discrimination in referrals, the State Employment Service refused discriminatory orders. The Regional Director in Cleveland ordered the directors of the State Employment Services in Michigan and Ohio to take similar action, but was subsequently instructed by Washington to conform with federal policy and rescind the order.

When it was suggested, in a more realistic vein, that the USES accept discriminatory orders but ignore the discriminatory specifications, the chief of the service was not responsive. Again, he indicated the possibility of antagonizing the employer and losing his business and again he expressed fear of embarrassment to the applicant so referred. In order to prevent such embarrassment and to comply with employers' preferences, he felt that the race of the applicant should be on his referral card. All the Washington office felt it could do in the fall of 1941 was to take steps to see that its personnel did not inject their own prejudices in their official acts, not take the initiative in raising questions about racial or religious preferences, and encourage employers to remove racial and religious specifications when such specifications prevented full utilization of the local labor supply. In a word, the USES was an agency to serve the employer, and, as a labor exchange, it should avoid, as far as possible, questioning employers' discriminatory requests.

Within the limited area in which it could be induced to act on the matter of minorities' utilization, the USES slowly began to effect changes. The first reform was relative to the classification of workers. In most areas outside the South, Negroes were generally being registered in their proper skills by 1942. The practice of inquiring about employers' racial preferences was more deepseated. Some state Employment Services, notably New York, took direct and effective action to correct this practice; but in general, although more regulations on this matter were issued, the practice continued until well in 1943. Even after that date, it still occurred in certain areas. In Philadelphia, for example, some USES staff members were still asking employers if they would accept Negroes as late as the spring of 1945. But FEPC has constantly put pressure on the United States Employment Service, and the practice slowly declined.

The USES in New York State has been the most effective branch of the agency in securing employment equality for minorities during World War II. Yet, as late as the spring of 1945, there were flagrant violations of the non-discriminatory executive order in local USES offices. At Niagara Falls, many registration cards contained racial and religious identification, despite the fact that such labels were prohibited by regulations. The local officials were unfamiliar with the WMC policies of the region and did not seem anxious to correct violations of these policies. In Buffalo similar bad practices were followed in at least one USES office, and the local manager, when questioned about his failure to refer Negro registrants properly, expressed fear of losing employers' business if his office attempted to enforce the federal non-discrimination policy.

Although some feeble efforts were made to do away with the Negro offices, many still existed on V-E Day, and they occasioned protest. In January, 1945, for example, a vigorous complaint of Jim Crow practices in the Birmingham USES was reported. Manpower requirements and official pressures caused some southern cities to expose Negro registrants to skilled and semi-skilled jobs, but the system permitted of evasion, and such evasion often existed. Investigation of the Savannah, Georgia, USES in 1944 indicated that orders for skilled workers were centered in the white office and practically no skilled or semi-skilled workers were referred from the colored office. Both offices placed workers who had completed defense training; the Negroes were placed in helper jobs where they were frozen. White trainees were so placed as to assure future up-grading.

Starting at the Washington level, the USES made efforts to sell Negro labor to employers. The initial steps were directed primarily at the employees of local and state offices. An issue of the Employment Service's monthly magazine was devoted exclusively to the need and methods for minority groups' placement. Led by New York City, many local Employment Services developed elaborate and effective regulations for interviews, and there have been definite and unambiguous regulations setting forth the responsibilities of the Employment Services' personnel. As the War Manpower Commission assumed direction of the United States Employment Service, it extended these activities.

In order to prevent the Employment Service's being used as a tool for hiding employers' discriminations and violations of Executive Orders 8802 and 9346, FEPC induced the USES to require a report on each case of discrimination which came to its attention. The regulations provided instructions for attempting to overcome discriminatory specifications and required individual reports for each instance where the employer was guilty of discrimination. Few such reports had been filed before 1943. Even at that late date, some states did not report a single case of this discrimination. Field investigations indicated that many offices failed to discuss discriminatory specifications with employers; others simply did not refer Negroes to firms which indicated orally their preference for white workers. There had been some improvement by 1945. For the most part, this was a result of the WMC order of July 1, 1944, requiring that all essential employers would thereafter be able to get new male (and sometimes female) workers only by referrals from the USES or under arrangements made by USES. At the same time, WMC stipulated that because of manpower shortages, no essential employer would be permitted to refuse any qualified applicant because of race, color, creed, or national origin.

In the spring of 1945, the southern USES offices were still generally practicing discriminatory acts. In many cities Negroes continued to encounter difficulties in securing proper classification in Employment Service offices which were often manned by white clerks who had definite concepts of the Negro's place. This problem occasioned much negotiation between WMC and FEPC in the southeastern region and adjustments were being made in Georgia, Florida, and Alabama. In these three states and in Texas, the USES submitted reports on employer discriminations. Elsewhere in the South, such reports were rare or non-existent. Seldom in the South were colored registrants referred freely to skilled work, and Negroes were usually sent only to those firms which had used colored labor in the past. In New Orleans, for example, a war contractor was induced to modify his discriminatory hiring specifications. When, however, this employer placed an order for workers, the local USES directed him to specify whether he wanted white or colored workers. And this occurred in December, 1944.

In many cities of the South and often in the North and West local USES personnel had verbal agreements with employers engaged in war production not to refer colored workers to certain plants or for certain types of work. Since the few Negro USES employees in the South have no contacts with employers, these agreements were seldom challenged or brought to light in that region; elsewhere, they were constantly being challenged in 1944 and 1945. There was little real effort in most southern USES offices to encourage employment of Negroes except in traditional types of work; despite the labor shortages in textiles, for example, USES in the South accepted the industry's traditional discrimination and made no real effort to introduce Negro workers.

This brief resumé of the United States Employment Service's approach to Negro placement indicates that the agency hesitated to face the problem squarely. It instituted some reforms, and the situation outside the South in 1945 was vastly improved over that which existed prior to the war. But even when the United States Employment Service became the exclusive referral agency for war plants, it often failed to take aggressive action to secure compliance with the federal policy of non-discrimination.

As the only consumer of war material, the federal government could have insisted upon full utilization of minority groups from the start of the defense program. Such an approach, however, would have been inconsistent with the over-all method of securing war production. At the outset, few things were required of war contractors, and the initial defense agency was advisory. As time went on, controls were introduced, but most problems of labor supply were dealt with through negotiation and voluntary agreements. Beneath these agreements were many controls and the threat of more. Yet few controls were exerted to get fair racial employment practices. Those responsible for the earlier over-all problems of labor supply were hesitant to insist upon Negro employment in war industries. They believed that economic forces would eventually require it, and they were waiting until the necessity became greater.

But the Negro people who suffered from this situation were not so patient. They insisted upon and got more positive action. The result was a non-discriminatory executive order and a Committee on Fair Employment Practice to enforce it. This machinery and the economic necessity led to the employment gains which Negroes made during the war. They also occasioned some real improvements in the United States Employment Service. Since the latter agency is continuing a program of education for its personnel, some of these changes may persist after the war emergency has passed. It is regrettable, however, that little of the good training material and few of the training courses developed by USES were being given in the South where the need for them was greatest.

CHAPTER X

LOCAL TRANSPORTATION–A SPECIAL CASE

FOR MANY years prior to World War II, Negroes in northern and western urban centers had attempted to secure jobs as motormen and conductors on street, elevated, and subway cars. Such work had become a white man's job; and when busses were introduced, their operation, too, was exclusively limited to whites except in a few cities where certain lines served Negroes exclusively. At the same time, however, most local transit systems employed a large number of Negroes as maintenance workers, and often in skilled capacities which did not occasion contacts with the public. As in retail and wholesale trade and in other distributive and service industries, it was assumed that the public would object to colored people's employment in such types of work. The initial use of whites exclusively, the resulting development of a vested interest of whites in these jobs, and the assumed public acceptance of whites only had created formidable barriers to Negro employment as platform operators in local transportation systems.

During the latter 1930's, two important developments occurred. In Detroit, where the city owned and operated the local transportation system, many Negroes were used as motormen and conductors. In New York City, after the completion of the municipally owned subway, colored workers achieved similar job opportunities. And with this base, the Negro community and the Transport Workers Union pressed for and achieved platform jobs on the independent traction lines. In Cleveland and a few other cities, Negroes were employed as motormen and conductors. In December, 1941, a Negro passed a civil service examination for a motorman's job on the municipal traction system in San Francisco. He faced extreme difficulties in securing training, and, had it not been for the fair and inflexible attitude of the civil service system and the traction management, he would not have been able to stay on the job. Once the ice was broken, however, others followed, and by January, 1945, over 700 Negro men and women were operating street cars and busses in San Francisco.

With the new demands of war production and the movement of millions of workers to industrial centers, local transportation systems became crowded and over-strained. At the same time, Selective Service and war jobs made serious inroads upon the operating personnel. Equipment remained idle because there were no operators, and war workers and others could not get to and from their places of employment. There was much dissatisfaction and criticism of management. Women and older workers were appealed to in intense recruitment programs, but established racial occupational patterns persisted and no Negroes were accepted. Colored Americans in many communities pointed to this situation and its inconsistencies; they renewed their efforts to get platform jobs. Finally, local transportation was classified as an essential industry subject to the provisions of Executive Order 8802. By the spring of 1945, FEPC had been successful in securing the employment of colored motormen, conductors, and bus drivers in Philadelphia, Chicago, and Los Angeles. It was preparing to act in Washington, D. C., and Oakland, California, and test cases were developing in Baltimore, Maryland, Columbus, Ohio, and many other cities.

The number of Negro workers employed as platform operators on local transportation systems during World War II was small, yet the events leading up to this employment are significant. They illustrate the tenacity with which management and labor cling to established color occupational patterns, and they illustrate that the public has little concern about who serves it as long as its needs are met. Recent events in a few cities indicate how management and labor can act in collusion to delay and complicate Negro employment and how that employment can be effected if sound principles of personnel administration are applied. These developments also offer an insight into the way in which governmental machinery operates to enforce the non-discriminatory executive orders.

The employment of Negroes as platform operators on street, subway, and elevated cars, and as drivers on busses warrants special attention for another reason: it represented a departure from the usual wartime emphasis upon minority group placement on production jobs. It was an outstanding instance in which the color-caste occupational pattern in a public service industry has been broken down. As such it has implications for the future; for, if real progress is to be made in establishing racial employment patterns favorable to Negro employment in the post-war era, there will have to be further infiltration of Negroes into those industries which are sure to expand at the close of hostilities. Included in this group are wholesale and retail trade, amusements, public and semi-public services, and kindred industries. In all of them, the exclusion of Negroes from most types of jobs has often been justified by referring to the alleged public resistance to colored persons' serving in operating or sale capacities where they have direct contact with the public. It is interesting, therefore, to see how this and other problems incident to Negro employment in local transportation systems were met.

THE PHILADELPHIA STORY

The efforts to secure operator's jobs for Negroes on Philadelphia's busses, street-cars, and subway-elevated trains were successful only after a system-wide strike had tied up all public transportation in the city for nearly a week. Investigation of the company's history and its labor relations strongly suggests, however, that anti-Negro prejudice on the part of white operators was only a minor causal factor in the strike. The work stoppage was essentially the result of a long-standing bitter struggle over financial power and the control of the Philadelphia Transportation Company's employees.

The origins of the strike lie in events which took place as long ago as 1911 when management of the local traction system set up a co-operative wage fund for employees at the same time that it established an Employees' Co-operative Association. For the next twenty years all employees were required to invest 10 per

cent of their salaries in the Co-operative Wage Fund, and ultimately employee investment exceeded $17,000,000.

By the middle '20's the wage fund, which invested employees'
savings almost exclusively in voting stock of the traction company, was well on its way to gaining actual voting control of the
company. This eventuality was avoided when management set
up a holding company and persuaded the employee wage fund
to trade its traction company stock for holding company stock.
In the last frenzied years before the 1929 stock market crash,
the holding company invested in a great many highly dubious
enterprises, and subsequently it, as well as the co-operative wage
fund and the traction company itself, became involved in extended court suits. It was finally determined that the assets of
the holding company had shrunk from $38,000,000 to less than
$5,000,000 and that the employees' wage fund had lost over
$16,000,000 of its total $17,000,000 capital. This final deflation
occurred in December of 1943, only two and a half months before the PTC employees turned away from their old, unaffiliated
union and chose the CIO Transport Workers Union as their
bargaining agent.

In 1911, management of the traction system, then known as the
Philadelphia Rapid Transit Company, gave workers the opportunity to choose between the Employees' Co-operative Association, the A. F. of L. Amalgamated Association of Street and
Electric Railway and Motor Coach Employees of America, and
the Brotherhood of Railroad Trainmen. Management specified,
however, that in order for either of the two large unions to become the bargaining agent for employees it would have to receive a two-thirds vote of all workers. Neither international
union was able to achieve this preponderance and consequently
the Co-operative Association became the bargaining agent.

All during the boom years the Co-operative Association continued as the only union for transit workers in Philadelphia and
played second fiddle to the Co-operative Wage Fund. During
the 1930's, when the transit company was in the course of under-
going reorganization, strong efforts were made by two separate
factions within management to gain control of the corporation.
At this time the lawyers for the Co-operative Wage Fund and

the Co-operative Association took sides in the fight for control of the company. They not only appeared in court as representatives of the employee-stockholders, but also organized masses of workers to sign petitions for this or that faction. During these struggles it is difficult to find reports of any activities on the part of workers as such in either of these organizations. Amalgamated likewise joined in the battle for control of the company at a time when efforts were being made to change the composition of the board of directors. Within a week after the attempted ouster occurred, Amalgamated began well-publicized efforts to organize the employees. When the ouster failed, the organization efforts of Amalgamated ceased, thereby lending credibility to the rumor that the Amalgamated had made a previous agreement not to attempt organization of traction workers as long as the existing management was in control.

In June of 1937, after the constitutionality of the Wagner Labor Relations Act had been upheld, management of the transit company notified all of its employees by letter that the old Co-operative Association was no longer a legal bargaining agent and that the employees would have to form a union to represent them in negotiating with management. On the day this notice was distributed, the 118 employees who served as members of committees in the Co-operative Association met and received membership blanks. These forms were handed out by a representative on the general committee of the Co-operative Association and a member of the board of the Co-operative Wage Fund. The multigraphed application blanks listed one of the distributors as business agent for a new union, the Philadelphia Rapid Transit Employees' Union, and the other as secretary-treasurer. Committee members were instructed to sign up the employees.

Meanwhile, organization drives among transit workers had been started by the CIO Transport Workers Union, by Amalgamated, and by the Brotherhood of Railroad Trainmen. The bargaining election was won by the Philadelphia Rapid Transit Employees' Union—a new organization which had sprung from the ashes of the Co-operative Association. Although this election was repeatedly challenged, it was approved by the judge who was then hearing the bankruptcy proceedings of the transit company and by the State Labor Relations Board.

The PRTEU continued to represent the transit employees without any further bargaining election for four and a half years. During this period charges were made several times of co-operation between union officials and management for the latter's benefit. The suspicion of team-work between union leaders and management was broken up only when TWU was elected as the bargaining agent for the Philadelphia Transportation Company employees in March, 1944.

The Negro up-grading issue first entered the muddy current of PTC labor relations in the summer of 1941, when a three-year period of buck-passing by management and by the officials of the PRTEU was initiated. In the fall of 1942, when the company was facing extreme labor shortages, management took the position that Negroes could not be put on jobs they had not hitherto held unless the proposal for the change was made by the union. In support of this position, management cited a clause in its contract with the PRTEU which made no reference either to up-grading or to Negroes. This clause stated:

Except as herein specifically covenanted, all existing rules, regulations and customs bearing on the employer-employee relationship shall continue in full force and effect until changed by agreement between the parties.

At a later date when management and officials of PRTEU were questioned about the origin of this clause, they explained that it was inserted in the 1937 union-management contract. Its purpose, they said, was to summarize a number of informal agreements reached in discussions between management and workers in the old days when the PRT Co-operative Association was the bargaining agent. Both management and union officials, however, admitted that the subject of up-grading Negroes to operating jobs had never been discussed at meetings between management and workers until after the pressure for such up-grading began in 1941. In other words, this subject was not one of those which the catch-all clause was designed to cover. When the issue arose, this clause was simply seized upon as the only possible item in the contract on which refusal to up-grade Negroes could be based.

In February, 1943, the Committee on Fair Employment Practice entered the case. Management continued to reaffirm that it was powerless to act upon Negro up-grading and that the matter was a union responsibility. The union, in turn, repeatedly denied that it had any control over the hiring of Negroes. Meanwhile, the company began employing women as car loaders, conductors, street car motormen, and subway operators. There was, however, no reference to the catch-all clause in the union agreement when management decided to use white women.

On November 16, 1943, the FEPC issued directives to the Philadelphia Transportation Company and to the Philadelphia Rapid Transit Employees' Union instructing them to cease and desist from discriminating on the basis of race in hiring and up-grading. The delegates of the PRTEU transportation division met that evening for six hours to discuss the directive but adjourned without taking any action. By November 23, union officials had concluded a series of delegates' meetings concerning the FEPC order, but there was no representation of the maintenance department (where most Negro employees were concentrated). The outcome of these meetings was a decision by the union to request a public hearing before FEPC.

This hearing was held in December, 1943, and the old arguments were reiterated. The union also brought forth a new one, namely, that the FEPC was attempting to destroy the departmental seniority which is common in traction companies and which was traditional in PTC. Under its terms, a man accumulates job seniority only in the department where he works. Thus, if an employee with twenty years' service in the maintenance department were to transfer to the transportation department to become an operator, he would be unable to carry his twenty years' seniority in the maintenance department with him but would start as the lowest ranking member of the transportation department.

The charge that FEPC was attempting to tamper with this seniority plan was entirely without basis in fact. It stemmed from a slightly confusing use of the date June, 1941, in FEPC's order. This was explained to the union officials at the public hearings when it was indicated that the specified date referred to the time President Roosevelt signed Executive Order 8802 and had no reference to seniority rights. It seems evident, however, that union officials did not transmit this fact to the rank and file of PTC employees but continued to use the false seniority issue as a means of rallying employee resistance to the up-grading of Negroes.

These hearings roused a storm of public pressure on PTC management and public officials, urging them to abide by FEPC's hiring directive. The CIO Central Labor Council went on record favoring immediate acceptance of the directive. Church groups joined in, and their efforts were climaxed on December 14 when a petition favoring fair employment practices on the local transit lines and bearing the signatures of over 12,500 substantial Philadelphia citizens was sent to the company.

In spite of this public pressure the PRTEU, which at this time had taken the lead in the mutual resistance of union and management to the up-grading of Negroes, remained adamant in its stand. Union officials made an appeal over a local radio station in which they again aired the false seniority issue and questioned the constitutionality of FEPC. On January 11, 1944, they hailed FEPC before the House Committee to Investigate Administrative Agencies under the chairmanship of Howard Smith of Virginia. This predominantly anti-administration committee challenged the authority of FEPC and, in general, encouraged the PRTEU officials to continue their defiance of that agency's order. In these hearings, as well as during the public hearing in Philadelphia, attorneys representing management joined the union in opposing the proposed change in employment policies. The PTC management seized upon this situation to state:

The company will consider itself bound by its contract [with the PRTEU] and will not take action in violation thereof unless and until the validity of your committee's [FEPC] directive now challenged, shall be finally established.

While the resistance of management and the PRTEU against obeying FEPC's directive had been coming to a head, a hot organizing campaign had been under way to elect a new bargaining agent for the transit workers. Participants in this contest were the PRTEU, the Amalgamated, the Brotherhood, and TWU. During the early phases of this campaign, the issue of Negro up-grading had been injected by PRTEU's adamant stand against the measure. TWU took a forthright position in favor of equal job opportunities for all employees of the company. Neither Amalgamated nor the Brotherhood made any public statement on this issue. It was known, however, that the Brotherhood's by-laws limit its membership to white males.

During the later stages of the bargaining election campaign, when the Brotherhood of Railroad Trainmen had withdrawn from the contest, political issues came to the fore. Amalgamated charged that TWU was "Communist-dominated" and professed a fear that if TWU got into Philadelphia, Michael Quill, its president, would set up a local branch of the American Labor Party. TWU countered by charging that the leadership of Amalgamated was venal and ineffective. The rejoinders grew so bitter that they embroiled all of the local A. F. of L. and CIO unions. Name-calling finally resulted in the dissolution of the United Labor Committee in which A. F. of L. and CIO had co-operated for eight years.

TWU won the right to represent both the maintenance and transportation workers, receiving 61 per cent of the votes among the maintenance workers and 53 per cent of the votes among transportation workers. (The small office force of PTC remained in PRTEU because neither Amalgamated nor TWU had sought to organize it.) Contract negotiations between TWU and management were scheduled for April 7. On the previous day FEPC urged the company to proceed immediately to up-grade Negroes without awaiting the outcome of the contract negotiation. FEPC had a most persuasive set of arguments on the basis of which to urge this step by management. Management had been maintaining for over a year that it had no objection to up-grading Negroes and failed to do so only because of the "customs" clause in the old PRTEU contract. That contract was now void and left management without any basis for continuing to resist the up-grading of Negroes to operators' jobs. Moreover, management would not have to worry about the reaction of the Transport Workers Union because that organization had repeatedly gone on record with public statements favoring full opportunities for all PTC employees, including Negroes. The company, however, refused to take the initiative in up-grading Negroes, arguing that if it took such action, TWU might think it was trying to undermine the union's prerogatives. This argument was also specious because under both the old contract and the one eventually negotiated with TWU, the selection of individual employees for advancement was a prerogative of management. Company officials were, however, able to persuade the FEPC office to let the Negro up-grading issue be settled during the contract negotiation with TWU.

During the period of negotiations, which lasted through June, the Transport Workers Union was urged to insist upon the insertion of a clause specifically barring any form of discrimination in hiring or up-grading in the new contract. This was not done. The TWU negotiators did arrange, however, to omit the old "customs" clause on which hiring and up-grading discriminations had formerly been based. TWU took the position that since the union stand in favor of non-discriminatory hiring and up-grading was a matter of public record, there was no need to insert a specific clause on this issue in the contract.

On July 1, 1944, the War Manpower Commission established employment ceilings and priority referrals which required most employers in essential war production to secure male, and, in some tight labor markets, female workers by referrals from the United States Employment Service or under arrangements made by USES. WMC stated that because of the manpower shortage no essential employer would be permitted to refuse any qualified employee because of race, color, creed or national origin. PTC management posted copies of this order in all its carbarns and work locations and stated that the company would comply with it. Notices also indicated that Negro employees of PTC would be given an opportunity to transfer to operating jobs before new colored applicants would be interviewed.

A frenzy of undercover activity by reactionary elements among PTC employees followed. Many meetings were held during the last three weeks of July, on and off company property, at which certain employees agitated in favor of a strike if the utilization of Negroes as operators was attempted. One of these meetings was called by the president of the former PRTEU at a company carbarn. This individual, who had been one of the bitterest opponents of Negro up-grading and of the TWU, urged the seventy-five employees in attendance to institute a work stoppage if Negroes were up-graded. His recommendation was that all white operators should report "sick" and stay "sick" until Negro operators were withdrawn. The chief organizer of the TWU was present and spoke strongly against the move proposed by the former PRTEU official. The meeting nevertheless voted in favor of the work stoppage plan.

Eight Negroes were selected by PTC management for training as street-car motormen and began their instruction during the last week of July. They operated school cars on the company's practice tracks at one of the carbarns and were scheduled to take cars out on the Philadelphia streets with instructors. Interviews with the trainees at this time indicated that their instruction was proceeding without incident and that all employees detailed to train them were co-operating fully. Both the union and the management said they did not expect any serious difficulty and estimated that at most 10 per cent of the white operators might attempt a temporary work stoppage.

Less than two hundred bitter men succeeded in organizing the strike which tied up all public transportation in Philadelphia for nearly a week. True to the threat made to management the night before, the work stoppage began when the 4:00 A.M. shift was scheduled to go on duty August 1, 1944. The time for commencing the strike was shrewdly chosen in light of the fact that street-car operation is at a minimum at that hour, and consequently, it was comparatively easy for the small group of leaders and their flying squads to persuade the few operators who came on duty to report sick. The choice of the street-car system as the first unit in which to engineer the stoppage was also well thought out. Street-cars are stored in carbarns and yards in long lines on a few tracks. In order to tie up street-car transportation it was only necessary for the strike leaders to persuade the men whose assigned cars were at the head of these lines to stop work. When these few cars failed to move out of the barn, it was virtually impossible for the operators who reported for work later to get their cars out. This maneuver could not have been successfully employed either on the bus lines or on the subway-elevated systems.

Bus drivers who took their early morning runs out were met at the starting points of their routes by flying squads who informed them that the street-car operators were reporting sick. Almost unanimously the drivers followed suit. The subway-elevated trains stayed in operation until almost noon. Even then the operators were willing to continue working but company officials shut off the power on the lines claiming they feared there might be violence if they did not do so.

The strike also spread quickly to the maintenance men. According to PTC officials, no mechanics appeared for work at its two trolley repair shops and six bus maintenance depots on August 1. The maintenance men, however, were back on the job on the following day and did not participate in the strike thereafter. This is significant in light of the fact that the maintenance department had the highest proportion of Negro workers in the PTC system and that this department also voted much more strongly for TWU in the bargaining election than did the transportation department.

The strike was immediately opposed by the Transport Workers Union and by all the federal agencies in Philadelphia. TWU officials, accompanied by army and navy officers, toured the various work locations during the first afternoon of the strike and tried to persuade the operators, on patriotic grounds, to return to duty. These appeals were met with jeers. The federal agencies involved issued statements on the first day of the strike pointing out its illegality and castigating its leaders. They also commenced a series of conferences which resulted in the presentation of a solid front against the strikers and culminated, two days later, in the seizure of the transit properties by the United States Army on an order from President Roosevelt.

The PTC management and board of directors refused to oppose the wildcat strikers despite tremendous pressure from civic groups and citizens of Philadelphia. Their one attempt to deal with the strike was made on the first morning. The director of industrial relations for the company appeared at a conference attended by representatives of the various federal agencies involved with a notice that had been mimeographed during the preceding night in which the company offered to rescind the War Manpower ruling on non-discriminatory hiring if the strikers would go back to work. Federal representatives told the company that it was free to post any notices it wanted but that the government would not support the proposed scheme to flout the War Manpower Commission's nation-wide order of July 1.

Except for one afternoon, management left its carbarns open before and during the strike and permitted employees to gather in them and, in some cases, even to hold strike meetings there. The one time when the barns were locked occurred on the second day of the strike, immediately after 200 TWU stewards had unanimously voted to make every effort they could to persuade employees to return to work. The barns stayed closed that afternoon and were open again the next morning.

The executive committee of the PTC board of directors was scheduled to hold its regular monthly meeting on the day the strike was precipitated. This committee was empowered to handle emergency questions and to make binding decisions. It had often held special meetings on matters far less pressing than a complete stoppage of transportation. On this occasion, however, the regularly scheduled meeting was canceled, and the executive committee did not convene until several days later, after the army had taken control of the property, and then only to issue a statement recognizing army control. No public statement condemning the strikers or urging them to return to work was made during the strike by any member of management or the board of directors.

Local political leaders, although subjected to as much public pressure as was management, likewise refused to make any effort to terminate the strike. Mayor Samuel and three other public officials were members of the Philadelphia Transportation Company's board of directors, appointed to represent the public interest. The mayor refused, however, to request a meeting of the PTC board of directors during the strike. His one known official act to deal with the strike occurred on the first day when he ordered all taverns and bars to close and also persuaded the governor to close all state liquor stores.

The most publicized leader of this wildcat strike was a subway motorman with over twenty years' seniority in the company who had long been the chief organizer for the Brotherhood of Railroad Trainmen among PTC employees and had never been a member of the PRTEU. The second most important leader of the strike was the last president of the PRTEU. Other strike leaders included various officers and members of the PRTEU and of both the Brotherhood and the Amalgamated. Three members of TWU who had been chosen by workers as stewards were also implicated. The strategy of the strike leaders was a blatant appeal to anti-Negro sentiment among the operators and a reiteration of the untruthful statement that the up-grading of Negroes would endanger the seniority of white operators including those on leave with the armed services.

During the month since TWU had won the bargaining election among PTC employees, the men who were now leading the strike had been working assiduously to create distrust of that union among the rank and file of the PTC operators. Since very few workers had actually read the contract negotiated by TWU, they were not in a position to know that the contract provided for the same departmental seniority that had become traditional in the PTC system. The distrust of TWU which had been developed by the divisive forces among PTC employees, plus the individual worker's unwillingness to be called a scab, was sufficient motivation to prolong the work stoppage for nearly a week after the leaders had successfully initiated it during the slack hours in the early morning of August 1.

On the first day of the strike TWU issued a statement charging that the work stoppage had been engineered by subversive groups and enemy agents. The union sent a telegram to Attorney General Biddle urging immediate investigation by the Department of Justice. The union also issued a statement refuting the strike leaders' claim that an issue of seniority was involved. Throughout the strike, TWU officials made strenuous efforts to line up union members behind a back-to-work movement. When these efforts proved fruitless, the TWU officials were among the first in Philadelphia to ask for army intervention and to welcome the army when it arrived.

Federal agencies, notably WLB, the Department of Justice, and the army, were unanimous in their stand that the War Manpower non-discriminatory hiring order would not be set aside. With one exception (the regional director of WPB) they also refused to regard the strike leaders as valid bargaining agents on this or any other issue. As a result of rapid moves on the part of these agencies, the PTC strike was referred to President Roosevelt on August 2, 1944. In the early evening of August 3, word reached the commanding general of the Third Service Command that the President, then in Pacific waters on a naval inspection trip, had signed a proclamation authorizing the army to take control of the transit company.

Within an hour after receipt of this notice, army officials formally took possession of the system and posted notices that the army would operate it "for purposes connected with the war emergency as long as needful or desirable." The army had decided, however, to attempt to resume operations without a strong show of military force. The plan was to use policemen or, if necessary, state militia to protect the transit properties and the operators who took out equipment. The police failed to supply sufficient personnel to act as guards for individual operators, and there was consequently no large-scale resumption of operations on August 4.

When the strikers' committee saw that the army was not displaying any real force, they took the position that the army summons to PTC workers to return to their jobs was not an order but a request. This stand by their leaders plus their fear of personal injury kept the strikers away from work for another day. The back-to-work movement which the army tried to initiate was likewise prevented by flying squads of strikers. According to General Hayes, who was in command of the Philadelphia situation, the strikers threatened injury to any workers who might take equipment into the streets.

From almost the beginning of the strike, Federal Bureau of Investigation operatives had been moving quietly among strikers and at strike meetings, gathering evidence for the attorney general. The day after the army had taken control of the transit company, FBI agents identified themselves at various strikers' meetings and informed those present of the penalties they might incur under the Smith-Connally Act if they continued to support the strike in the face of presidential seizure. On the evening of Saturday, August 5, when the strikers were still defying the army order to return to work, the four most publicized leaders were arrested on the basis of evidence gathered by the FBI.

On this same afternoon, the army had moved approximately 5,000 troops into Philadelphia to enforce its back-to-work order. These troops appeared with full battle equipment and were dispersed to the various work locations in sufficient numbers so that one or two soldiers could be sent out with every public transportation vehicle. In addition to these guard troops, several hundred soldiers with previous transit operating experience were gathered from various military camps east of the Mississippi River to operate the Philadelphia transit system if necessary. At 5:00 P.M. on August 5, a few hours before the four strike leaders were arrested, General Hayes announced an ultimatum that unless the strikers returned to work by Sunday midnight the army would take over the direct operation of the transit system, using its trained soldiers as operators. General Hayes invited all strikers to return to work on their regular shift, beginning at the deadline. He further stated that those who did not respond and failed to show a doctor's certificate of sickness would be dropped from PTC payrolls and would be unable to get jobs in any essential industry for the duration because they would not be given referrals by the War Manpower Commission. Such men were to receive no unemployment compensation and, if they were of draft age, were to be immediately classified 1-A and given physical examinations for immediate induction. General Hayes added that any strikers who continued to influence or coerce other workers into continuing the strike would be prosecuted under the Smith-Connally Act.

The army show of force and the support given the army ultimatum by the federal civilian agencies quickly broke the back of the strike. Before midnight of August 5, men had begun to form lines at the various work locations in order to take out their

regular shifts on the next day, a full twenty-four hours before
the deadline set by the army. On Monday, August 7, all transit
lines were again operating at full capacity, and the absentee rate
for that day was only about a quarter of what it had averaged for
the last several months preceding the strike. The army continued
to send fully uniformed and equipped soldier guards out with all
vehicles for several days after the strike ended. On August 17 the
transit system was turned back to the Philadelphia Transportation Company and the army withdrew from the city. Before the
military left, Negro trainees resumed their instruction.

Two days after the conclusion of the strike, PTC officials
finally signed the contract with TWU which had been approved
by the union membership on June 30. No explanation was offered
by company management, at least publicly, to account for this
long and unusual delay. This is especially noteworthy since it co-
incided with the enforced up-grading of Negroes and the strike
which resulted from the inadequate way in which this matter was
handled.

Bitter opposition to TWU was carried on by small minorities
within the body of PTC workers for some time after the conclusion of the strike. Under the terms of the union contract, members of TWU were entitled to withdraw from that union at any
time before midnight of August 23. Those who remained in the
union after that date were required to continue in it for the one-
year life of the contract. The die-hard opponents of TWU began
a strenuous campaign during this period in an effort to induce
PTC workers to withdraw from the union. Hundreds of small
cards were distributed among PTC workers around the middle
of August which read:

FRANKLIN TO ELEANOR

You kiss the niggers and I'll kiss the Jews
And we'll stay in the White House as long as we choose.

Accompanying these cards were forms, apparently drawn up by
a lawyer, signifying that the individuals who signed were with-
drawing from TWU.

On the last day before the deadline for withdrawal from the

union, three men who represented themselves as TWU stewards attempted to present what they claimed to be over a thousand withdrawal cards at the union headquarters. TWU officials denied that any of these three men were members of their union and said that one of them had been a delegate in the old PRTEU. TWU also said the number of withdrawal cards was smaller than the three claimed and that many of them were duplicates. Observers felt, however, that TWU was greatly weakened by loss of members, and its subsequent loss of an election to secure a check-off supported this assertion.

At an election of officers held by TWU on October 11, however, the number of votes cast was about the same as the number by which TWU had originally been chosen as the bargaining agent for PTC employees. This vote would seem to indicate that by this time TWU actually had more members than at the time of the bargaining election. It is also significant that the union members elected a Negro to one of the four vice-presidencies of the local union.

Another aftermath of the Philadelphia Transportation Company strike was an investigation by a federal grand jury which resulted in the indictment of thirty PTC operators on the charge of violating the Smith-Connally anti-strike statute. The grand jury did not find any evidence of conspiracy involving men of public importance, although the federal judge who charged them intimated that such conspiracy might exist and might be connected with the impending national election.

On March 12, 1945, twenty-seven defendants who pleaded no defense in the PTC strike were fined $100 each in a federal court in Philadelphia. According to the March 13, 1945, edition of The Philadelphia Record, Judge George A. Welsh, before whom the case was tried, expressed amazement that no outcry had been made by the company for public or government interference during the strike. The defense counsel repeatedly referred to "sinister influences" and characterized the strike as follows: "It was so well planned—and I say this with the utmost respect for my clients—that not one of these men in this courtroom today had the mental capacity to formulate such perfection of plans as was accomplished."

A WEST COAST VARIATION

Rivalry between labor unions and intervention by management in the selection of a bargaining agent for employees complicated the matter of up-grading Negroes in the Los Angeles transit system, as they did in Philadelphia. In Los Angeles, however, the relationship between company management and the official bargaining agent of the employees was apparently not as closely knit as in Philadelphia. The bargaining agent for the Los Angeles Railway employees, the A. F. of L. Amalgamated Association of Street and Electric Railway and Motor Coach Employees of America, has a clause in its national charter barring discrimination. The Los Angeles local could not, therefore, take an official stand against the up-grading of Negroes, nor could it and management quote a catch-all clause in a bargaining agreement, as did the Philadelphia Rapid Transit Employees' Union. Some of the top leaders of the Los Angeles local, nevertheless, did agitate against the up-grading of Negro employees and thus hampered and delayed the ultimately successful efforts of local and federal agencies to accomplish this up-grading.

Another important factor in the background of the Los Angeles transit situation was that since 1942 Los Angeles street-cars and busses had been grossly overcrowded and service had been inadequate. This critical situation in public transportation created an insistent and vociferous public demand that the company make full use of the skills of its employees and that it hire any qualified individuals who were available, regardless of race, creed, color or national origin. In the face of this demand, however, the company maintained its discriminatory hiring and up-grading policy until ordered by a federal agency to desist from such practices.

Until late 1941 the employees of the Los Angeles Railway Corporation were organized in an unaffiliated local union. At that time both the Amalgamated and TWU began active organization campaigns among the workers. Observers who were on the scene report that at the height of this campaign management representatives unilaterally prepared a new contract providing for a closed-shop for the Amalgamated. Although the exact nature of any such maneuver cannot be established, this much is known: there was no bargaining election in which workers had a chance to select their own union.

This alleged intervention by management aroused some immediate bitterness among employees and led to hard feelings between local A. F. of L. and CIO union members, feelings which were to have repercussions during the efforts to secure operating jobs for Negro employees. The circumstances surrounding the selection of the A. F. of L. union as the bargaining agent for Los Angeles Railway Corporation employees also led to accusations that the local officials of this union thereafter "played ball" with the management of the corporation.

Efforts were made by Negro employees of the Los Angeles Railway Corporation as early as 1936 to obtain up-grading, not only to operators' jobs, but also to levels in the maintenance department from which they were excluded. By the fall of 1942, the Negro community began to press vigorously for the use of colored workers as platform operators. The president of the Amalgamated local in Los Angeles at that time was apparently thoroughly in favor of equal opportunities for Negroes in the traction company and willing to take the lead in driving for this goal. He sent a telegram to the Labor Conciliation Service in Washington stating that public transportation in Los Angeles was currently curtailed because of lack of manpower and charging LARY with discriminating against members of his union on account of their race by refusing to promote them to better jobs. He pointed out that this action was contrary to national policy and appealed for an investigation.

Since FEPC had no Los Angeles office in 1942, the agency requested the Minority Groups representative of the Los Angeles War Manpower Commission office to take action to enforce Executive Order 8802. At an early meeting called by WMC, management predicted there would be serious repercussions among employees and patrons if Negroes were up-graded. The president of the union and the business agent of the mechanics' division of the union took the position that no serious difficulties would develop. The business agent for the bus and street-car operators opposed his fellow union officers and sided with management against the up-grading of Negroes.

When the president of LARY was informed that FEPC would probably issue a directive to the company, he asked for time to prepare a statement. Three days later, he stated that the company would employ Negroes in all its divisions and would up-grade them to skilled jobs. The company proceeded immediately to interview Negro applicants for operators' jobs and to plan for the up-grading of qualified colored personnel in the maintenance division.

In February, 1943, the War Manpower Commission in Los Angeles reported to FEPC that some union members had signed a petition objecting to the training of Negro platform operators and that the business agent for all operating employees was in sympathy with this attitude. FEPC was requested to ask the international president of Amalgamated to use his influence with the Los Angeles local to support the non-discriminatory national policy of the union. Two days later, the War Manpower Commission in Los Angeles made a direct appeal to the international officers of the union.

This request for help received immediate attention. First Vice-President Edward McMorrow wired the War Manpower Commission in Los Angeles that he had requested the international representative in California to intervene immediately in the local situation. He also indicated that wires had been sent to local union officials advising them that opposition to Negroes' training and up-grading was contrary to union laws and government policy. Shortly after this action, a statement prepared by the union was posted on all company bulletin boards quoting from Executive Order 8802 and stating that LARY and Amalgamated had been informed that this order banning discrimination applied to local public transportation. The training of Negro operators was then begun.

The Los Angeles Railway Corporation up-graded two Negroes at a bus station to the position of mechanics' helpers in February, 1943. Eighty white workers at this station thereupon suspended all operation for two hours. At the end of this time the company supervisor ordered the Negro workers back to their former jobs, whereupon the white workers resumed operations. A few days later another effort was made to up-grade three Negro employees from the cleaning force to mechanical classification jobs, and it was followed by a similar work stoppage.

Meanwhile, FEPC sent a telegram to LARY urging the company not to be intimidated by work stoppages but to proceed promptly with the program of up-grading qualified Negroes. The wire advised the company to call upon union officials to correct any refusal of employees to work and suggested that, if this measure failed, management should request the Regional War Labor Board for a conciliator to take jurisdiction in the matter.

In subsequent discussions, union officials were unable to give assurance that they could prevent a walkout if additional attempts were made to up-grade Negroes. They felt, on the contrary, that a partial work stoppage would result. Management stated that the company was willing to go ahead anyhow provided one or several government agencies would assume responsibility for the consequences, and it referred the case to the Regional War Labor Board in San Francisco. The War Labor Board indicated that the case was being referred to the Labor Department Conciliation Service which, the board stated, had to take action before the WLB would assume jurisdiction. Apparently both the War Labor Board and the Labor Department Conciliation Service were reluctant to be drawn into this controversy or to take a stand on the issue of up-grading Negroes; no action was taken on the referral by either of these federal agencies.

In the spring of 1943, management announced that the problem of labor turnover was so great that it planned to join with the union in requesting an upward revision of hourly wage rates, hoping that this step would stop the flood of resignations and attract new employees to the transit company. When FEPC learned of the proposed request for a wage increase, it suggested to WLB that any modification of existing contract terms approved by WLB be made conditional upon acceptance by the union and the company of a non-discriminatory hiring policy wholly in conformity with Executive Order 8802.

WLB agreed that the discriminatory employment practices of LARY had a bearing on the wage issue and requested that FEPC appear at the hearings to give evidence on the employment situation at LARY and to make appropriate recommendations. FEPC made the requested statement at the hearings. Its comments were interpreted by the counsel for Amalgamated as indicating that the FEPC opposed wage increases for LARY employees. Such an attitude was denied by FEPC. The incident nevertheless created a lingering distrust of FEPC among both local and international officials of Amalgamated and increased the difficulties of achieving Negro up-grading in the Los Angeles transit company.

Subsequently, the War Labor Board granted certain wage increases, but nothing was said about making these increases contingent upon the acceptance by the company and the employees of a non-discriminatory hiring policy such as FEPC had recommended.

During all these months of negotiations the service of LARY street-cars and Los Angeles Motor Coach Company busses had been steadily deteriorating. An official summary of LARY operations as of January 1, 1944, indicated that whereas 800 street-cars should have been operated at peak periods, only 493 were actually in use. LARY and its associate, the Los Angeles Motor Coach Company, were at that time operating regularly only 212 busses while 144 stood idle through lack of operators and maintenance personnel.

With the deterioration of public transportation, pressure increased for a solution of the transportation crisis. Resolutions and demands from organizations began to appear in ever increasing numbers and with greater and greater insistence. On December 31, 1943, the city government of Los Angeles intervened directly in the transit situation when an official spokesman indicated that the mayor felt that the use of members of minority groups as motormen, bus operators and conductors should be encouraged in the interest of improved public transportation and amicable race relations.

In February, 1944, the Central Labor Council (A. F. of L.) at a regular session adopted a resolution pointing out that public transportation was a bottleneck which seriously threatened the war effort, that it had become necessary for the War Manpower Commission to grant LARY number one priority in recruitment of workers, that LARY refused to utilize all possible manpower, and that the Central Labor Council thereby put itself on record as urging LARY to utilize all available manpower regardless of race or color. This resolution was important because it meant that the top A. F. of L. body in the region was putting the Amalgamated on the spot. The transit company was put in an even worse position by this resolution because, assuming that Amalgamated members would abide by the edict of the A. F. of L. council, the resolution meant that LARY stood alone in its refusal to up-grade Negroes.

On March 7, 1944, the Los Angeles council of the CIO officially applied pressure in the LARY case when it petitioned the Southern California manpower director to revoke the manpower priority which LARY had enjoyed since early November, 1943. The council demanded that LARY be denied referral and recruitment services of the United States Employment Service until such time as the company made proper use of existing manpower in the Los Angeles area. The council took the position that there was a sufficient number of available men and women in the Los Angeles area to make up the deficiency in LARY operating personnel if the company would cease to discriminate against certain groups. The council's letter to the WMC director charged that CIO members were losing time in war plants because of poor public transportation.

By this time FEPC had decided to begin arrangements for a public hearing. At a conference between FEPC, members of the executive committee of Amalgamated and top LARY officials, the union representative expressed resentment against FEPC and WMC activities in the LARY situation, particularly against the intervention of FEPC at the War Labor Board wage hearing in September of 1943. The attorney for LARY intimated that the CIO wanted to undermine Amalgamated and take over LARY employees. (It is notable that the first gun in this particular barrage was fired, not by CIO, but by the A. F. of L. Central Labor Council on February 28, 1944. The first CIO blast came on March 7.) No progress was made at this meeting because neither management nor union agreed to take any initiative in the matter of up-grading Negroes.

In a few days, the Los Angeles CIO council issued its second blast, a three-page resolution concerning the state of public transportation in Los Angeles. The resolution charged that LARY made a greater profit by over-crowding an inadequate number of street-cars and busses than it would by giving full service and that this was one of the main reasons for its refusal to hire all available manpower to operate its rolling stock. The resolution charged the company with falsification in alleging that the white members of the A. F. of L. union would not work with minority people and in support of this contention pointed to the Central Labor Council resolution of February 28 in which the A. F. of L. condemned the discriminatory hiring policies of LARY. It denied that the CIO was attempting to take over the employees of LARY, declaring that the CIO "does not now nor will not in the future entertain any intention of doing organizational work among LARY employees."

When the mayor learned that FEPC had scheduled a public hearing on the LARY case, he appointed a Committee of Six to develop a definite educational program to be conducted among the rank and file of LARY employees and the community. This committee consisted of one representative from each of the following agencies: the mayor's office, the Office of Defense Transportation, War Manpower Commission, Fair Employment Practice Committee, Los Angeles Railway Corporation and the Amalgamated union.

The Committee of Six held its first meeting on April 11. The framework within which it operated was a general agreement among interested parties that Negroes were to be up-graded by LARY. They agreed that their task was to devise ways and means to do this as promptly as possible and to plan an educational program for the purpose of preventing any untoward events from occurring as a result of the change in LARY employment policy.

While city officials were attempting to effect a local solution, pressure was applied on FEPC to persuade that federal agency to lessen its insistence that management hire and up-grade Negroes. An official of the Los Angeles Chamber of Commerce and a member of the local Bureau of Public Utilities separately urged

FEPC not to compel LARY to employ minority groups. Both these individuals felt that the effect of such a move would be merely to force the company's hand and might result in work stoppages. They likewise agreed that the approach should be gradual and that particular efforts should be made to secure acceptance for Negro operators before any attempt to force their up-grading was made.

At the request of city hall, the date of the FEPC hearing on the case was not publicized so that the Mayor's Committee of Six could handle the matter locally. The Los Angeles representative of FEPC and the mayor's office worked out an ambitious program for the union meeting scheduled for April 28. Labor relations officers for both the army and navy agreed to speak and so did three famous movie actors and actresses. War Department films were obtained to be shown at the meeting. The speeches of the motion picture people were professionally written and all pointed out the need for democracy at home as an essential feature of waging a democratic war. These speeches were submitted to union people the day before the scheduled meeting, and the latter succeeded in emasculating the speeches by removing any reference to the race question and eliminating the Hollywood people from the program. As a result of the union leaders' attitude, the main point of the program, the integration of Negro workers into operating jobs on the local transit company, was not directly mentioned at any of the three meetings which were attended by a total of 1,500 LARY employees.

The situation deteriorated rapidly. This was due in part to the fact that the union began negotiating a new contract with LARY in early May, and relationships between the union and management became very strained during this period. Around the middle of the month, the Amalgamated published a threat to strike and applied to NLRB for a strike vote because the company had not begun contract negotiations on May 15, as agreed. Negotiations had commenced by May 20, but by this time there was so much mutual suspicion between union officials and management that neither side would co-operate with the other in seeking a constructive solution of the Negro up-grading question.

The local union first promised to take a strong position forcing the employment of Negro operators; then it bluntly refused to co-operate further in this program. International officers of the Amalgamated accused FEPC of not acting in good faith in the LARY situation. They objected to FEPC's effort in September of 1943 to make a wage increase at LARY dependent upon the full utilization of Negroes. They also charged that it was unfair for FEPC to attack discriminatory practices of the Los Angeles Amalgamated local while nothing was being done about identical practices of the Brotherhood of Railroad Trainmen on another transportation line in the Los Angeles area. These A. F. of L. officials further charged collusion between government agencies and the CIO in Los Angeles for the purpose of embarrassing the Amalgamated. On this occasion, the international Amalgamated officials refused to take any further action in the Los Angeles situation. They stated that in their opinion the Los Angeles local would not obey a directive from the international, from FEPC, or even from the President of the United States.

In the midst of this discouraging impasse, and after more than a year and a half of fruitless negotiations, the FEPC conducted a public hearing on the LARY case on August 8, 1944. Early in the hearing testimony by an employee of the United States Employment Service indicated that well qualified Negro applicants referred to LARY by USES had been refused operators' jobs by the company and had been told it was contrary to company policy to hire Negroes in that capacity. The area director for the War Manpower Commission testified that LARY had been given hiring priority from November 8, 1943, until May 24, 1944. He indicated that the priority rating was removed because WMC was convinced that LARY was not employing all qualified labor available in the local market.

Management freely admitted that it had refused to hire Negroes for platform service or to up-grade them to mechanics' jobs. The only defense offered for the company's discriminatory policy was the allegation that, with very few exceptions, employees would refuse to work with Negroes. It was alleged that this was a "circumstance entirely beyond company control." Management testified that LARY believed that any unilateral effort on its part to conduct education among employees would have been destructive rather than constructive.

The Los Angeles local of the Amalgamated union was represented at the hearings by its president. He said: "Our position is in accordance with our constitution and by-laws of the international association. Our union does not discriminate against race, creed, or color." He testified that before the up-grading attempt in February, 1943, the union had held stewards' meetings and membership meetings at which the President's Executive Order 8802 was discussed and at which it was stated that Negroes would be up-graded. He also indicated that when the work stoppage occurred, the business agent for that particular department "got on the benches that day and begged them to go ahead and work."

During the hearing both management and union representatives intimated that a federal directive would have to be issued before Negroes would be hired as operators or up-graded to jobs for which they were qualified. In a conference with FEPC following the hearings, both management and union officials asked that a directive be issued immediately and stated their belief that the up-grading of Negroes could be successfully accomplished if the attempt was based on a definite order from the federal government. As a result of the hearings and of this conference, FEPC did issue a directive to LARY, ordering the company to desist from its discriminatory hiring and up-grading policy. At the same time, FEPC recommended to WMC that it restore to LARY the manpower priority which had been cancelled on March 24, 1944.

The willingness of the company and of the union to accept a government directive, and the orderly integration of Negroes into platform jobs in Los Angeles which ensued, must be attributed in considerable measure to the determined federal handling of the wildcat strike on a similar issue in Philadelphia. This strike had been broken only two days before the Los Angeles public hearings were held. While the effect of the Philadelphia affair on the Los Angeles situation cannot be accurately determined, it seems clear that management and union officials as well as the rank and file of transit workers in Los Angeles were convinced by the determined federal handling of the Philadelphia strike that further resistance against the up-grading of Negroes in Los Angeles was useless.

The first Negro operator began training on August 23, 1944. He and two colored conductorettes were instructed by the chief superintendent of one of LARY's carbarns. All relationships were reported as cordial and the trainees were greeted by other operators with the traditional clanging of bells. By August 30, fifteen Negro operators were running street-cars in Los Angeles under supervision. Some of these Negroes operated out of the shop where walkouts had occurred when up-grading was attempted in February, 1943.

Only one white employee quit over the issue of Negro up-grading. Employee turnover at LARY did not increase with the up-grading of Negroes. There was no effort to develop organized opposition to the new hiring policy. Both union officials and management seemed to act in good faith to facilitate the up-grading of Negroes, once the federal government had demonstrated its insistence on the policy of non-discrimination. By September 14, the new Negro operators were running cars without supervision on the streets of Los Angeles.

CHICAGO'S SUCCESS STORIES

Before Negroes were finally employed as operators by the three traction companies in Chicago in 1943, the colored population of that city had long resented its inability to obtain equal job opportunities in this field. Unorganized efforts were made as early as 1931 to secure transit employment for Negroes. These efforts slowly gained support and organization when the drive was adopted by local branches of the NAACP, the Civil Liberties Committee, the Urban League, and the National Negro Congress. Their efforts, starting slowly at first, culminated in an organized drive which began in the summer of 1943 and was reinforced when the President's Committee on Fair Employment Practice opened a Chicago office in September, 1943.

In the early 1940's, the Chicago city council passed an ordinance concerning the regulation and unification of the city's public transportation systems. During consideration of this ordinance, testimony was taken concerning discrimination against Negroes in the hiring policies of the three existing companies, and a clause favoring equal hiring opportunities for individuals of all races, creeds, and colors was incorporated into the unification ordinance.

Shortly after the hearings, telegrams were sent to the chairman of FEPC, calling his attention to the discriminatory hiring policies of the Chicago transportation system. These telegrams indicated that transportation service was poor because of manpower shortages and that this fact impeded war production in the Chicago area. The telegrams argued that since public transportation was vital to war production, the public transportation companies properly came under FEPC jurisdiction and urged that the committee plan immediate steps to enforce the President's Executive Order 8802.

The pressure of civic groups for equal employment opportunities on the Chicago Surface Lines continued and intensified during the summer of 1943. In August, local Negro groups staged a series of meetings and demonstrations as a part of their drive to have transit lines in Chicago employ Negroes. A Sunday late in the month was designated as "Jobs for Negroes on the Street-Cars Day" and additional mass meetings were held on this occasion.

Shortly after the middle of September, by which time the local FEPC office was in actual operation, the regional director of that agency informed the general manager of the Chicago Surface Lines of the complaints that had been received about the discriminatory hiring policy of the company. A meeting was arranged for September 23 between FEPC and high officials of the Surface Lines. At this meeting, the general manager of the Chicago Surface Lines stated that his company had no policy of discrimination because of race, creed, color, or national origin. He admitted, however, that no Negroes had ever been employed on the Surface Lines as street-car conductors or motormen. He also stated that this matter had been under consideration since he had recently joined the management of the Chicago Surface Lines and that it had been considered by other officials of the company prior to his coming. He stated that the company was at that time studying the whole question and hoped to arrive at a feasible solution.

The general manager of the Surface Lines had experience in the employment of Negro platform operators since he came to Chicago from the Detroit transit system where a large number of colored workers had been hired successfully in such capacities for several years. He asserted, however, that initiation of non-discriminatory employment in Chicago would be more difficult than it had been either in Detroit or in New York, giving as his reason the fact that in Chicago the transit lines were owned by private companies, whereas in both Detroit and New York they were municipally owned and operated under civil service. His specific fears of the Chicago situation were that the public would react unfavorably to the employment of Negro street-car operators and that the white operators might occasion an interruption in services unless Negro employment was handled very carefully.

Management saw another difficulty in the way of up-grading Negroes in the growing frequency with which Negro car riders were attacking white operators. It argued that this tension would increase the white operators' resentment against the up-grading of Negroes, and it felt that something had to be done about that problem before Negroes could be employed as operators. FEPC rejoined by suggesting that as soon as Negroes felt there was a chance for them to be employed as street-car operators, there would be a tendency toward the reduction or elimination of these violent incidents.

On October 5, 1943, management stated: "The Chicago Surface Lines, in the normal course of business, will accept applications from Negroes for the positions of trainmen and feels that as the problem is worked out by patience and understanding ever-increasing opportunities for such employment will be afforded." Meanwhile the Chicago Surface Lines had apparently been training a Negro candidate as a conductor. On October 21, the same day management indicated to FEPC that the Surface Lines definitely would employ Negro platform men, the first colored conductor went on regular duty. Chicago newspapers carried a story based on a news release from the Chicago Surface Lines, indicating that Negroes with proper physical and mental qualifications stood an even chance with white men in getting platform jobs on the street-cars. The stories further stated that Negroes under forty-five years of age who were employed would be considered permanent employees and would not be subject to dismissal at the conclusion of the war. By July 26, 1944, the Chicago Surface Lines employed 128 Negroes as platform men, and it reported that their work was entirely satisfactory and that there had been no difficulties in putting Negroes on platform jobs.

The integration of Negro operators on the Chicago Surface Lines was thus successfully carried out without delay, apparently primarily on the initiative of management and without special educational efforts to prepare white employees to accept the innovation. It is to be noted, however, that the local officials of the A. F. of L. Amalgamated union greatly facilitated this move by their ready acceptance of it and their firm stand in its favor. The president of the Amalgamated local informed FEPC that there had been absolutely no problem resulting from the employment of Negroes on the street-car lines of Chicago. He said the whole operation had worked out extremely well and that relations between white and colored workers were harmonious.

Although there had been a little opposition to the idea in the beginning, which took the form of a few men declaring they did not wish to go out of the barn with a Negro as the other half of a two-man car crew, the union president said that he made it a point to talk personally with these men and that they finally accepted the innovation without causing any real trouble. Despite efforts to bring up the subject as an issue at a union meeting prior to the introduction of Negroes, the union president refused to discuss the matter and took the position that everyone has a right to work regardless of his color and that this right is not a debatable issue in the Amalgamated union. He said that from that point on, any opposition which may have existed in the union vanished completely.

When the discussion turned to the difficulties which local unions elsewhere in the country had experienced in integrating Negro members on a non-discriminatory basis, the local president stated that the problem was predominantly one of union leadership. He said trouble was bound to result where union leadership was weak or indefinite on this issue.

As a result of negotiations between management and FEPC, plans were developed for the up-grading of Negro workers on the Chicago Rapid Transit lines. On December 8, 1943, management informed FEPC that eleven Negroes had successfully passed their physical and mental examinations and had been instructed as trainmen on the elevated lines. By July 18, 1944, twenty-three Negroes who had been up-graded from porters were working as regular and extra trainmen on the elevated lines. The company reported that their services were satisfactory and that the Negro operators had been accepted by their fellow-workers. Management explained: "We attribute this to the fact that all of them have been in the employ of the company in other capacities prior to their taking trainmen's jobs and were familiar with the railroad and its operation, acquainted with members of the organization, and also familiar with the objective all employees have of giving full service to the public."

By the end of October, FEPC was informed by the Chicago Motor Coach Company that five Negroes had entered its school of instruction; in December, ten Negroes were working as bus drivers. Management stated: "We are pleased to advise you that our experience with Negro drivers has been very satisfactory from the company's as well as the public's standpoint. We plan to employ a few additional Negroes as drivers in the near future." By July 25, 1944, the bus company was employing thirty Negro drivers in addition to seventy-seven other Negro employees in its shops and garages. Negro employees of the bus company on that date totaled about 11 per cent of its personnel. This figure was above the average of Negro job holders in Chicago industry and slightly larger than the proportion of Negroes in the city's population.

The operating vice-president of the Motor Coach Company was interviewed in the fall of 1944 concerning the company's experience with Negro operators. He stated that there had never been any discrimination against Negroes in the Motor Coach Company during the twenty-odd years he had been connected with it. He said that Negroes had been used in all levels of work, skilled and unskilled. For many years Negroes had worked as shipping clerks, painters, and mechanics and some of them received higher wages than those paid to white bus drivers. He further said that the company would have used Negro bus drivers long before but that no Negroes had ever applied for such jobs until the summer of 1943. When the company was approached by a group of Negroes at that time, they were told that Negro applications for bus drivers' jobs would be treated the same as any others. This official said that most of the colored applicants for bus drivers' jobs were newcomers but that some were old employees. He said no efforts were made by the management to educate white bus drivers to train or accept Negroes. The company just put the Negroes on and "nothing happened."

One of the most striking things to be learned from the experiences of Chicago, Philadelphia, and Los Angeles is that there is no appreciable public antagonism to the employment of Negro platform workers. In both Philadelphia and Los Angeles, management and union officials claimed that the public would refuse to accept Negro street-car and bus operators. When the innovation was tried in these cities, however, there were no protests. Apparently little or no notice was taken of the change in Los Angeles, for a newspaperman there reported that his paper had not received a single communication from the public either for or against Negro operators after they were put on the cars. In Philadelphia, there was wide public demand from civic and church organizations as well as from individual citizens to give Negroes full employment opportunity on the transit system. Since Negroes have entered platform jobs in that city, there have been almost no unpleasant incidents between patrons and colored operators. In Chicago, where management feared public reaction to Negro platform operators, the employment of colored operators occasioned a brief flurry of laudatory newspaper publicity.

A comparison of the ease and success with which Negroes were integrated into platform jobs in Chicago, as contrasted with the difficulties which developed in Philadelphia and Los Angeles, strongly suggests that the attitude of positive leadership, exhibited by management in Chicago, is the most fundamental requirement for the successful accomplishment of Negro up-grading in the traction, or any other industry.

So far as the union situation is concerned, the Chicago case suggests that the introduction of Negroes into platform jobs can be much more readily accomplished if the union is a strong one whose officers and members mutually respect and trust one another. In neither Philadelphia nor Los Angeles, by contrast, were the unions as strong nor was the leadership completely trusted by the rank and file. The Philadelphia situation was particularly bad because of the long history of murky labor relations which had taught a great many employees to distrust their supposed leaders. The Philadelphia situation was further complicated by the fact that the Transport Workers Union was new on the scene and was still being bitterly opposed by all the men who had traditionally been the labor leaders among the employees. In Los Angeles the union leadership was under suspicion by a great many of its members because of the suggestion of a deal between that leadership and management. In the Los Angeles situation, moreover, there was the disruptive influence of a union official who used the race issue to defeat his opponents and win power for himself.

The attitudes of management in Philadelphia and Los Angeles differed strikingly from those of the managers of the three transit systems in Chicago. In Philadelphia the buck-passing and refusal of management to take any constructive step prior to the War Manpower Commission order of July 1, 1944, appeared to indicate that it was strongly opposed to the up-grading of Negroes all through the negotiations. In Los Angeles the traction company management appeared to be neither so opposed to the up-grading of Negroes as in Philadelphia nor as willing to take positive action to accomplish this end as in Chicago. In Los Angeles, management did try once to up-grade several Negroes into new classifications in the maintenance department. No preparation was made prior to this move, however, and when a work stoppage occurred over the up-grading, the supervisory staff had no plan of action. Instead, management weakly surrendered its prerogatives of hiring and up-grading employees to the pressure of

prejudiced workers by backing down at the first show of resistance. Thereafter, management was in a poor position even if it
had been willing to assume further positive leadership in up-
grading Negro employees.

Public officials in Philadelphia and Los Angeles also reacted in
strikingly different ways to the problem of up-grading Negroes
in the respective transit systems. In Chicago, no action by public
officials was necessary because management in each case immediately accepted the suggestion of FEPC to utilize Negro operators as one way of combatting the manpower shortage.

In Philadelphia, Mayor Samuel, although subjected to almost
constant pressure from a large number of civic groups over a
period of two years, refused to exercise any leadership in the
situation or even to commit himself on the advisability of reliev-
ing the manpower shortage by employing Negroes as operators.
His failure to act is even harder to explain when we realize that
he and two other public officials under his control were members
of the Philadelphia Transportation Company's board of directors, appointed to serve the public interest. Mayor Bowron of
Los Angeles, on the other hand, made a real attempt to help
achieve the up-grading of Negroes in the local transportation
company. The shortage of manpower in Los Angeles' transit
system was much more acute than in Philadelphia and this fact
undoubtedly gave greater impetus to the Los Angeles mayor to
act.

Protracted negotiations and delays occurred both in Philadelphia and in Los Angeles after federal agencies interested themselves in the employment policies of the respective traction companies and before the up-grading of Negroes was accomplished.
These long delays appear to stem primarily from the fact that
while both sets of negotiations were going on, the life of FEPC
was hanging by a slender thread. Several changes in top personnel occurred, and the agency was subjected to repeated attacks by anti-administration congressional groups. FEPC, moreover, had no real power to enforce its orders short of official
intervention by the President of the United States.

One further point may be made regarding FEPC activity in
the Philadelphia case. The order regarding the up-grading of

Negroes, originally issued to the company and the unaffiliated union in November of 1943, directed the company to cease and desist from discriminatory employment and also to reconsider all applications it had received from Negroes for operators' jobs since June, 1941. The use of this date was the flimsy excuse on which the union, adamantly opposed to the up-grading of Negroes, charged that FEPC was trying to destroy the traditional departmental seniority under which PTC employees operated. The union claimed that FEPC was trying to install Negroes as operators and give them seniority back to June of 1941. Actually, the only reason this date was used in the FEPC order was that it was the date of President Roosevelt's original executive order against job discrimination. This fact was explained to the union representatives at the public hearing, but the explanation was couched in somewhat obscure terms. No representative of FEPC said in simple words: "The FEPC is not interested in the particular type of seniority which exists in this company and has neither the authority nor the wish to make any change in that seniority plan."

The same confusion over this matter occurred at the Smith Committee hearing in January, 1944, and again the opportunity to explain the matter in simple and direct words was missed. The failure of FEPC representatives to eliminate publicly and with extreme clarity the issue of seniority had grave consequences when the company attempted to up-grade Negroes to operators' jobs on August 1, 1944. That issue was probably the only one the leaders of the wildcat strike could have used to persuade the rank and file of employees to strike in time of war. And the seniority issue was sufficiently beclouded in Philadelphia so that strike leaders were able to use it to persuade men to go out on strike. It seems probable that even as late as July, 1944, the strike could have been prevented if people in authority had widely publicized the falsity of the seniority issue in Philadelphia.

The relation of federal agencies other than FEPC to the problem of Negro up-grading also warrants comment in the Philadelphia and Los Angeles cases. In Philadelphia the only other agency involved in the transit case prior to the strike was the War Manpower Commission. This agency and the United States

Employment Service, which was under the War Manpower Commission, appeared to have co-operated fully and effectively in Philadelphia from the very start of negotiations. It was during the Philadelphia strike, however, that all the federal agencies involved showed special effectiveness. In a situation that serious, hesitation and false steps can easily occur but are also exceptionally dangerous. In the Philadelphia strike situation, however, the action of all federal agencies was prompt and courageous so that a solid front was presented in opposition to the strike. The only exception to this occurred when the regional director of the War Production Board attempted to negotiate with the leaders of the wildcat strike. His activities in this direction were promptly stopped by the Washington headquarters of WPB.

In the Los Angeles case, the unanimity of the federal agencies is not so readily established. The early stages of that case were handled by the Minority Groups representative of the War Manpower Commission. This unit of WMC acted in accord with FEPC at all stages. The United States Employment Office in the region appeared to be reluctant, however, to follow the lead of FEPC and the Minority Groups Division of WMC during the early months of the negotiations.

At one point when the War Labor Board was hearing a request from the Amalgamated union in Los Angeles to raise wages, WLB suggested that FEPC appear at the hearing and urge that any increase in rates be made contingent upon the adoption of a fair employment and up-grading policy in the Los Angeles transit system. FEPC representatives did testify to this effect but the War Labor Board took no account of the recommendation when it granted wage increases. Later developments in the Los Angeles situation suggest that it may have been unwise for FEPC to have appeared at this hearing. During the later stages of negotiations, just before the FEPC public hearing, the union representatives in Los Angeles and also the international union officials in Detroit indicated they felt great distrust of FEPC because, as they saw it, FEPC had tried to prevent the Los Angeles streetcar and bus operators from securing wage increases.

Once the decision to up-grade Negroes was taken in the transit systems of the three cities under discussion, certain techniques were followed which merit brief discussion. In all the cases under examination, the first Negro employees in the new job were selected with extra care. This point is in agreement with the accepted good personnel procedure and the reason for it is easy to see. The individual members of any minority group who are occupying a new job category represent the entire minority group to other employees and to the public. It is of the greatest importance, consequently, that such individuals be particularly intelligent, efficient, and well-balanced. If they do their jobs well and get along easily with fellow workers and the public, it will soon become an easy matter to add other members of the minority group to the work staff, using the same means of selection that are used for all other employees.

In three cases under consideration, the new Negro operators were given routes which ran through good, white neighborhoods, at least during part of their run. In all cases, the first idea discussed was to put Negroes on cars which would operate only in Negro districts. After giving the matter a little thought, both management and unions agreed that an attempt to set up such limited service would be impracticable.

The traction companies here under examination were also unanimous in their findings that there was no necessity to send out all Negro crews on two-man cars. Such a practice would complicate the choice of routes which depends on seniority in most transit companies, and the move was consequently opposed by unions. It was found in almost all cases, moreover, that a Negro motorman and a white conductor, or a white motorman and a Negro conductor, team up just as well in street-cars as two white men do.

The outcome of the three cases shows conclusively that Negro operators can, and should, be treated simply as operators and that efforts to give them special handling or special routes are unnecessary and inadvisable.

CHAPTER XI

THE ROLE OF MANAGEMENT

MANAGEMENT of American industry has rarely faced the problem of racial employment in the framework of any well-conceived plan. Practices which had emerged prior to World War II created the concept of the black worker as an untrained, unskilled laborer. Even democratic public education, wedded as it had been in the field of vocational training to the concept of preparing workers for specific jobs in a contracting labor market, had hesitated to train Negroes for mechanical work. Labor unions had often reacted violently against a group of strikebreakers with a high degree of visibility; and certain craft unions, particularly in the metal trades, had a decided prejudice against colored artisans.

The racial employment patterns which occasioned and, in turn, resulted from these circumstances made employers extremely resistant to the use of Negroes in capacities which had not become traditional. And it was traditional to use Negro labor only in heavy, hot, and dirty occupations. Supervisory staffs and foremen rapidly absorbed the attitudes of top management, contributed their own prejudices, and often became an almost insurmountable barrier to the occupational advancement of minorities. These patterns of industry created vested interest in certain jobs and industries on the part of white workers, an attitude which became more pronounced during the extreme job competition of the depression.

Although the general practices of management in 1939 were unfavorable towards introducing minorities into new types of work, World War II has indicated how modifications in the color occupational patterns can be achieved. Three groups are the deciding factors: top policymaking management, the supervisors and foremen, and the workers in the plant. Of these the first, top management, is by far the most important. In instance after instance, it has been demonstrated that, when management has developed a comprehensive and definite plan for dealing with this problem, the desired results usually follow. It is, of course, not enough for management to have an *inclination* to use Negro labor; it must have a *conviction* and transmit that conviction to its supervisory officials, foremen and workers. The attitude of the supervisory staff is important because this staff can, by its co-operation or lack of it, do much to decide whether or not a given program succeeds. When supervisors realize that a part of their job is to make a given policy work, they generally devise means to achieve such results. Workers, organized or unorganized, are influenced by management's attitude.

Where there is a well-developed, strong labor organization, the active co-operation of the union is normally sought by management when a new source of labor supply is about to be hired. This is a natural approach in a company where industrial relations have matured to the point that employment policies are changed only after they have been the subject of discussions between labor and management. In other instances, where management is not in the habit of conferring with its workers on matters of labor policy, postponing action on employing Negroes until the workers agree to such a policy can hardly be more than an attempt on the part of management to shun its responsibility and delay action on what it considers a difficult problem. This does not mean that the hostility of white workers has ceased to exist or that exclusionist policies and practices of labor unions and unorganized workers are unimportant. It does mean, however, that in most instances (save under closed-shop agreements) management exercises the right to hire workers and must take the lead in introducing new employees. Unless and until this is done, it is impossible to establish the responsibility of the workers, organized or unorganized, for any restrictive hiring policies. And until such responsibility is established little can be done to influence the policies or practices of labor. There are, for example, scores of instances where unions have capitalized on management's hesitancy to face the issue and have hedged. Increasingly, however, as these cases were brought to light, government was able to secure action by responsible union officials. At the beginning of the defense effort, most new plants and a large proportion of established firms with war contracts did not have closed-shop or member maintenance agreements with unions. Consequently, the choice of employees was largely a determination of management.

The most prevalent reason given by management for hesitancy or refusal to use Negroes in the early phases of the war effort was that white and colored labor would not work together. There were, however, long-established employment patterns in American industry which refuted this opinion. The record of the iron and steel industry in both its northern and southern branches, certain northern and southern shipyards, some establishments in the automobile industry, the leading plants in the meat-packing industry, the tobacco industry, and a few other important branches of manufacturing showed that white and colored labor could and did work together. Subsequent developments further illustrated the possibilities in this field. During the second World War American industry introduced scores of thousands of colored workers into new establishments and occupations in aircraft, ordnance, machinery, electrical goods, rubber, and shipbuilding. The fact that aircraft, which started out with a pronounced and announced color prejudice, had by the end of 1944 hired some 100,000 Negroes shows that management's attitudes and policies do change under pressure and that management can successfully introduce and up-grade Negro workers.

There is a discussion of segregation in almost every analysis of Negro employment, and it is usually presented as though the matter of expanding the use of Negro labor were unrelated to problems of labor supply and production. In a war economy, the discussion should have been centered around possibilities of securing maximum output and fullest use of available labor supply. The latter, in turn, usually requires greatest flexibility in use of this labor supply and maximum up-grading on the basis of individual merit. In a post-war economy these same objectives will remain valid. When the question is viewed with these criteria in mind, it becomes clear that in many types of production, the objectives outlined above cannot be achieved through setting up

separate divisions, units, or occupations for Negroes. In a period
when labor supplies were drying up, plans should have been
made for the best possible use in the quickest possible time of
each available worker on the basis of *his* aptitudes and abilities.
In most tight labor markets these objectives could not be achieved
when trained workers were held back until a group of similarly
qualified persons of the same race could be assembled. Possible
difficulties incident to the introduction of Negro workers were,
in such instances, more than compensated for by the additional
productivity which would have resulted from immediate maximum use of workers regardless of their race.

There were several schools of thought relative to how rapidly
colored workers should be introduced. There were those who
felt that a few workers should be employed as a first step, the
experiment watched, and then, gradually, the numbers increased.
There were others who stated that there should be no preparation but that large-scale employment should begin at once. This
latter point of view does not stand up under the scrutiny of good
personnel policy. As regards the first point of view, it is clear
that had we not been at war and faced with an extreme shortage
of manpower, we probably could have afforded the luxury of
such a slow pace of utilizing an important source of manpower.
During a manpower crisis it was costly and foolish to accept
such tactics of delay.

The following elements are basic to any sound approach to
this problem. The necessity for securing full use of available
Negro labor should be faced by management and plans should be
drawn up for dealing with it. Racial patterns of employment
should be conceived of in terms of the economic factors involved.
Once a decision has been made, a plan should be developed to
minimize any possible resistances and, at the same time, facilitate
speedy action on the matter. Such a plan should go hand in hand
with a program of education. It has been wasteful in the war
emergency to delay action until the educational program has
been completed. In many instances we indulged in such waste;
our manpower difficulties after 1943 were accentuated by these
earlier practices.

In 1942 the American Management Association and the New

York State Committee on Discrimination in Employment issued pamphlets on the techniques of integrating Negroes into industry. In order not to duplicate what has already been said, we will concentrate upon actual case histories of selected firms which have dealt with this problem. The earlier discussion of local transit systems has already served to present some material on the subject.

In the spring of 1941 the president of the Lockheed-Vega Aircraft Corporation wrote to the Office of Production Management as follows: "In the matter of employment for Negroes, we are aware of the problems involved and are sympathetic with the aims of utilizing all available skills and aptitudes in furthering the defense program. Our industrial relations department is making an exhaustive study of this subject."

When, in August of that year, the company was ready to act, the secretary of the corporation addressed the following memorandum to all executives and supervisors:

"I am sending you herewith a copy of an executive order issued by President Franklin D. Roosevelt which we propose to post on the bulletin boards for the information of all employees. While Lockheed Aircraft Corporation and Vega Airplane Company have never had any discriminatory policies with regard to race, color or creed, it is, nevertheless, a fact that no Negroes are now in the employ of either company.

"After giving full consideration to this fact, the management of Lockheed and Vega have decided that, in line with their policy of co-operating fully with the federal government in the national defense program, special effort will be made immediately to comply with the request of the President and the Office of Production Management that 'plans for their [Negroes'] training and employment in capacities commensurate with their individual skills and aptitudes should be undertaken at once.'

"It is my earnest hope that the subject will not be made an issue for excessive discussion and I am sure that it will not become an issue if all employees in positions of authority lend their full interest to this program.

"When and where a member of the colored race is employed, it will be with full consideration of his personality, character, aptitudes and skill, so that he should be given full opportunity to adjust himself to his job and associates.

"If all supervisors do their part, I am sure that the problems involved in the employment of Negroes will be handled effectively."

The following fundamental principles underlay the approach of the corporation to this problem: (1) the company proceeded after it had developed a comprehensive plan for dealing with this matter; (2) management instilled a feeling of co-operation and a sense of responsibility for the success of the plan in all executives and supervisors; (3) management was positive and firm in its statement and approaches to the problem; (4) from the outset management was committed to a policy of selecting carefully the workers who were to pioneer the way for Negro employment.

On August 15, when the company had 41,000 persons on its payroll, it announced in its employees' paper, The Lockheed-Vega Star, that Negro workers were to be introduced. The article which made this announcement contained an extract from the memorandum cited above and a direct quotation from a similar communication addressed to Aeronautical Lodge No. 727, International Association of Machinists. Then, in accordance with management's plans, Negro workers were interviewed and employed.

Shortly after this employment started, the director of industrial relations addressed a letter to the writer in which he said: "You may be interested to know of the progress we have made in employing Negroes since our 'statement of policy' a few weeks ago. During the last few weeks we have employed thirty-one Negroes, twenty-two of whom have been placed on mechanical work in various departments of the factory, five on stockroom and parts handling work, and four on common labor. As you see, we do not practice segregation of Negroes, and I am happy to say that our supervisors and employees are entering into this program with a wholesome attitude."

The degree to which supervisors felt responsibility for the success of the corporation's program for Negro employment is reflected in an unsolicited report from an assistant foreman who stated:

"Several weeks ago we received a Negro in this department. He is proving to be very satisfactory as a learner riveter and bucker on the swing shift, and most of the fellows are showing him 100 per cent co-operation. A few of the employees from the South may feel a little resentment toward his being among them but there has been no outward expression of such feelings.

"It is my opinion that regardless of color, Vega employees think and act mainly in terms of Americanism.

"As there will no doubt be more Negroes coming into this department, I thought perhaps you would welcome the knowledge that everything is going well with them and the old employees."

The success of the program was greatly enhanced by the development of good public relations. Thus, in the November 21, 1941, issue of The Lockheed-Vega Star, a Negro employee whose picture appeared had an article entitled "Color is No Bar to Employment at Lockheed and Vega." In that same issue of the paper, there was a picture and an article concerning the visit of Joe Louis to the Lockheed plant at the time that the hundredth Negro was employed.

By February, 1942, Lockheed-Vega employed more than 300 Negroes. Colored workers were used in various capacities, many of them on sub-assembly lines. In March, the director of industrial relations spoke at the twenty-first anniversary celebration of the Los Angeles Urban League. At that time he made a forthright statement of his company's policy relative to the employment of Negroes and again contributed toward the establishment of sound public relations between the Lockheed-Vega Corporation and the Negro community.

In the June 26, 1942, issue of The Lockheed-Vega Star, there appeared an article entitled, "Adherence to United States Employment Policy Restated." The article reviewed the company's earlier statements on Negro employment and concluded with a paragraph emphasizing the need for using local labor wherever possible regardless of sex. During the month of June, the first Negro woman was appointed as a production worker and on the third day of her employment received a promotion. As of August 28, 1942, the Lockheed Aircraft Corporation employed 400 Negroes, of whom approximately fifty were women. Vega Airplane Company employed 202 colored workers at that time. By the end of 1942 Lockheed and Vega employed over 1,000 Negro men and women as technical clerical, skilled, semi-skilled, and unskilled workers, and on March 31, 1943, there were over 2,500 colored workers in the two plants. In the summer of 1944, Negroes made up 5 per cent of the total employees at Lockheed-Vega.

The situation at the Douglas Aircraft plants in California presented the element of resentment of Negro employees by white workers. An extremely well-qualified Negro had been in the engineering department for years, and early in 1941 the company hired three Negro machinists. It was then that difficulties arose. Management, however, refused to release the colored workers and met the problem successfully by shifting them around in the plant.

During the early winter there was a gradual increase in Negro employment, and by February of 1942, sixty colored workers were on the payroll. At that time, the company stated that it would use Negro women on production, and in June the first colored female assemblers were employed. As the company was continuing to increase materially its Negro employees, the president issued the following statement: "No discrimination among employees of the company will be permitted in matters of place of work, character of work, wages, promotions, classifications, or other conditions of employment because of race, relationship, or political affiliation or any affiliation with, or membership in any union or labor organization." The public relations department of the company asserted that the statement was issued in the interest of production with the least possible interruption and maximum efficiency.

By the fall of 1942, there were 779 Negro workers on the company's payroll; 413 of these were men and 366 were women. Of the men, 377 were on production jobs while 297 of the women were so employed. By the close of 1942, the California plants of the Douglas Aircraft Company employed approximately 1,800

Negroes at all occupational levels. In the summer of 1944 Negroes were 4.5 per cent of the total labor force of Douglas Aircraft in California.

At the beginning of the defense program the New Jersey plants of the Western Electric Company did not hire Negroes. When management decided to change this practice, it determined that care should be taken to establish early occupational patterns which would permit widespread employment of Negroes. As a labor supply problem, it was clear that unless several categories of work were opened to colored applicants, it would be difficult, if not impossible, to make maximum use of this source of labor. Accordingly, the first group of colored workers included a stenographer, four electrical testers, an elevator operator, a janitor, a window washer, and three female light factory production workers. The company also requested colored machinists, detail instrument makers, screw machine operators, and electricians.

As soon as job opportunities were opened, many unskilled Negro applicants appeared. Management expressed its fear that its unskilled workers might soon outnumber its colored skilled employees. It was felt that should such results occur early in the program of introducing Negro labor, they would tend to establish a pattern which might well limit the occupational opportunities and numerical employment of Negroes.

Six months after the hiring of the first colored workers, it was obvious that the Western Electric Company, which then employed fifty-eight Negroes, had not accomplished much on the quantitative front. Management recognized this but felt that the then current use of Negroes in fifteen occupations and the inclusion of twenty-three colored women offered a sound base upon which to expand. Already the assignment of colored women in the personnel office had done much to establish in the minds of white workers the fact that the company was committed to a policy of non-discrimination in employment. The Western Electric plants in New Jersey reported that there were 326 colored persons on their payroll in September, 1942. Of these, 224 women were engaged in twenty-one occupations, the majority of which were skilled and semi-skilled production jobs. Negro men were used in nineteen occupations. The plants were training Negroes for new occupations. Only eighteen Negroes had left the company. Of these, one was fired, four secured military leave, and thirteen resigned. This low rate of turnover was due, in large part (as in the success of the program), to the careful selection of workers. The personnel office had recognized that Negroes—as all other workers—differ and that only by applying criteria for selection of Negroes impartially and objectively could it hope to secure desirable workers. The employment of Negroes continued at the New Jersey plants of the Western Electric Company. In October, 1942, there were 800 Negro men and women in these establishments; by 1944 the number had increased to about 3,000.

No doubt the experience of the Western Electric Company in New Jersey was useful to its plants in Baltimore. As of January, 1942, the Maryland establishments hired only ten unskilled Negroes; nine months later the number of Negroes in the plants had increased to 600 men and women who were engaged in a variety of occupations.

In commenting upon their experience in the summer of 1942, management observed that the plants did not discriminate, and all qualified applicants had opportunity for employment; Negroes were employed in semi-skilled and unskilled capacities; Negroes and whites were doing similar types of work and there was no segregation; white workers had presented no serious objections, and it was customary to see Negro and white men and women working together.

This had been accomplished in response to economic needs in the city of Baltimore, where Negroes are usually segregated in public places, and where, prior to the defense effort, colored labor had not been hired for production work except in heavy industry. But the experiment was not without difficulties. In the summer of 1943, there was agitation in the plants relative to the joint use of toilet facilities by Negroes and whites. It resulted in a work stoppage which occasioned hearings before the WLB, and that agency refused to "order any change in the company's present policy of providing common facilities for white and Negro employees in the plants . . . involved."

Following this ruling, the United Electrical, Radio and Machine Workers, CIO, began an intensive organization campaign. It initiated a broad program of education relative to the realities of race relations by means of a comic strip in its official paper, The Western Electric News. The strip was entitled, "There are No Master Races," and it presented the most advanced scientific thinking about race in an attractive form.

The P. R. Mallory Company is located in Indianapolis, Indiana. As late as January, 1942, this firm employed its first colored worker, a janitor. It had in its employ at that time over 1,500 workers, of whom 40 per cent were women, and there was a bargaining agreement with the United Electrical, Radio and Machine Workers union. Early action on the employment of colored workers was delayed because, under union agreement, some 150 displaced female workers had priority on employment. Obviously, this agreement had to be respected, and it would have been a mistake to use the occasion of introducing Negroes as a means of abrogating seniority rights of former employees. By the spring of 1942, the displaced workers had been absorbed and hundreds of new employees had been added. Only a few Negroes were then hired and those on the payroll were classified as janitors and maids.

A program for hiring Negroes was carefully worked out by the company and representatives of government. Five Negro men and one Negro woman were first employed for house service work. The company then planned to employ additional colored men and women for a variety of jobs throughout the plant; they were to be carefully selected on the basis of their competitive qualifications. Great care was used in the selection of Negro workers in order to secure desirable individuals and, thus, encourage the co-operation of older employees with the company's program for Negro employment. Acceptance for colored production workers was encouraged by management's decision to use Negroes in the front office. Also, management decided to place a letter on the bulletin board indicating its new policy and the reasons for it.

In September, 1942, the firm employed twenty-seven Negroes in the following classifications: one male baromatic machine operator, three male and three female inspectors, six male steel storeroom workers, one male tumbling machine operator, eight male and one female service workers, one female record clerk, one female clerk, one male mechanical designer, and one male electrical engineer. The director of personnel stated that his company was continuing its program of expansion in the employment of Negro workers and that there had been no difficulties as a result of the integration of Negro workers throughout the plant. He felt that its program for the employment of Negro workers had been made possible by the acquisition of individuals of outstanding ability. By March, 1943, the number of Negro employees was 125; eight were skilled, eighteen semi-skilled, sixty-five unskilled, and thirty clerical, technical and miscellaneous. In 1945 the plant hired several hundred additional Negro women.

In January of 1942, the RCA factory in Indianapolis employed approximately 2,900 workers, of whom 1,400 were women on light assembly. There was only one Negro in the plant, and he was a janitor employed by the athletic association. The International Brotherhood of Electrical Workers, A. F. of L., represented the workers in the plant. The local production manager stated that in accordance with company policy, the Indianapolis plant would begin to hire colored workers in the near future. It was feared that the union might object to such a development, however, and a conference was arranged between government, management, and labor. The international representative of the union was invited to attend and did so. He affirmed management's fears but agreed to the union's responsibilities in the matter although he stated that the white workers might walk out on an unofficial strike if colored persons were hired.

After objections of both labor and management had been overcome in an extensive discussion, a plan was developed for introducing Negroes into the RCA Indianapolis plant. The production manager promised to send a letter, similar to the one issued by Lockheed, to all foremen and supervisory personnel, pointing out that the firm would abide by Executive Order 8802 and give employment to Negro workers. A similar letter was to be addressed to the international representative of the union. This letter was scheduled to be presented to a meeting of the day shift on January 20 and the night shift on January 27. (It was suggested that the plant be closed down for one shift so that a combination meeting might be held. This was decided against on two grounds: the loss of a day's work and pay would not dispose the white workers kindly toward the subject of the meeting which had occasioned an economic loss to them, and calling a special meeting would give undue importance to the question.)

Following these preliminary steps, government representatives agreed to address a letter to the international representative of the union indicating that the company had given commitments for the employment of Negro workers. This letter would state further that the union was expected to abide by Executive Order 8802. Then, management and the union were to work out a program for the integration of Negro workers, and the union was expected to develop an educational program for its members.

Management, however, expressed some fear that even if the co-operation of the union were secured, a problem might arise due to the refusal of individual white workers to work with Negroes or even use the same sanitary and other facilities. It felt that this was more of a problem with women than with men. Management had not, however, sent the letters to foremen and supervisors, and such action was again urged. A meeting was arranged between government, labor, and management. At this meeting, it was disclosed that the employees had voted to give the executive board of the union authority to deal with all matters relating to the employment of Negroes except two. The union had voted in favor of segregation of Negroes in the use of sanitary and eating facilities in the plant, and it had withheld from the executive board any authority to deal with the matter of segregation of Negroes.

It was decided that the first Negroes employed were to be messengers. This was justified on the ground that messengers, not being confined to one department or section and having many contacts with workers in other departments, could break down the resistance of white workers to Negro employees; and that, since messengers come under the supervision of the administrative office, interference by plant employees with such workers could be more easily controlled than in the case of workers assigned to a department or section of the plant.

As for segregated facilities, it was decided that whatever form of segregation might be agreed upon was to be considered as a concession to the expressed will of the white workers for the purpose of achieving the introduction of Negroes. It was anticipated that as soon as Negro workers had been accepted by white employees, segregation would not be necessary and the pattern initially established would be gradually dispensed with.

On February 16, two Negro messengers were employed and management sent out the statement to supervisors and foremen. By late summer of 1942, the RCA plant in Indianapolis was in the process of integrating Negro workers. Colored men and women were, according to management, scattered throughout the plant in production and in office work. Colored women were employed as secretaries and clerks, and a Negro man was in the shipping and receiving department. In March, 1943, the plant hired 182 Negroes: eighteen were skilled, ninety-nine semi-skilled, twenty-nine unskilled, and thirty-six clerical, technical and miscellaneous.

The company continued gradually to place Negro workers throughout the factory. On one occasion when two Negro girls were introduced into a new department, several supervisors resisted this move and threatened to resign but the personnel office stood its ground and the supervisors became reconciled to the new development. (This illustrates that the education of supervisory officials is a continuing process in which the announcements of company policy and employees' responsibility are but first steps.) The personnel manager of this plant appeared before personnel men in Indianapolis and discussed the employment of Negro workers in war industries. He made these significant observations:

"Industry is finding . . . that it is more profitable to up-grade Negro janitors to semi-skilled or skilled jobs than to train white workers from outside the plant. Likewise it is more profitable to use the unemployed Negroes of the community than to import white workers from other cities. Gradually we are becoming aware that the production demands of this war can be met only by skills and by manpower—recruited, trained, up-graded, and fully utilized regardless of race, creed, color, nationality, sex, or age. . . .

"The demonstrated success of Negro employment and, beyond that, the social needs of the nation indicate the need for a program of action on the part of personnel management. My recommendations would be these: Survey the skills of Negroes now employed; find out what they can do, what they want to do; train, up-grade, and promote them. Survey the Negro population in each community for skills, trained or potential, and hire and train these men and women before seeking white labor elsewhere. Help educate against racial discrimination on all fronts—government, housing, schools, entertainment, vocational training, and in the plant. Enlist the co-operation of civic, educational, and business leaders in the community to plan for a long-time program."

The effect of foremen education and feeling of responsibility for the success of Negro employment is illustrated by two additional cases. On Long Island, New York, there was a plant employing about 300 workers engaged in war production. When a Negro janitor was up-graded and placed on a machine, a large number of white employees threatened to quit. An assistant foreman assembled the disgruntled workers at lunchtime and made a short speech which was quoted in the press. "You see that bridge over there and these docks?" he asked. "Who do you think is guarding them? And who is guarding all of the vital areas in New York? *Negro soldiers!* Do you kick about that? No! Then why in hell have you got so much nerve as to walk out when a Negro is put on a machine the same as you are? He can't help it if his skin ain't white. But, by God, he's an American citizen and if Negroes are good enough to guard this city and keep you safe, then Negroes are good enough to work and earn a living the same as you men."

The next morning, every worker returned to his machine and the abortive strike was ended.

A Negro worker at the Denver Ordnance Plant tells this story of his induction into production work: "The plant was just opening up, and they hired ten of us in the first hundred men.

Before we went into the shops the first day, they broke the whole bunch up into gangs and put at least one Negro into each crew. Then as each crew stepped into the plant for the first time, each foreman made a short speech, saying: 'It is the policy of the Remington Arms Corporation and the United States Government not to discriminate against any worker because of his race, religion, or color. And this company expects each worker in its employ to abide by its policy.' There were a number of white boys from the South, and I was afraid something might happen. But nothing did. And we've been working side by side ever since."

Bad practices of up-grading and introducing minorities have been all too common in the industrial history of the nation; during World War II they were more prevalent than ever before because economic necessity and government pressure forced the entrance of Negroes into new occupations and industries. Such employment was contrary to past practices and inconsistent with most employers' concept of the Negro's place in industry; consequently, many managements were hesitant and needlessly apprehensive. Below are a few case histories which illustrate some bad techniques in handling the introduction or up-grading of Negro workers.

At a General Motors plant in up-state New York, 180 Negroes were employed in non-defense work in 1942. When the plant was converted to war production, the question of up-grading these workers in accordance with the six-point agreement between management, labor and government was raised. Management decided to take action. It selected about fifty of its Negro employees and sent all of them to the heat-treating room—about seventeen or eighteen on each of the three shifts. As soon as this happened a rumor circulated that the white workers employed in the heat-treating department were either to be discharged or transferred elsewhere in order that the department could be an all-Negro division. This caused resentment among the white employees, who issued a petition saying that they did not want to be replaced by Negroes. The petition went to management and a copy went to the local UAW-CIO union. Fortunately, the union involved had a definite policy and, by the spring of 1942, an accumulation of experience with regard to the up-grading of colored workers. Officials of the union went to the white workers and explained the dangers to organized labor in such action. The white workers in the heat-treating department prepared a second petition stating that they not only wanted Negros in that department but in every other department within the plant—as long as no one who had a job was displaced in the process.

Management then moved most of the Negroes out of the heat-treating department. The employment director stated that he was anxious to up-grade the Negro porters but did not know quite how to go about it. A government representative then suggested that each colored worker who felt that he was capable of doing other than service work be given a chance to request a transfer to the section of the plant in which he felt he would best fit, and in the case of workers seeking production work but having no training or experience, there be temporary assignment to learners' jobs. Such workers would be given the same training and employment opportunities as white trainees.

This program was followed. Many of the 180 old Negro employees were up-graded, and a larger number of new colored workers were employed. Colored workers were no longer restricted to service jobs and their presence was generally accepted. Had there not been immediate educational and remedial action on the part of the union at the time when Negro up-grading was concentrated in one department, the resentment of white workers would have increased. In such a situation the hasty, misdirected action of management would have delayed any possible program for full use of labor and, in the end, restricted production.

In the fall of 1941, there was a strike at the Curtiss-Wright aircraft plant in Columbus, Ohio. According to press accounts, the cause of the work stoppage was the assignment of a Negro to one of the more highly skilled production divisions. There was no recognized bargaining agency for the workers although an industrial union was in the process of organizing the plant. About 75 Negroes were employed, nine of whom were on production work. Management stated that it intended to carry out the President's executive order with respect to employment without discrimination as to race, creed, color, or national origin.

In this case, a thorough investigation disclosed that management had, wittingly or unwittingly, introduced the issue of Negro up-grading at a time when relations with the union were most unsatisfactory, that management had failed to set forth its policy in this regard, and that the Negro issue had not been the chief cause of the walkout although there had been some misunderstanding incident to the method used to introduce Negro workers. At the same time, certain union officials, in an effort to organize workers, had capitalized on the racial question and used it as an issue to bring workers to drastic action.

There were the seeds of a prolonged conflict and great impediments to the full use of Negro labor in this situation. Fortunately, the disputing parties were brought together, and the international union moved its representative who had accentuated the race issue. A settlement was soon reached. It provided for the return of the men to work, agreement by the company to post the proper notices, and (in accordance with union demands) carry out the terms of the non-discrimination policy literally—including the employment of Negroes in all departments of the company, office and engineering as well as production and service. The employee representatives (only a part of whom were union men) agreed to these points and went back to their departments to explain this situation to the workers. Other grievances were adjusted at the same time and the employment of Negroes progressed. By 1944 several thousand colored men and women were working at many levels of skill throughout the plant.

There was a well-established firm located in the center of machine-tool production in Cleveland, Ohio. It had never used Negro labor, although for the last twenty-five years there have been many thousands of Negroes in the city. Other local industries—especially the foundries—used colored workers in all capacities.

When the employment of colored workers was first discussed, management was none too enthusiastic, stating that its labor force was static. Production records and hirings soon disproved this assertion, and management then stated that it would discuss the matter with the employees' association. Later it reported that the association was opposed to the move and suggested that a letter be addressed to the association. Such a letter was prepared and dispatched in the fall of 1941. The president of the association replied indicating that it was a social and a benefit organization as well as an employees' representative for "bargaining with the company under the Wagner Act." The club further stated: "If the company wants new men now and then we have friends, relatives and connections, some on WPA yet, that we are duty bound to look out for and are qualified. Bringing in Negroes to fill up vacancies has been opposed by most of the members, because they think it would damage the social program of the club, and that helps keep the good feeling and morale in plant. Also, they think that close contact at work would cause discontent and dissatisfaction using the same washrooms and other facilities." The association had no objection to the employment of Negroes in a separate division.

A conference was arranged between management and the officials of the employees' association. During the discussion a government representative pointed out that employment in a defense plant was not the sole right of connections of present employees, that such attitudes as the association expressed were extremely dangerous in a democracy, and that sooner or later labor scarcity would force the admittance of Negroes. The nature of the product and its methods of fabrication made separate production units impractical, and the general racial pattern of mixture in schools and other public places made such a proposal entirely unacceptable to Negroes. Management, with the detachment of a parent who shakes his head at a bad child while indulging it, agreed with these arguments but indicated that it was helpless in influencing the "independent" union.

The degree of this helplessness soon became apparent. In the early part of 1942, management signed a contract with its employees' association which contained a clause providing that the "independent" union should be consulted before any change in hiring policy was undertaken. In light of the stated policy of the association, it was obvious what the position of that body would be when the question of Negro employment was again raised.

In this case management had, with the active support of the

association, attempted to postpone the "evil" day when it would have to employ colored workers. It is doubtful if the day can be postponed indefinitely. In this company, management had encouraged, by its evasive actions in the past, an attitude on the part of its white workers that they and their "connections" had a vested interest in the available jobs and that the employees' association was above and beyond announced government policy.

One of the methods used by management in dealing with the problem of introducing Negro workers has been the employment of Negro personnel men. Unfortunately, historically and emotionally such appointments are associated with the Negro welfare officers of the first World War. As rural Negro workers from the South were inducted into industry, certain plants added Negro social workers to their payrolls. The duties of these employees were to look after the welfare of colored workers and to assist them in their process of urbanization. More than occasionally they sold to Negroes a feeling of personal gratitude to the employer and an anti-union bias. Thus, they have become associated with welfare programs, anti-unionism and company paternalism.

Since the Negro personnel man is their lineal descendant in the minds of many, it is important to realize the psychological handicaps which surround such an appointee. It is also important to emphasize that the older type of welfare worker is passé today. If the notion of wet-nursing colored workers to a goal of paternalism is the object of such an appointment, it is the worst possible means from the point of view of establishing good relations between Negro and white workers. At the same time, if such an appointee is assigned to the task of keeping Negro workers "happy" and "satisfied," without having authority or will to influence employment opportunities or working conditions affecting Negroes, he will lose the respect of colored workers.

There is certainly a job which a Negro personnel man can do. In plants where management has had no experience with the introduction of colored workers and in instances where large numbers of colored workers are to be inducted over a short period of time, the appointment of a Negro in the personnel office has proved to be most helpful. The degree of success has varied directly with the caliber of the man and the support which management has given him. It would be a mistake to create such a position in every plant where colored persons are about to be introduced or up-graded. Where there are no special problems foreseen, the very appointment of a specialist might in itself create problems. If the existing personnel department is capable and resourceful, often there is no reason for having such an official assigned to deal with Negro employment.

If a special personnel man is selected to work on problems incident to Negro employment, he must have authority as well as responsibility. His job must be clearly defined, but usually it is not defined at all. *His should not be a separate employment office but rather an integrated office which sees that the operations branches in the personnel office function in accordance with company policies.* He should be in a position to open new and better jobs for Negroes and to adjust, through channels, valid grievances of workers. He should see that the methods and procedures of selecting colored personnel are sound and fair. He should participate in separation interviews. He can serve as a counselor and assist in the development of recruitment programs. If he can do these things, he can secure the co-operation and respect of colored and white workers. Unless he does these things, he cannot have such confidence and respect and is, in the long run, of no real usefulness.

Out of the experience in integrating Negro labor in World War II, management has learned much. Applying accepted personnel standards it has, in many instances, arrived at sound and effective approaches to this problem. The American Management Association has captured and collected material on this subject. It has summarized management experience and opinion on the employment and integration of the Negro. Some of its most important conclusions are as follows:

"Negroes *can* and *have* been trained for occupations requiring all levels of skill, as the lists of jobs on which colored men and women are now working indicate. These lists combine the data especially prepared for AMA by employers with plants located throughout the country.

"The first requisite in the program of Negro integration is a firm declaration of company policy. This will sound the keynote for the attempt to enlist the co-operation and support of supervisors, union officials, and the workers in the ranks.

"The way has to be paved solidly for the introduction of the first colored recruits into the plant. Supervision must be 'sold' on the idea. This can be best accomplished by means of conferences and discussions which provide an opportunity for 'clearing the air.' In all these meetings, bias must be parried with facts, not with emotion.

"To the personnel executive often falls the task of presenting the case for Negro employment to management. Personnel men now know there is as much danger in *not* dealing with the problem of the Negro worker as there is in dealing with it ineptly.

"Both the CIO and the A. F. of L. are officially committed to the policy of non-discrimination. While a number of affiliates of both these organizations have violated the official stand of the parent bodies, there is much evidence of union co-operation and initiative in securing a wider and more fruitful use of colored labor.

"The interpretation of management's policy of non-discrimination to labor is the responsibility of supervisors and foremen. How well they do this will determine the receptiveness of the white workers to the introduction of the Negroes. With the first colored employees rests the greatest responsibility for setting the standards for the group. Their attitude and productivity will influence their number and the types of jobs to which they will be assigned.

"Successful integration of colored workers is predicated on a planned program of selection, induction, training and up-grading. Intelligent use of the services of federal, state and local agencies as a source of selected Negro applicants and strategic placement of colored manpower in the plant will yield a substantial dollars-and-cents return to industry."

CHAPTER XII

RECENT EVENTS IN NEGRO UNION RELATIONSHIPS

THE SECOND World War and its manpower requirements forced the government to face the problem of securing full use of all available labor. One of the most difficult issues incident to this objective has been the employment of Negroes on contracts where there are closed-shop and other bargaining agreements with labor unions which have excluded Negoes from membership or otherwise limited their work opportunities. In its immediate incidence this problem does not necessarily involve the matter of Negro membership—the traditional hurdle facing colored workers in shops under the control of certain unions. It becomes clear, however, that, when clearance or auxiliary-union affiliation is arranged, the questions of membership status and full participation in unions are sure to become issues. These questions may be raised by the minority affected in its opposition to second-class membership and work permits (sometimes at first-class membership fees), or they may be initiated by white members who cannot see why a group of new workers should have union clearance at no cost or at reduced rates.

In a period of full employment and national programs to encourage men and women to enter defense industries, it was inevitable that there should be deep resentment against the payment of work-permit fees to organizations which will not extend full membership to the group affected. In the case of the Negro worker, opposition to special unions or to second-class union status is but a part of his effort to achieve full American citizenship rights.

In order to appreciate the nature of trends in Negro-union relationships during World War II, it is necessary to sketch briefly the background of the problem. The color line in certain

American labor unions is deeply intrenched. As early as 1834 the New Orleans Typographical Society forbade its members to work with free journeymen of color, and some international unions (principally in the metal trades and railroads) have denied admission to Negroes practically from their inception.

The National Labor Union was the first national federation of labor unions to deal with the race problem. At its initial session in 1866 it stated that the interests of labor demanded the inclusion of all workers without regard to race or nationality and that organization should be encouraged among colored people. Action, however, was postponed until the next session. At that meeting a committee on Negro labor reported that it was inexpedient to act on the matter. This recommendation was accepted, and the tradition of making liberal declarations and taking no action on Negro participation in labor unions was born. The 1869 convention admitted Negro delegates and disclaimed race discrimination by resolution. This, too, established a precedent, for the declaration or resolution was little more than a benevolent utterance with only moral force at its back; it could easily be disregarded or nullified by either a national or local union disinclined to organize Negroes.

The official attitude and actual practices of the American Federation of Labor and its affiliates relative to Negro workers have often been presented. The federation soon relaxed its early liberal policies and emphatic opposition to affiliates which excluded Negroes from membership by constitutional provisions and accepted a compromise which provided for the organization of Negroes into separate locals or their direct affiliation with federal unions in instances where they were refused admission to regular unions because of color. The A. F. of L. Executive Council is theoretically the international for federal locals which are thus attached directly to the headquarters of A. F. of L. and not to any of the internationals, where most of the power in the federation resides. But actually, it usually refers matters pertaining to these separate federal locals to the national union whose policies of exclusion or discrimination have made a federal local necessary. Negroes relegated to such locals have seldom had adequate grievance machinery, effective means of contract negotiation, or protection against the encroachment of white workers. Nor has the A. F. of L. Executive Council prevented strong national unions from absorbing federal locals and making them subordinate auxiliaries.

Until there were large government-financed programs of construction and war production, the principal issue raised by Negroes in the A. F. of L. was the right to membership—a question which constantly arose at the federation's annual conventions. When large-scale construction projects were initiated by PWA, Negro building trades craftsmen faced a new problem. Where there were separate Negro locals, colored men were usually denied clearance or referral to the public-financed projects. In other crafts, white unionists objected to the employment of Negroes, opposed their affiliation with the union, or discriminated against them within the organization. Government and labor cooperated in devising procedures to meet the situation. In some instances numerical increases in Negro union membership resulted; in others work permits and union clearance were arranged. In every instance the key to corrective action lay in the policies, practices, and controls established by the internationals and effected by union leadership on the local levels.

While these developments were creating a more realistic attitude on the part of Negro building trades craftsmen toward their unions, a new unionism, which ultimately blossomed forth as the CIO, arose among industrial workers. It departed from the dominant craft structure of the A. F. of L. and organized workers on an industrial basis. Following the practices of the Knights of Labor and the United Mine Workers of America, when they embarked on mass organizational campaigns, it afforded the Negro a chance for widespread participation. Negro workers embraced this opportunity in many areas and in large numbers.

At the outset the position and responsibility of unions in the matter of Negro employment and up-grading should be outlined. It is clear that a union is directly involved wherever closed-shop, union-shop, or any other type of bargaining agreement between management and a labor organization exists. The American Management Association has stated that, as the first tactic in counteracting union resistance to the employment or up-grading of Negroes, management must emphatically indicate that it regards its policy of non-discrimination as fixed. Once management announces its favorable policy toward accepting colored workers, the attitudes, policies, and actions of the union are extremely important. It is, of course, always possible for unions to take the initiative, as some of them have done. When a labor organization, acting in good faith, declares that it is in favor of full integration of Negro workers, discriminatory hiring policies cannot then be ascribed to union opposition. This is the one sure way for the union to establish its position clearly.

In the past, labor unions have impeded the employment of Negroes in the following ways: withholding membership from Negroes by means of constitutional provisions, by means of a provision of the ritual, or as an unwritten policy of the international or the local union; accepting Negro members but discriminating against them in referrals; hindering the up-grading of Negroes; championing the up-grading and employment of Negroes in plants in which the union has no bargaining agreements, while taking no action to correct discrimination in plants in which the union has an agreement.

Contrary to popular opinion, relatively few important unions outside the railroad industry have constitutional provisions barring Negroes from membership. The establishment of racial restrictions in rituals and the creation of Negro auxiliary unions are much more important factors in manufacturing industries. This follows because the International Association of Machinists has a ritual provision barring Negroes and the Brotherhood of Boilermakers, Iron Shipbuilders, Welders, and Helpers, which reported a similar bar against Negro membership, has provided for their organization in auxiliaries under the control of white locals. The influence of these two metal trades unions has grown, since they no longer restrict their jurisdiction to craftsmen and have often limited Negro employment not only in skilled but also in semi-skilled production work. Their wartime strength in shipbuilding and aircraft (where they have been, in effect, industrial unions during the war) gave them control over segments of the two largest defense industries. The exclusion of Negro workers, until late in 1942, at the Boeing Aircraft Company in Seattle, was due largely to the policy of the machinists' union; and the continuing difficulties at the Kaiser shipyards in California and Oregon have been occasioned by the local boilermakers, who stood first for occupational limitation and finally for the relegation of Negroes to auxiliary locals.

Negro auxiliary unions take varied forms in practice. A few are said to operate as separate locals with complete autonomy and direct lines to internationals. Such a situation is contrary to the terms under which they are established and rarely exists. Usually, Negroes in auxiliary locals do not control their own affairs, nor do they have effective means of influencing the general policy of the parent organization. Certainly, Negroes attached to such locals do not have first-class union membership. Often the auxiliaries are used as a means of limiting the number of colored workers, and in every instance they can be instrumental in depriving Negro workers of seniority rights. Negro auxiliary members complain that they do not benefit from grievance protection through the aggressive action of the supervising locals. (In the railroad industry, where auxiliaries have a long history, this is a long-standing complaint.) In the case of the numerically important Brotherhood of Boilermakers, Iron Shipbuilders, Welders, and Helpers, the second-class status of Negro workers in auxiliary unions has become increasingly controversial.

The pre-World War II situation in the A. F. of L. was summarized in a bulletin issued by the United States Department of Labor: "The race issue has presented difficult problems and has created serious situations from the beginning of the organized-labor movement. The American Federation of Labor has since its inception declared for the organization of all workers without regard to 'race, creed, color, or sex.' At the same time some of the most important and powerful organizations affiliated with the federation specify that applicants shall be white, others exclude orientals; still others admit Negroes but not on an equal footing or on the same terms as white workers. The American Federation of Labor has no control over the internal policies of its affiliated international organizations, hence cannot apply to them its own rules in this matter even though it admits the element of inconsistency in the situation."

The manpower requirements of war production and government's action to ban discrimination on defense contracts altered the responsibility of the A. F. of L. for policies and practices of its affiliated internationals. The position of the federation in demanding from government certain recognition and rights for all A. F. of L. unions implied a responsibility for securing compliance with federal policy. A part of this policy was the executive order which banned discrimination in war production. The action of President William Green in securing work permits and clearance for Negro machinists on the West Coast and the action of the Metal Trades Council in influencing the policies of the boilermakers in Portland, Oregon, indicated gradual acceptance of this responsibility by the A. F. of L.

The positions of the A. F. of L. during World War II can be summarized as follows: although on occasions the A. F. of L. actually interceded in effecting the clearance and employment of colored workers through its affiliates, it has since 1895 maintained the fiction that it is powerless to control the internal policies of its affiliated international organizations. Apparently, the actual situation was this: in response to economic and governmental pressures, the A. F. of L. has influenced the practices of internationals and secured clearance for Negroes. It has not, however, taken official cognizance of Negroes' membership status in affiliated internationals.

The Congress of Industrial Organizations, because of its structure, its mass-organization program, and the large participation of Negroes in it, has from its inception done a more effective job than the A. F. of L. in facilitating the employment of Negroes. But this is a relative statement. In many instances CIO unions have been slow to act. Opposition to the acceptance of Negro workers on the part of CIO unions has found its most striking expression in the work stoppages occasioned by the introduction of Negro workers into plants and occupations where they were formerly not used. National officers of the CIO have issued unequivocal statements on this matter, many of the international unions have specific constitutional provisions banning race discrimination, and an increasing number of internationals have established machinery for enforcing their announced policies. The stronger central authority in the CIO, the absence of constitutional or ritual bars to Negro membership, and the recent appointment of able Negroes to the executive board are facilitating the transmission of statements of policy down to the local levels. To implement its policies and facilitate their enforcement, the CIO established a National Committee to Abolish Racial Discrimination. This committee has a full-time, competent director and has established similar anti-discrimination committees in local, county, and state industrial union councils. By the end of 1944 there were eighty-five such local committtees.

The intrenched nature of the color line in certain segments of the labor movement makes it difficult to get at in an old and conservative organization such as the A. F. of L. On the other hand, the early blanket indorsement of all CIO unions by certain elements among Negroes often led to an uncritical attitude toward them. This, in turn, occasioned a policy of paying lip service to non-discrimination in certain unions. At times these activities developed into tactics of evasion. During the war, the pressure of public opinion and economic necessity forced many unions to deal with the matter of Negro employment and upgrading. In some instances the approach has been spontaneous and forthright; in other cases, it has been forced, hesitant, and half-hearted.

Local No. 1225 of the United Electrical, Radio, and Machine Workers of America, CIO, in New York City, established a Fair Employment Practice Committee and set up the following procedure: questionnaires on the status of minority-group employment were sent to all shops; the local referred Negroes, Jews, and persons of foreign extraction to all shops; if these persons were refused employment, the business agent investigated and reported to the committee; if management continued to discriminate, a meeting of the shop committee and the union's Fair Employment Practice Committee was called to pass a resolution against discrimination; after the resolution had been passed, the local sent a qualified worker of the race, color, or creed discriminated against to the plant in question; if this worker was refused employment, the case was sent to the President's Committee on Fair Employment Practice.

Other New York City locals followed this lead. Results were

soon forthcoming. In May, 1942, there were only 172 Negroes in forty-one selected electrical machinery plants in the city. By January, 1943, the number was over a thousand. In May, non-white workers constituted but 1 per cent of those employed; eight months later they made up 3.7 per cent of the total. For the nation as a whole the proportion of non-whites in electrical machinery increased, during the same period, from 1 to only 1.5 per cent.

The up-grading of Negro workers from janitorial to production jobs at the North American Aviation plant in California had been the occasion of many conferences. At first the union took little interest in the matter, but as manpower shortages became critical, organized labor pressed for Negro employment and up-grading. Management, however, stated that it hesitated to up-grade Negroes freely because of the possibly unfavorable reaction of the white workers. In order to supply the final impetus for action, a conference was arranged with Aircraft Division of local No. 887 of the UAW-CIO, which had a bargaining agreement with the plant. In February, 1942, the executive committee of this union addressed a letter to the company, requesting management to give colored persons in the plant equal consideration for production work and to publicize the above policy so that future Negro applicants would be fully informed. By the fall of 1943 the California North American plant hired about 2,000 Negroes—the majority of whom were women on production, and in the summer of 1944 Negroes constituted slightly over 7 per cent of those in the plant.

The most widely known and in many ways the most difficult problem involving Negro union relationships in the CIO arose in the conversion of the automobile industry in Michigan from civilian to defense production. Developments in the automobile industry are most instructive in that they illustrate the complicated interrelations between management and unions in expediting up-grading for Negroes in plants where there is intrenched opposition among a minority of white workers. At the outset, both management and labor were not inclined to face this problem and act, since it was clear that there would be difficulties. The constant pressure of Negro union members to secure the enforcement of constitutional provisions by the international made the union join government in urging management to act. When the employers did act, it became obvious that many of the local unions would not or could not control their members. Then management and labor slowly evolved a program of joint action. It was not until both were convinced that they had to face the problem that anything worthwhile was accomplished. The really effective action took place when management and labor simultaneously issued statements of policy and developed programs for disciplinary action.

Had there not been constitutional provisions in the CIO prohibiting discrimination, the Negro union members would have had less support in their demand for equal up-grading. Had there not been firm conviction on the part of both labor and management that the problem had to be solved, much more time would have been wasted in trying to establish which of them was responsible for the situation. When management took steps to upgrade Negroes, and white workers refused to work with them, it became clear that the responsibility for initiating corrective action lay with the union. The international and its officers had to face the problem of establishing machinery for facilitating and enforcing the policies of the organization. When these steps had all been taken, Negro workers won the right to up-grading—a right which theoretically had always been theirs. The Detroit experience of the UAW and the position of its president, R. J. Thomas, in his international and in the councils of the CIO did much to encourage the establishment by other CIO unions of workable machinery to deal with subsequent problems involving the employment and up-grading of Negroes during the war.

As the necessities of war production occasioned the up-grading and introduction of Negroes into many new occupations and plants, the number of walkouts of white workers in protest to the introduction of Negroes increased. There seemed to be a wave of such occurrences, and the Negro press characterized them as "hate strikes." Many of the plants involved had contracts with CIO unions. An example of an early instance is offered by developments in the Westinghouse plant at Essington, Pennsylvania. In January, 1942, a Negro was hired as a machine shop learner. His presence was strongly resented by white members of the United Electrical, Radio, and Machine Workers. Management promptly laid him off and reported that he had been threatened with bodily harm. Local No. 107 of the UERMW attempted to avoid the issue. Finally it reached the international. That body took a realistic view and stated that "it [securing the up-grading of Negroes] is primarily a question of getting our own members in some localities to meet the problem honestly and deal with it in accordance with the policy of the national organization." By June, 1942, district council No. 1 of the Philadelphia industrial area had drawn up and unanimously approved a program for facilitating and encouraging the employment and up-grading of colored workers.

In the spring of 1943 the epidemic of "hate strikes" hit the Middle West. Detroit seemed to have the largest number of cases, but the walkouts spread to near-by industrial Ohio and elsewhere. The United Steel Workers were involved at the Timken Roller Bearing Company in Canton, the UERMW at the Hoover Company in the same city, and the Industrial Union of Marine and Shipbuilding Workers in the Bethlehem shipyard at Sparrows Point, Maryland. In each of these instances and in a score of similar situations, the appropriate international either co-operated fully or took the initiative in enforcing its non-discrimination policy.

When, in the fall of 1943, it was alleged that a foreman of a government project refused to hire Negro workmen referred by a local of the International Union of Operating Engineers, A. F. of L., on the ground that a number of white workers had threatened to walk off the job if colored were employed, the organization reaffirmed its opposition to race discrimination. The foreman involved was informed by the local union that any operating engineer who carried out this threat would be replaced. The union's president reported to the President's Committee on Fair Employment Practice as follows: "I can assure you that our local unions are open to membership for those who qualify as operators . . . and our local unions have been instructed that discrimination against applicants because of race, creed, or color will not be tolerated."

In the San Francisco bay area of California there was much difficulty relative to the placement of Negro skilled and semi-skilled workers in the shipyards during the earlier years of the war. One of the established firms, the Moore Drydock and Ship-building Company, had used Negro mechanics during World War I and was ready to expand their use. Other yards would accept colored workers. These shipyards had closed-shop agree-ments with the boilermakers' union. Despite the fact that the international had modified its regulations and authorized the es-tablishment of Negro auxiliary lodges, the bay area lodges would not clear Negroes for employment.

In response to continuing pressure from government, the inter-national had assumed a degree of responsibility in the matter early in 1942, and jobs in many categories were opened to col-ored workers. Negro workers, however, were placed in an auxil-iary in accordance with the rules of the organization. At the close of 1942 that auxiliary had several thousand members; and by March, 1943, there were over 20,000 Negroes in the shipyards of the bay area. It has been repeatedly charged, however, that the number of Negro workers employed in the area has been limited by the actions of the boilermakers' union, and there has been dissatisfaction on the part of Negro shipyard workers on the West Coast with their second-class union status. In Los Angeles, for example, a Negro worker in the California Shipbuilding Cor-poration refused to pay dues to the auxiliary and announced that he intended to test the legal right of the union to insist upon his discharge while it refused to accept him as a full member.

Although Negroes object in general to their restriction to seg-regated unions, the issue in the boilermakers involved more than the relegation of Negroes to separate unions. In this case colored workers were restricted to auxiliaries which were subordinate to the main (white) lodges in the area. Thus, the Negro worker who was required under a closed-shop agreement to pay first-class dues for second-class membership claimed that he suffered from discrimination as defined in Executive Orders 8802 and 9346.

At the Kaiser yards in Portland, Oregon, a similar situation arose. It was the occasion of much negotiation and finally reached the Metal Trades Department of the A. F. of L. The president of the department dispatched a strongly worded telegram to the secretary of the Portland Metal Trades Council, stating that its action was contrary to sound judgment and patriotic duty, the President's executive order, and the declaration of the A. F. of L. and Metal Trades Department against racial discrimination. Later the president of the Metal Trades Council and the secretary-treasurer of the boilermakers' international joined government representatives in establishing the right of Negroes to work in all capacities in the Kaiser yards. Here again, however, auxiliary lodges were established, and Negroes immediately began to work to achieve first-class membership within the union.

The whole matter of membership status of colored workers in the boilermakers' union has been constantly challenged on the West Coast during World War II. Negro shipyard workers in the Portland area refused to pay union dues to the colored auxiliary and stated that if they were to continue to contribute toward the support of the organization they wanted full membership and the security and protection thereof. A large number of Negroes who refused to pay dues for membership in an auxiliary were discharged under the terms of the closed-shop agreement between the Kaiser yards and the union.

This matter and similar cases involving the boilermakers on the West Coast were referred to FEPC. They became the occasion for hearings and resulted in the committee's finding that the auxiliary unions were in violation of the executive orders banning discrimination. FEPC then issued directives to the union and to management instructing them to remove discriminatory conditions. In March, 1945, four of the five large shipyards cited by FEPC agreed to comply with the committee's directives. Accordingly, they promised to cease firing Negroes who refused to pay dues to separate auxiliary unions.

The traditional opposition of the International Association of Machinists to Negro membership inevitably limited the use of colored labor in war industries. Early in the defense program the international took the position that the Negro did not present a problem to the organization because there were so few skilled Negro machinists. As a matter of fact, of course, the exclusionist policy of the union was the largest single factor limiting the number of Negro machinists. When, however, the IAM assumed jurisdiction over semi-skilled production workers as well as craftsmen, large numbers of qualified Negro workers were affected by the union's restrictions.

At the Nashville plant of Vultee Aircraft Incorporated, at the Boeing Aircraft Company plants at Seattle and Wichita, and at several shipyards on the West Coast, local machinists' unions declared they could not clear or refer colored men to defense jobs because of the ritual provision banning non-white persons from membership. Then, in October, 1941, at the California hearings of the President's Committee on Fair Employment Practice, cases were presented alleging that local lodges No. 68 and No. 751 had refused to admit Negroes to membership or clear them for employment at the Bethlehem shipyard in San Francisco and the Boeing Aircraft plant in Seattle. These cases were referred by the committee to President Roosevelt. He, in turn, discussed them with President Green of the A. F. of L., who conferred with Harvey Brown, president of the IAM, urging him to act upon the complaint "quickly and decisively." The effect of this action was to establish the precedent of issuing work permits to Negroes by these lodges of the machinists' union. Other local lodges on the West Coast followed a similar procedure.

One of the problems encountered under the work-permit system was the matter of fees. The original agreement with the Boeing local in Seattle provided for the issuance of thirty-day renewable work permits. These cost $3.50, and the annual fee for Negro non-members thus cleared was $42.00. Full members, however, paid only $25.00 initiation fee and $1.50 dues per month. This meant that members paid $43.00 the first year and $18.00 per annum thereafter; Negroes on permits would continue to pay $42.00 per annum. Naturally, the colored workers objected to this arrangement. It was reported that an adjustment had been made whereby Negroes who work on permits paid $3.50 for the first twelve months, and thereafter $1.50 per month.

Following the pattern on the West Coast, Negroes have been cleared by the IAM in other sections of the nation, principally in aircraft plants. But the most significant development in the IAM occurred in Cleveland. In March, 1943, local lodge No. 54 accepted Negro employees at the Warner and Swasey plant into full membership, apparently with the tacit approval of the international. In connection with this development, Peter Gencope, organizing chairman of the shop committee of the plant, stated to colored workers: "I am reminded that no matter where you go, if you have your union card with you then you will be recognized as a member of the machinist lodge No. 54. . . . There will be no separate meetings of white and Negro. You will sit in our regular meetings, with full voice and voting rights. . . ."

These developments in the boilermakers' and machinists' unions indicate that the internationals can take effective action to facilitate clearance of Negro workers. They also show that, when sufficient pressure of public opinion, government persuasion, and economic necessity are exerted, these organizations will take such action.

There are two principal developments which are responsible for these events: the manpower requirements of war production and the shift of the machinists' and boilermakers' unions from a craft to an industrial basis. The first of these occasioned the breakdown of skills, the concentration of war workers in single-skilled and semi-skilled jobs, and government's policy of non-discrimination in employment as finally expressed in Executive Orders 8802 and 9346. It also resulted in many tight labor markets and the economic necessity for removing barriers to Negro employment in new industries, occupations, and firms. The second brought the two largest metal trades unions face to face with the problem of dealing with a large number of colored workers who were needed in war production.

The issuance of work permits to Negroes, the acceptance of them in auxiliary lodges, and their clearance to war jobs without the payment of fees did not solve the old problem of full union membership for colored workers. They have, however, established a modus operandi for facilitating the utilization of Negroes on government financed jobs. These developments demonstrated that the A. F. of L. and the international unions involved can influence the policies and practices of their locals. Internationals can, when economic, public, and government pressures require it, modify long-standing practices of barring Negroes from employment in plants under their jurisdiction. While it is true, as others have observed, that the IAM could, in accordance with its ritual, dismiss its colored members, the international cannot again sustain the fiction that it is powerless, because of its ritual, to expedite the use of colored workers in plants where it has bargaining rights or closed-shop agreements. Nor can the machinists or boilermakers sustain the assertion that white and colored workers under their jurisdiction cannot work together. They did so during the war by the tens of thousands.

In the future it will be possible for government to point to the war experience to show that these unions can effect compliance with federal non-discrimination policy. It can point to the internationals as the appropriate agencies to effect such results. If the practice of securing the employment of Negroes in shops controlled by these unions is extended long enough, or if the government's non-discrimination policy is expanded to include contracts involving interstate commerce, it will be good business for the unions to admit colored members. Indeed, there were signs during the war that white union members will often take the lead in demanding such action. It has been difficult for many of the new unionists to understand why Negro workers should not pay full membership fees, and colored workers have constantly objected to first-class fees and second-class membership. Most of the wartime inflated membership was new and not permeated with the craft union-mindedness of much of the leadership. In September, 1943, for example, the Providence, Rhode Island, Urban League reported that local No. 308 of the boilermakers' union unanimously went on record against the formation of an auxiliary local for colored workers and in favor of accepting such workers into full membership.

The auxiliary structure in the boilermakers' union has been giving way under the continuing pressure of FEPC and litigation. The directives of the committee set forth specific instances in which the Negro auxiliary lodges actually discriminated against colored workers and violated the spirit and wording of Executive Orders 8802 and 9346. Following the Portland and Los Angeles hearings in the fall of 1943, President Roosevelt addressed a letter to the officers of the boilermakers and to President Green of the A. F. of L. making a personal appeal to the boilermakers to do away with racial discrimination. Despite this action, the international voted unanimously to keep Negro members in auxiliary lodges. The boilermakers did, however, make a few concessions which reduced the degree of second-class status of Negro auxiliary membership.

Just prior to the hearings mentioned above, the National Association for the Advancement of Colored People had filed a brief with the National Labor Relations Board contesting the right of a union, which denied Negroes full union membership, to become the bargaining agent for workers covered by the non-discrimination executive order. The NLRB found, in the matter of Bethlehem-Alameda Shipyards, Inc., that Negroes in the boilermakers' union were segregated into separate auxiliaries and expressed grave doubts "whether a union which discriminatorily denies membership to employees on the basis of race may nevertheless bargain as the exclusive representative in an appropriate unit composed in part of members of the excluded race." Although in the case before it the board evaded deciding this question, it did state that it expected the local Metal Trades Council (including the boilermakers) to comply with Executive Order 9346.

This was a straw in the winds. In January, 1944, a court in Providence, Rhode Island, declared that the purpose of auxiliary lodges of the boilermakers was to segregate Negroes in a position less favorable than that of white members. It then ruled illegal and void a union election in which the international had challenged and refused to count the votes of colored members. Negro auxiliaries were ruled illegal and void insofar as they involved racial discrimination, and members of the auxiliary were declared members of the supervising lodge.

In California a similar decision was in the offing. In February, 1944, a court in San Francisco enjoined a local of the boilermakers from compelling colored workers to join an auxiliary, and the company and the union from excluding Negroes from employment because of non-membership in the union. The local was then ordered to accept Negroes into full membership. This decision was appealed and in January, 1945, the Supreme Court of California, in James versus Marinship, ruled that a labor union must admit Negroes to full membership or not try to enforce a closed-shop agreement. Meanwhile, the United States Supreme Court had rendered an important decision. In the case of Stelle versus Louisville and Nashville Railroad Company mentioned in Chapter VII, the court ruled that the Brotherhood of Firemen and Enginemen must represent Negro firemen without discrimination.

These court decisions and the constant pressure of government had their effect upon the boilermakers. The international informed FEPC in January, 1945, that the executive council of the union had authorized the dissolution of Negro auxiliaries and stated that these auxiliaries would become regular (though separate) lodges with full autonomy, subject to controls defined in the constitution and other rules governing all lodges.

These developments were significant as wartime gains and as steps toward the ultimate goal of full and equal participation of Negroes in all labor unions. As far as the boilermakers are concerned, they represented a movement toward greater status for Negro members. But it must be remembered that according to the new policy of the boilermakers' international the Negro was still relegated to a separate (but, according to the new policy, no longer a subordinate) lodge. Colored members could not transfer their cards except to other Negro lodges. If there is mass unemployment, as there is sure to be in shipbuilding, Negro lodges will probably find little chance to secure jobs for their members. Still, if there is a peacetime policy of non-discrimination in employment enforced by a federal agency, it will be possible to put more direct and effective pressure upon the employer to hire colored workers who are members of local boilermakers' unions. The grave danger, in such a situation, is that due to general unemployment, Negro boilermakers' lodges will lose their charters during the transitional period. There is also the possibility and probability of discrimination against such locals within the union and by management.

The machinists have a somewhat different policy. In a few places, Negroes have been taken into full membership, in other places they have been organized into auxiliaries, in still other places they were on work permits. In every instance, however, they were either members in violation of the white clause in the ritual, or they were on temporary permits. As wartime necessities and government pressures pass, the IAM can, and in most cases probably will, invoke the ritual and rid itself of Negro members or do away with temporary permits and auxiliaries.

The recent action of the CIO in effecting the up-grading of Negro workers is significant because it, too, involved the establishment of a modus operandi. In this instance, international officers demonstrated that they can influence the actions of recalcitrant locals. In the future it will be difficult for these officers to justify to an increasing number of Negro members their failure to enforce non-discriminatory constitutional provisions and statements of policy. In the post-war economy, when unions will insist upon the retention of workers in accordance with seniority, the application of non-discriminatory policies will be of great importance to Negro unionists, although it will involve many difficult problems.

The growth of Negro populations in industrial centers and the development of industrial unionism have changed community attitudes. When, for example, the CIO solicited Negro membership and guaranteed no discrimination on account of race, creed, or color, many Negro liberals saw in the new industrial unions the complete economic salvation of colored Americans. Here, at long last, they found a labor movement which not only accepted but courted Negro labor. After years of failure in this field, Negroes who were in accord with the ideology of the labor movement and tormented by the practices of some unions and the resultant jibes of anti-union leaders of the race, rejoiced that their theory had justification in fact. Many despaired of securing any relaxation of exclusionist and discriminatory practices in certain craft unions; others saw in the CIO the automatic and complete economic emancipation of the black worker. As would be expected under such circumstances, indorsement and hopes went too far. Disillusionment was sure to follow such all-out support of a new and, at times, undisciplined organization.

There were, however, several important developments in the

field of Negro union relationships incident to the rise of the CIO. The resulting wider participation of Negroes in the labor movement and the inclusion of occupations in which Negroes were concentrated in organizational campaigns brought to the Negro community more actual contacts with labor organizations than it had ever had before. Large numbers of Negroes became conscious of labor unions, and the movement became accepted among them as they became accepted by the movement. Thus, in most of the larger industrial areas of the nation, there was by V-E Day a conviction on the part of the vast majority of articulate colored citizens that the Negro workers should and must become a part of the forces of organized labor. A decade earlier only a small minority of colored citizens shared this belief.

A part of the difficulties which faced Negroes in labor unions were due to their inexperience and unfamiliarity with organized labor. This deficiency often led to a lack of participation on the part of Negroes in the affairs of local unions. In some instances Negro workers requested or accepted separate seniority lists—a feature of certain CIO contracts which froze colored workers in a limited number of semi-skilled and unskilled occupations. In other instances Negroes who had been separated from white people all their lives did not feel free to attend union meetings with them.

During the depression these patterns developed in industries in which there was a slack demand for labor and in which the union was in no position to deal effectively with the problem of up-grading. In such industries the organization was usually held together by a minority of members who were thoroughly schooled in the ideology and methods of unionism. Few Negroes were so qualified in the basic industries. There were, however, a few outstanding exceptions. In the meat-packing industry, for example, under the able leadership of experienced colored unionists, Negroes participated in union activities and secured significant occupational advances. This was a consumers' goods industry, and it never suffered the degree of unemployment which typified durable goods production. The economic factor combined with able Negro leadership (developed chiefly in the

United Mine Workers of America) to illustrate how labor organizations can effect new and better job opportunities for colored workers. This lesson was most important in World War II. The emergence of the Negro as a powerful factor in local No. 600 of the UAW-CIO at the Ford Motor Company, in the industrial unions in the Columbus, Ohio, area, and in the National Maritime Union indicated that further progress is being made in this field. But the Negro was not sufficiently active as a union member in 1945 to assure his being able to affect union seniority policy in a large number of local organizations.

The experience of Negro workers in the conversion of the automobile industry and similar experiences with labor unions in other areas of war production have created a much more realistic attitude of Negroes toward organized labor. No longer are labor unions damned or praised without reservation. Rather, they are being analyzed carefully on the local level and evaluated in terms of their performance. In instances when they are not fair, it is being realized that their behavior is a reflection of the prejudice of a segment of the rank-and-file membership and some officials. Negro workers no longer turn en masse against all labor unions in such situations. They have demanded from unions, as they have demanded from employers, the right to work in war production. They will continue to fight to gain admittance and to secure all the rights and privileges of membership.

Despite this obvious gain in attitude, there is still need for much education among Negro workers and the community relative to the problems of unionism. Colored workers must learn more about the structure and operations of labor organizations. It is in their interest to participate more actively in local and international business meetings and to become better informed of the policies and practices of the local and international unions. Progress is being made in these directions. The fact that there are about a million Negroes in labor unions is the most significant single development. Recent conventions of the United Automobile Workers, the Oil Workers International Union, the United Steel Workers, the United Rubber Workers, the United Electrical, Radio, and Machine Workers, the National Maritime

Union, as well as those of the national CIO, indicate that more and more colored union members are active participants in the affairs of these organizations. Likewise, the courageous and intelligent stand of the UAW and its president during and after the Detroit race riot did much to impress the Negro community with the significance of a strong labor organization as an ally; and the aggressive action of NMU to secure ship command for qualified Negroes, the union's outstanding educational program for intergroup understanding, and its fight for the Negro's right to work have given Negroes a new concept of the role of labor unions in the Negro's economic struggle.

Competent observers have noted the failure of Negroes to produce a large number of effective labor representatives in many of the new unions where they were numerically important during the war. To a degree, such observations are superficial; Negroes were relatively new to these unions, and their numerical strength was of most recent origin. Those locals in which Negroes have a long history of participation have often had serious internal political upheavals, and the relatively few established colored union leaders were, for the most part, eliminated in the process.

There was, however, one development which troubled many students of the problem. It was the rise of extremely vocal, but not especially able, Negro leadership in some local unions. This has been due to three principal factors. First, any minority group can be corralled by a champion who hollers "race discrimination." And in most American institutions and situations, there is ample evidence of discrimination to give basis for such an appeal. More important, however, were the occupational distribution and the geographic concentration of housing of Negro industrial workers. Most Negroes were still in dirty work. They either hesitated or were discouraged from eating near the plant or place of union meeting. When they went home to change and eat, they were usually miles away from other workers and union meetings. Few were willing to take the long car ride again. The ones who did go to the meetings were often those who had the least ties in the Negro community and who found the union meeting a forum for expression and a symbol of belonging. Often they were most active and vocal; often they did not have full appreciation for the larger issues involved in union activity. It is doubtful if colored workers will ever have their full share of real union leaders as long as they are concentrated in ghettos and their working lives and off-the-job activities are in two separate worlds.

CHAPTER XIII

THE NEGRO WORKER COMES OF AGE

THE ECONOMIC fate of the Negro has never been and will never be dissociated from that of all labor in the nation. Traditions and practices occasioned by the occupational color-caste system increase the intensity of the Negro's wants in times of depression and delay his gains in periods of expansion; but his status, no less than that of his white prototype, is determined primarily by the general economic health of the nation. Nevertheless, there can be no real appreciation for developments affecting the black worker without an analysis of the influences of these changes upon the status and attitudes of white workers and of the white community.

Any period of great demand for labor would ultimately occasion a demand for minority groups' workers. World War II was such a period, and it brought job opportunities to most Negroes in the labor market. Yet the war years have been unique in the Negro's economic history. This is due to several factors. In the first place, a social revolution (an inevitable result of a total war) occurred at a time when Negroes had been exposed to education for three generations and more. It was, therefore, no less inevitable that in a war devoted to the Four Freedoms Negro Americans wanted and demanded more of these freedoms here. Nor was this all. The war occasioned a rapid acceleration in the trend toward an increase in the proportion of trained workers in American industry. Consequently, the Negro clamored for new types of employment; his labor could be utilized effectively for war production only if he was given much greater opportunity to participate in skilled, single-skilled, and semi-skilled jobs. The second World War required the industrial employment of millions of women, most of whom had never been in a factory.

Negro women wanted to participate in this new trend toward greater utilization of female labor.

For the past thirty years, the black worker has been on the move. His first mass exodus from the South occurred during World War I, and it continued throughout the boom years. Even in the depression years, there was a constant movement of colored workers from the farms of the Southland. Many went to southern cities, but the trek to urban centers of the North never ceased. These movements were in response to many factors such as the social advantages of urban living and the added protection to life and property which it afforded. The most important single motivation, however, was the greater adequacy and higher rates of relief in the cities, and in the North as contrasted to the South. When the defense program began, the black worker had, like the white worker, become mobile. The chief impetus to his migration was the same as that for other workers—job opportunities. In contrast to World War I, however, there were sizable Negro populations in most industrial communities, and these darker Americans had become urbanized and accustomed to the requirements of industrial employment.

The relief and public works programs of the New Deal had often made fairly successful attempts to assure wide participation of Negroes. Policies and techniques had been developed to reduce racial discrimination and encourage minority groups' protection. As a result of these developments, Negroes had come to believe that the federal government could be effective in promoting (if not protecting) their right to work on government financed programs. And, of course, war production was such a program. It was natural, therefore, that colored citizens looked to Washington for aid in their quest for full participation in the war effort. When such participation was not forthcoming, they were resentful and they became militant. Their exposure to education, their greater urbanization, and their growing political power enabled them, under the guidance of able and effective leadership, to make their protests felt.

These developments and the production requirements of war created a significant change in the economic position of the black worker. This took the form of a modification in the color occupational system. With it, there occurred changes in employer attitudes and practices and a definite change in the position of Negroes in organized labor. Such changes, representing as they do distinct variations from patterns of long standing, incurred resentment and opposition. There were tensions and conflicts. But, for the most part, these difficulties were healthy, though dangerous and costly manifestations of progress. In a society which had become conditioned to the concept of white men's jobs and black men's jobs, it was inevitable that occupational advancement for the Negro would be resisted. The significant development is not the hundred or so conflicts but the fact that century-old patterns have been modified in five years without more opposition and more frequent clashes.

The issuance of Executive Orders 8802 and 9346 and the subsequent operations of the Committee on Fair Employment Practice have illustrated that the federal government can do much to change racial employment practices. Naturally, there were dire prophecies of the dangers of federal intervention in this field. Some saw a violation of the employer's "God-given" right to choose his own workers; others cried violation of state rights; while still others declared that the final result would be race war. The most violent and intemperate statements emanated from the South, where the color-caste system was most firmly intrenched. Leading southern citizens reported incipient riots throughout the area at the time of the Birmingham FEPC hearings. Others were greatly agitated by the fact that a Negro member of the committee had stated that Executive Order 8802 superseded the traditions of the South. Some asserted that the committee was determined to wipe out the "fixed" policy of segregation in the South and that the peaceful relations between the races in the region (in accordance with the color-caste system) were being dangerously threatened by "outside influences" which were attempting to create a new position for the Negro. It was further stated that any attempt to have black and white labor work together would lead to violent racial conflict. Many responsible southerners expressed a belief, in the summer of 1942, that there was a well-planned and concerted effort to incite an uprising of Negroes against all whites. Most of those who were of this opinion readily asserted that the impending strife was due chiefly to the activities of the federal government, and especially FEPC.

Outside the South, the reaction to changes in racial patterns was less violent but often extremely critical. Many local chambers of commerce were alarmed by the new "militancy" of the Negro and the government's "encouragement" of it. The non-discrimination executive orders were blasted, usually in confidential letters or memoranda. The Negro press was severely scored, and Negro leadership was accused of being interested chiefly in self-aggrandizement and monetary gains. Some representatives of management dogmatically stated that Negroes and whites could not work together and that governmental efforts to force them to do so would result in widespread violence and serious loss of production.

These prophecies occasioned much opposition to FEPC. The committee was crippled by inadequate appropriations, insufficient staff, and excessive administrative controls. During its earlier existence, the committee was plagued by inexperienced and at times inept administration. Yet it survived and its efficacy increased. Economic necessity combined with the work of the committee and that of other agencies to modify the color-caste occupational system. Negroes and whites have worked together; Negroes were in new occupations, plants and industries, and federal regulations had done much to accomplish these changes.

As a result of the success of FEPC and the earlier successes of non-discrimination regulations in many New Deal agencies, the Negro became committed to press for a federal policy of non-discrimination in post-war employment. As early as 1943 there were movements for a permanent FEPC. In the 1944 election both political parties advocated a permanent FEPC, and bills were introduced in Congress to set up such an agency. The legislatures of many northern states had considered FEPC bills by 1945.

Employers, too, were forced to change some of their attitudes as war and governmental pressure forced them to modify their racial employment patterns. It is obvious that in a situation such as existed in 1945, employers had developed varying attitudes toward their Negro workers. Some were pleasantly surprised at the efficiency of colored workers and the ease with which they had been introduced; others were resentful at being forced to take a step the soundness of which they still doubted; a few were holding on to their old attitudes and anxiously awaiting the return to "normalcy" and the chance to rid themselves of all colored workers.

In a situation as complex as this, no sound generalizations can be made. This much can be said. Many employers had, through necessity, been compelled to take on Negro workers; many will, if the general economic situation permits, retain a fair representation of Negroes. By V-E Day, a declining number of industrialists in the North and West, or their spokesmen, openly stated that they did not want to hire colored help; a declining number reiterated their old statements that Negroes cannot do skilled and production work.

Some insight into the significance of these developments in Negro employment can be gained by comparing the position of the colored worker in the first World War with his status in 1945. One of the characteristics of the Negro worker in the earlier war was the fact that he was considered a threat to organized labor. In World War II, progressive unions in many plants had either taken the lead in facilitating wider utilization of minorities or had actively co-operated with such developments. Where there was an official policy or a practice of excluding Negroes on the part of certain unions (in the metal trades and the railroad brotherhoods, in particular), the reason was not the fear of Negroes as a potential group of strike-breakers; it was usually an expression of the unions' desire to exclude Negro competition in a future economy which they believed would offer a limited number of jobs, or the expression of deep-seated, traditional race prejudice.

Several factors had effectively reduced the danger of the Negro as a strike-breaker. The first and most important was the growing power and strength of the labor movement. The vast majority of war contracts were with firms which had bargaining agreements with labor unions; consequently, there was little incentive to use any group of workers to break strikes. At the same time, for the duration of the war at least, there were grave limitations upon the use of the strike as a mechanism for union action.

During the first World War, official cognizance was given to racial wage differentials. The Shipbuilding Labor Adjustment Board established wage rates in conformity with existing regional patterns, and southern yards were authorized to pay white common laborers ten cents more an hour than colored common laborers. The leading southern yard using skilled and semi-skilled Negroes was permitted to pay rates below those established for other yards on the East Coast. While this may have facilitated the employment of a large number of Negroes, it implied that they were less efficient, and it nurtured the white worker's concept of the colored worker as a potential threat to the current wage rate, and ultimately, to the white worker's job.

The refusal of the National Recovery Administration to approve wage differentials obviously based on race was the first important step in reversing this trend. Later, the expansion of public-financed construction programs further weakened the wage differential in the South. The operation of the Wages and Hours Act and the growing importance of labor unions in war production have had a similar influence. In June, 1943, the War Labor Board, in the matter of Southport Petroleum Company, Texas City, Texas, and Oil Workers International local No. 449-CIO, unanimously ruled that wage classifications based solely on difference in race were without validity and ordered the abolition of pay differentials between white and Negro workers performing equal work. These developments have done much to challenge the dual wage system of the South and thereby modify the basis for the fear of Negro labor as a force undercutting the wage structure.

The attitudes of the Negro community and the Negro worker towards labor organizations have undergone great changes in the last decade. Because of their dominant rural background, their constant dependence upon white bosses, and their exclusion from and displacement by certain craft unions, Negroes had often opposed organized labor. This attitude was, in part, a reaction to racial discrimination in the labor movement; it in turn led to further anti-Negro sentiment in unions. The recent growth of Negro population in industrial centers and the rise of industrial

unions which welcomed Negroes brought about a change of attitude. During World War II, most Negro workers in industrial centers accepted labor unions about the same as their white
prototypes.

Racial wage differentials have been gradually disappearing in
the larger industries of the South, and they are most infrequent
in industries of other regions. These developments will reduce
the incentive of certain industries to hire Negroes as a source of
cheap labor and an insurance against unions, and they may tend
to break down Negro domination of certain occupations. But, at
the same time, they will furnish an additional economic basis for
the spread of labor unionism in the heavy industries of the South.
They will also establish a wage pattern favorable to the Negro's
participation in this unionism. More important, however, is the
fact that these events are contributing toward a wage system
favorable to better understanding and greater co-operation between white and Negro labor. Already, there are a growing number of CIO unions in the South with white and Negro membership. So deep is the fear and hostility between the races in the
South that tangible results will be gradual and, as elsewhere,
largely dependent upon the abolition of general economic and
social insecurity. But as they do evolve, they will be based upon
a solid and lasting mutuality of interest; they will offer an instrument through which the racial occupational caste system can be
modified.

Outside the South, the significance of these developments is
more apparent. The growing participation of Negroes in labor
unions has afforded a basis upon which the continuing advance
of colored labor may be projected, provided full employment
typifies the post-war economy. In the past, the white worker's
ever-present fear of the colored worker as an economic competitor has been one of the most serious obstacles to the expansion of Negro employment. It still exists, but the growing contacts between the two groups on the job (in increasing instances
under conditions of equal occupational status) and, more important, in the union were slowly breaking it down during the war.
Industrial unions in the past few years have had to deal with the
opposition of certain members to the occupational advancement

of colored workers. After attempting to evade or postpone meeting the issue, they established machinery for handling it. This machinery and this experience will be of great importance for the post-war period. The growing Negro membership in these organizations, Negroes' new knowledge of the operation of unions, and Negro unionists' gradually increasing importance in the direction of local and international affairs will often exert a continuing pressure upon the organizations to translate their non-discrimination pronouncements into fact. Unless there is a prolonged period of unemployment during or after reconversion, this pressure should be effective in preserving many of the Negro's occupational gains.

All of these developments and others have made the Negro worker much more realistic than he was a decade ago. He has tasted of new status in industrial employment and wider union participation. At the same time, he has received more training so that he is better prepared to function as a citizen and to work on production jobs in modern industry. Nor is this all. Negroes have become more mature politically and socially, as well as economically. A generation of Negroes has participated in the political life of scores of cities. The hundreds of thousands of colored migrants who entered northern and border cities found experienced and effective Negro politicians who often made their votes felt in municipal, state, and national elections. Nowhere is this political maturity better illustrated than in the presidential election of 1944. The Republicans offered the usual platform promises and stressed the traditions of the party. When, however, the old-line Negro political orators appeared to speak, few Negroes came to hear them. The Democrats promised less, but they cited the record of the New Deal, and they presented political leaders who had more support in the grass roots of the communities from which they came. The principal factor in swaying the pivotal Negro vote in industrial cities, however, was probably the economic appeal of Franklin D. Roosevelt. CIO-PAC presented this appeal to all workers; it stressed the basic needs of working people; it won response from many Negroes who realized that their security was tied up with that of all working elements in the nation.

This same maturity is ever-present in many fields. No longer can Negroes be won over to any issue by a few pet phrases or by kindly reference by whites to "your people." An increasing number of colored people have been inquiring into the basic factors in social issues. They have been concerned with world events and the place of darker peoples in them. Despite a growing race consciousness, few Negroes were attracted by the active pro-Japanese propaganda which flooded the black ghettos of the North at the beginning of the war—a propaganda which stressed the mutual problems of colored peoples, capitalized upon the color segregation and discrimination in America, and presented the Japanese as the hope of the colored races. Negroes realized then—as they affirm today—that a dictatorship, regardless of its color, is destruction or potential destruction for a minority.

This maturity has another side. It finds its expression in a cynicism and a distrust of promises. Negroes as a whole have begun to realize that fine phrases mean nothing and that a minority group must be well organized if it is to achieve recognition. Consequently, they are demanding results, and at the same time, they are better trained to know how to get these results. The appointment of a few Negroes to well-paying jobs is not enough. Colored America is much more concerned about effective action to assure equal work opportunities, decent housing, and social security than about "important" appointments.

At the same time, leaders among Negroes are constantly being challenged. They, too, are judged more by their deeds than by their words. Unless they are prepared to fight forthrightly for the economic, social, and political rights of colored Americans, they are soon exposed and deserted by those whom they profess to represent. Colored persons, hand-picked by whites, are distrusted and soon become impotent to corral any real following among the masses of Negroes. At times, and in a few places, this maturity and cynicism has gone to extremes; the result has been black chauvinism. This is a danger for the future, and it can be offset only by giving recognition and support to those Negro leaders who are militant, honest, sincere, and wise.

America faces the future with a great, unsolved social problem. It is the problem of Negro-white relations. In the past, we have referred to it as the Negro problem, but that is misleading. As a matter of fact, it is largely a white problem. For in our democracy we have failed to apply the basic principles we profess to follow when colored peoples are involved. But we have followed one precept of democracy; we have given our color minorities an exposure to education. Some of it has been inadequate, but all of it has made the Negro want more—more of a real American democracy. At the same time we have failed to educate the majority of our citizens to realize how traditionally American it is for Negroes to resent second-class status. The Negro is wanting, thinking, and acting like the rest of Americans, and the rest of Americans can't understand what has happened to the Negro.

There are many forces which have produced this situation. It is sufficient here, however, to outline some of the economic factors. The Negro has had his first chance to approach economic equality in many areas. His earnings have been more nearly equal to those of white workers than ever before; he has experienced equal working conditions in many plants. He has made a frontal attack upon the occupational color-caste system, and he has won the first battle.

These, then, are developments which can be extended and made the basis for greater equality of opportunity and more participation in industrial life. There are many factors which will determine whether or not such results will follow. Most of these variables are basic economic and social factors of our post-war world. We can only speculate about them. But this much we know. The Negro in America will not return to his prewar economic status without a constant and loud complaint. He will accept the casual, the occasional, the low-paying and the confining job, regardless of training, only if there are no other work opportunities open to him. If he is forced into such employment exclusively, he will be more disillusioned than ever before. He will be a potential source of weakness in our society, for his frustration will be great. Together with his white unemployed companion, he will be vulnerable to the promises and false leadership of demagogues and extremists. He is no longer patient.

This is a situation which should be faced by our nation. If we prepare to deal effectively with post-war economic problems, we can create a framework within which great progress can be made to establish intergroup understanding. If we evade the issue, if we attempt to ignore it, or if we stubbornly delude ourselves into believing that Americans will again accept ten to fifteen millions unemployed, we are in for troubled times ahead. One of the most serious possibilities is the pitting of race against race and the inciting of intergroup conflicts out of group and individual insecurity.

PART III

IMPLICATIONS FOR THE FUTURE

CHAPTER XIV

FULL EMPLOYMENT

I<small>F</small> <small>DISCUSSION</small> and wishing achieved economic and social gains, the United States would surely have full employment in the post-war era. But no modern nation has ever hoped its way to prosperity; and in our complex and closely interdependent world, jobs for all will not automatically materialize from good will. There must be understanding of the issue and planning to bring about the desired result. Nor is this all. Workers have long and sometimes bitter memories. The post-World War I events are still vivid reminders that a war can be followed by a depression. Consequently, American labor is alive to the possibility and probability of mass unemployment in the years to come. Because of these circumstances, labor fears the future. Workers are apprehensive about their job prospects in peace, and their fears are being fanned by those who speak of protecting veterans' rights or of protecting employment opportunities for special groups. With the exception of organized labor, few have had the statesmanship to indicate that employment opportunities for any group cannot be secured without regard for the volume of total employment; no group can hope for job protection unless there are enough jobs for all.

There seems to be a retreat away from a forthright stand for full employment. The Committee on Economic Development, while concerned, does not always appear to be convinced that we can maintain full employment; other groups representing management shy away from clean-cut expressions on the issue or imply that full employment is unobtainable in a free society. Mr. Eric A. Johnston, president of the United States Chamber of Commerce, for example, had this to say in the March 31, 1945, issue of the widely read Saturday Evening Post:

"I am for *steadier* jobs in America. . . . But I do not want to raise false hopes. I know that economists and business leaders have been trying for years to solve the problem of periodic depressions. I do not hold that steady employment is the only answer, *nor do I believe that it is completely obtainable* . . . we must not strive for more security than is compatible with the preservation of freedom." (Italics mine.)

Congress, in the Wallace-Jones controversy, has repudiated aggressive action to assure the highest possible levels of employment. And, worst of all, as late as the summer of 1945, few local communities were laying plans to face their future needs. In Portland, Oregon, for example, the population had grown appreciably between 1940 and 1945; tens of thousands of war workers had come in to man the shipyards, but only a small post-war program of employment had been conceived. Yet, in that city, shipbuilding, the principal industry during the war, will be greatly reduced in 1945, and perhaps eliminated, in the post-war period. Most of the city fathers were indulging in the false hope that the majority of the new war workers, and especially the Negro workers, would soon return to their old homes. As a matter of fact, while a small number of recent migrants will leave Portland, current surveys indicate that the majority intend to stay—the proportion of Negroes who will not elect to move will be greater than for whites. And if these migrants' home towns have been taking no more action than Portland to plan for post-war employment, there will be no economic incentive for this movement away from Portland.

Throughout the country similar problems were appearing in the spring of 1945. Conversion to peacetime production will occasion the displacement of a large proportion of war workers in many areas, particularly on the West Coast. It has been estimated, for example, that in California half the entire labor force will be displaced as a result of cancellation of war contracts. The availability of unemployment relief, for veterans at least, and the climatic advantages of the region will certainly combine to discourage movement away from California. And since there may be no great immediate demand for workers "back home," a large proportion of the recent migrants will stay on the Coast—many will be colored.

These developments have serious implications for our future. It is doubtful if Americans will again accept the philosophy that economic laws cannot be influenced and that the volume of employment is determined by forces beyond the control of man. Rather, they will demand that government take steps to increase the number of jobs in the nation. If this is done as the result of sound and well-conceived planning, it will result in socially desirable activity; if it comes as a result of pressure when mass unemployment is upon us, there will be emergency programs which will be inefficient and wasteful. Just as the New Deal was not able to restore prosperity, so a future program for recovery *after* the spiral of unemployment has started will be faced with great if not insurmountable difficulties.

No element in the community will suffer more from our failure to secure full employment than our color minorities. As in the recent depression, economic factors will combine with racial ones in intensifying their displacement from gainful employment in a subsequent period of mass unemployment. At the end of World War II, however, the Negro will have more to lose than he had after the first World War and the post-war boom. He will face the prospects of losing a great deal more occupational advancement; he will be subject to forfeiting a place in a vastly larger number of industries and individual plants in a much larger number of urban centers. Nor is this all. The color-caste occupational system will tend to re-establish as white men's jobs those desirable types of work in which Negroes have just obtained a foothold. These developments will combine with the general competition for work to make white labor fearful of black labor as a real threat to the white worker's chance to earn a living.

Negro-union relationships, too, will be affected. Where unions are prone to foster racial discrimination, an economic depression is sure to promote additional policies and practices of exclusion and discrimination. The opposition to Negro membership in the rapidly expanding boilermakers' and machinists' unions during the war was due largely to traditional policies of the internationals and old-line local union officials. As we have noted, some of the new membership has questioned these attitudes. If, however, there is a serious depression, and if jobs are scarce, it will be easy and natural for the vast majority of the new membership to become inoculated with the attitudes of the old leadership. It will see in the Negro a threat to its job, and the gains in Negro participation in these unions will be quickly destroyed.

Even the industrial unions which have non-discriminatory policies and successful experience in pressing for fair racial employment practices will be adversely affected. In the past, such unions have been relatively ineffective in maintaining occupational advancements for Negroes in periods of general unemployment. The United Automobile Workers, who were so helpful during the war in facilitating the up-grading of colored workers, were impotent during the depression and the earlier phases of the defense program when problems of Negro up-grading arose. Likewise, the United Mine Workers, despite their generally successful approach to equal treatment for minorities, were unable to prevent a reduction in the proportion of colored workers when machine loading was substituted for hand loading in the southern fields during the thirties.

During World War II, some of the most significant and far-reaching education in intergroup relations took place in certain industrial unions. In some plants, such as the leading meat-packing establishments in Chicago, and in certain industries, such as freight handling on the San Francisco bay docks, the proportion of Negroes had, by 1945, increased to a phenomenal degree. The unions involved had long insisted upon fair employment practices, but persistent rumors and implications that Negroes were about to "run the white workers out of the industry" aroused new racial animosities. The unions faced this issue, and they intensified their programs of education. These programs have a chance to succeed and have a lasting value as long as there are enough jobs to go around. If, however, there is general unemployment, and if, in accord with a strict adherence to seniority regulations, a large proportion of Negroes remains employed in good jobs, many displaced whites will clamor for the right to work and will want the Negroes discharged. In such a situation programs of education for intergroup understanding and co-operation will be endangered.

In industries and plants where the proportion of colored

workers is smaller than in the examples cited above, the problem will be no less difficult. In a period of mass unemployment, the white workers, who are the majority, can easily be incited to demand preference in employment. Even if the international officers are sincere in their desire to be impartial in the application of seniority, there will be a real danger that the white membership can be induced to support a program for reducing the volume of Negro employment so as to increase the white worker's chances for a job. If such appeals should be successful (and the newer unions are usually controlled by the will of their membership), the Negro members will surely resent the results. Here again, programs for intergroup understanding will be endangered.

There is still another possibility. Some employers will welcome any move calculated to weaken unions. In a period of mass unemployment, the racial issue can easily be used for such a purpose. Management can, if it wishes, appeal to the disgruntled white or Negro workers and state that, were it not for union regulations governing re-employment, it would hire a larger proportion of them. Such a program would, in some instances, give rise to serious divisions within the organization on the basis of race.

These are not problems affecting Negroes alone. They have grave implications for all workers, and they present serious potential difficulties to labor unions. If, in a post-war period of unemployment, the basic issue of providing a larger volume of jobs can be confused by the injection of group antagonisms, there is less chance to secure effective action for economic recovery. Throughout our history, successful attempts have been made to color economic issues with racial situations. The inevitable result has been an avoidance of constructive action and the generation of intense color consciousness. In the end, the white worker has joined his darker brother in want and misery.

Labor unions will be faced with other crucial tests. Many progressive labor organizations have taken forthright stands on fair racial employment practices; they have centered their appeals to minorities around this issue, and they have secured a large following. If, in response to economic pressures (and resulting political pressures) within the unions, they reverse their stands, or if they attempt to straddle the issue, they will alienate a half million members and a community of thirteen millions. The political support of Negroes, which in the 1944 election gave strength to CIO-PAC, will be largely lost. These results can only weaken labor; they will surely do much to destroy the solidarity of workers and the effectiveness of labor unions. Such a development would threaten the most potent progressive force in American life. It would also place the Negro masses in a vulnerable spot for economic exploitation. And when any large segment of labor can be exploited, all of labor will ultimately suffer the same fate.

Management, too, has troubles ahead if there is a serious, sustained post-war depression. Much of labor and a large segment of the general population will be distrustful of the existing economic system if there is mass unemployment at the same time that the failure of the economic system to produce and distribute much-needed goods leads to want and misery. Many groups will respond to appeals for political (and direct) action which promise to offer an easy road to economic security. This will represent a threat to the vested interests of those who control industry, and it will constitute a real danger to the system of private enterprise. If and when full employment is re-established, industry again would have to face the problem of utilizing minorities. During World War II, however, some managements have spent much time, energy, and money to introduce Negroes on the production line. These efforts would be largely lost, were the volume of employment to decline to a point where Negroes as a group were displaced.

From the point of view of race relations, one of the most serious consequences of mass unemployment is the fact that it will create an economic situation in which gainful employment for the Negro can and will be interpreted as a menace to insecure white workers. It will lead to general down-grading of Negro workers and the strengthening of the occupational color-caste system, so that the losses in employment status would be institutionalized. And these developments will occur at a time when Negroes are dedicated to establishing equal opportunity for themselves. The personal lives of a half million black wage-earners who are prepared to do skilled, single-skilled, and semi-skilled work will be affected. Several million Negroes in the nation will be unemployed. These colored Americans and their friends will not accept such a situation with grace. They will press to change it. Whites will press to drive Negroes out of the jobs they have. Conflict will surely follow.

Complete eradication of unemployment in an industrial nation which does not have a controlled economy is an impossibility. The more complex and diversified the economy, the larger the industrial system, and the more advanced the technological processes, the more difficult it is to match man and job in a free society. Those workers who are idle because of the mechanical difficulties of getting the right man at the right place for the right job are victims of frictional unemployment. In addition, certain industries, such as the production and distribution of toys, are subject to varying degrees of activity at different periods of the year. Those who depend upon such industries for work are periodically unemployed. When they are so temporarily out of work, they are said to be victims of seasonal unemployment. But there is a third type of unemployment. It is not due to maladjustment between the man and the job, nor is it due to the seasonal nature of production; it results from a general decline in industrial activity and job opportunities. It occurs when we have economic depressions which come in waves and are described as phases of the business cycle. Those who are displaced from gainful employment during the down-swing of the business cycle are said to be suffering from cyclical unemployment.

Prior to the depression of the 1930's, it was generally believed that we could escape the scourge of unemployment if we mobilized the labor supply (so as to reduce frictional unemployment) and regularized industry (so as to minimize seasonal unemployment). When, however, significant progress had been made in achieving these two objectives, the industrial nations suffered from the most violent depression the world has ever known. It then became crystal clear that cyclical unemployment is by far the most important of the principal types of job dislocations, and, unless we are able to control it, we will be exposed to long periods of mass unemployment.

By the end of 1944 we had achieved full employment in the United States; yet almost 1,000,000 persons were looking for jobs in the nation. But in 1944 there were well over 1,000,000 jobs looking for people, and there was no cyclical unemployment. Those out of jobs and employable did not face the prospect of permanent inability to find work: some of them, under the labor market conditions then current, could have found jobs if they had moved to other localities; others could have been employed if they had taken training for the types of work in which there were openings; still others would have found jobs in the normal course of events had they done no more than stay in the labor market. And a sizable proportion of the unemployed in 1944 were not qualified to meet the minimum standards of industry. As the employable individuals in the unused labor pool were absorbed, others took their places. It is doubtful if the economic system of America, even in war, could have less than between 750,000 and 1,000,000 unemployed at any given time.

The minimum number of unemployed workers in our peacetime economy will be appreciably larger than during war production. While the estimates vary, it can safely be said that full employment in peace will be achieved at a time when there are from two and a half to three millions out of work in the United States. Such a situation will exist because in a peacetime economy the work standards are more exacting than in wartime, there is more temporary displacement due to seasonal fluctuations, there is greater dependence upon a fluctuating demand for exports, and individual workers spend more time between jobs.

The exact number of jobs required to achieve full employment as here defined cannot be estimated since we have no way of knowing how many persons now in the labor market will voluntarily leave it or how large a peacetime army and navy the United States will maintain. One group in particular, married women, is sure to lose many of its representatives. Other groups, such as young people and the older workers, will have smaller proportions gainfully employed. While we cannot say statistically what full employment will involve in numbers of jobs, we do know that the volume of employment will have to be much higher than we had ever thought possible in civilian production. Indeed, it will probably be higher than the employment figure at V-E Day.

Most businessmen, economists, and labor leaders agree that we can achieve full employment in the post-war world. The man in the street shares the same opinion although he has arrived at his conclusions usually without benefit of economic analysis. To the average American, it is a rather simple matter. In response to the demands of a war, we had need for more workers than were available in the labor market; we have many needs for consumer goods, such as washing-machines, radios, automobiles, clothes, houses, and household equipment; and we should be able to direct our energies and resources toward supplying these needs. Such direction would result in full employment.

Businessmen are most vocal as champions of full employment in peacetime when they are defending "private enterprise" and demanding removal of government regulations as soon as the war is over. Most of the analyses and calculations employed to illustrate the probability of post-war full employment presuppose full employment and then demonstrate where, under such a state of demand for labor, workers will be needed. These calculations tell how labor, under a condition of full employment, would be distributed; this is true on the local level, on the regional level, and then on the national level. The final sum adds up to full employment, and it is thereby assumed that because the total is adequate, jobs for all would follow. Mathematically, this method is probably sound, but it is certainly not convincing as a mode of economic reasoning.

There are, however, less optimistic analyses which stress the need for an effective demand * in order to sustain levels of production and question whether the accumulated demand for consumers' durable goods will ensure the re-employment of war workers and those demobilized from the armed forces. Those following this line of reasoning warn against the accumulation of excessive inventories in the post-war economy, such as developed after the first World War. And they are emphatic in

---

* Effective demand means the desire to purchase and the money to translate the desire into reality. It is a want backed up with dollars and willingness to spend these dollars at the current price levels.

their insistence upon the critical need for a large construction program. Also, they call our attention to the fact that the consumers' goods industries, which are usually cited as the ones which will expand to meet the accumulated needs of citizens, will, in fact, discharge many workers.

Professor Gunnar Myrdal, the Swedish economist who is well versed in the social and economic problems of America, is less optimistic than most Americans. In an article in the November, 1944, issue of The Atlantic Monthly, he has noted that outside of nations which have centrally directed economies, there is no historical precedent for the stabilization of a boom. He is particularly concerned about what will happen when the pressures for expansion (war contracts) are withdrawn at the same time that balancing controls are relaxed. Myrdal notes the achievements of American business to expand when backed by unlimited effective demand. But he sees great difficulties ahead in view of the pressure for orthodox financing (in the sense of an annually balanced budget). The Swedish economist aptly observes that many businessmen are promising jobs for all under private enterprise in order to divert the people's demand for full employment from radical expression. But he points out that if private enterprise should fail to live up to its promises, extreme radicalism will appear.

Myrdal justifies his pessimism on several grounds. The following are the most important: although the men who control business believe in full employment in general, they assume that others' post-war production levels will assure it; they do not seem to be prepared to accomplish their own share of production. He also observes that employers are ready to reduce wages and thereby withdraw the foundation of purchasing power needed to assure and sustain full employment. Myrdal doubts if consumers will elect to increase their standard of living sufficiently in volume or rapidly enough to maintain full employment, even if they have the purchasing power. This doubt is based upon the belief that even if there are dollars in the hands of the public, past spending and consumption habits may be so strong that people will not elect to spend at a sufficient volume to take off the market a quantity of goods necessary to require the con-

tinuing employment of all labor. In light of the recent technological progress in America, this is a real danger. Myrdal doubts
if the post-war level of exports from America will be as large
as the wartime volume sustained by lend-lease. He stresses the
strategic importance of construction and the dominant role that
housing must play in such a program.

Myrdal believes that political considerations will render a large-
scale construction program impossible of achievement. He re-
minds us also that the post-war period will be characterized at
the start (due to dislocations and unemployment incident to conversion) by a steep decline in effective purchasing power. Very
important in his analysis is the attention he gives to regional unemployment. There will be depressed areas in America after the
war. Unemployment in these centers, unless speedily corrected,
will affect the rest of the economy. This last factor and a series
of problems incident to the disposal of government-owned war
plants and consumer goods can, according to Myrdal, make
America's conversion become a depression. Even if this is avoided,
it seems likely that within a period of from six months to three
years, America will face a slump—a slump which may grow in
a self-generating fashion into another great depression. Myrdal
does not deny the theoretical possibility of establishing an economic plan productive of full employment, but he believes it is
politically impossible.

Out of what has been said certain principles emerge. Full employment is attainable. It will not come, however, by wishing
for it, or by assuming the existence and spending of adequate purchasing power to assure full production, and then piecing the
picture together by adding up how many workers would be
needed by each industry under an *assumed* condition of full employment. Such figures have their place; they indicate the types
of shifts in our labor supply which may occur. As such, they are
interesting in an analysis of changes which will begin to appear
with the move back to peacetime production.

No discussion of effective demand and future consumer habits
can ignore the psychological factors. Reconversion to peacetime
production will involve the lay-off of millions of workers. If this
is concentrated in several short periods of time, many prudent

individuals may decide to postpone the purchases which they had contemplated under conditions of wartime full employment at high wages. Others will catch the fever in their fear of possible displacements from jobs. Out of this, a general deflationary psychology may sweep the country and existing purchasing power in the hands of consumers may not be spent. Such developments would be extremely serious because they would occur at a time when there would be much unemployment incident to the reconversion. This latter process can lead to a major depression. If such an eventuality is avoided, the depression could come as soon as the abnormal demand for consumers' goods abates, the increases in export trade cease and the accumulation of inventories passes.

Full employment during the war had been achieved through government participation and government regulation of our economy. From the outset of the defense program there was the prospect of effective demand (in the sense of dollar purchasing power ready to be spent) for the production potential of the industrial and agricultural system of the nation. Soon this was translated into an actual effective demand, and the enormous purchasing power of a gainfully employed population joined the vast resources of a nation at war to create more effective demand than there were goods to satisfy. American ingenuity did marvels in production. And in order to assure that the most important goods for the prosecution of the war were produced before the less essential, governmental regulations were developed. The most important of these were controls of prices, raw and processed materials, and manpower.

The war economy did away with the cyclical fluctuations in the demand for labor and afforded full employment for the first time in a generation. *Such a volume of employment was possible when, in the emergency of war, there was sufficient assured outlay* * *to take a maximum output of needed goods off the market.* War wiped out depression; it did so because no one questioned the wisdom of appropriating money to pay for matériel for the protection of the nation and the prosecution of the war. The

---

* Outlay is spending for goods and services currently produced.

budget was conceived of in terms of national resources, and the only limiting factors were raw materials, manpower, and organizational ability. In order to be most efficient and in order to save time, the nation accepted controls over these limiting factors. And in order to assure that such controls would be effective and save the nation from inflation, price ceilings were established.

Many persons assume that the significant feature of our war economy has been its controls. As a matter of fact this is not true. Such governmental controls as we have had accelerated the movement toward full employment and enabled the necessary part of our productive capacity to be concentrated upon the main purpose of the nation, prosecution of the war. But it was not these controls which brought full employment; rather, it was the creation of effective demand for the full productive capacity of the nation. *Governmental participation in creating and assuring expenditure for the maximum current products of industry, rather than governmental controls, enabled us to achieve a new high in the volume of production.*

Between the two world wars, there was a violent economic depression which resulted in worldwide, mass unemployment. When this chronic situation was corrected during World War II, it became apparent that governments' expenditure for war matériel had occasioned unlimited outlay; this, in turn, resulted in the creation of more jobs than there were workers to fill, and full employment followed. Even minority groups ultimately found work in this society of jobs for all. The deficiencies in total outlay in our peacetime economy are usually due to the fact that savings and investment (spending savings for factories, machines and the like) do not always keep in step. The result is a deficiency in purchasing power (effective demand) and a failure to take goods off the market. From this, a decline in production and the demand for labor follows. If we are to have an adequate volume of peacetime employment, there must be effective demand for the maximum potential production of industry. In order to achieve this objective, society must take measures to assure that although savings and investments are made by two different sets of people and in response to different motivations, the amount saved will be compensated for by investment or other action.

Unless the amount saved is somehow offset, income will decline, goods will not be taken off the market, and unemployment will begin its spiral of expansion.

Sir William Beveridge in his recent book, "Full Employment in a Free Society," has observed that three basic factors determine the volume of employment. They are the quantity of effective demand, the direction of demand, and the manner in which the supply of labor responds to the demand. Consequently, he proposes three lines of attack upon unemployment: maintenance of adequate total outlay, control of location of industry, and securing the organized mobility of labor. Of these, the first is the most important. In order to achieve it there must be a new approach to the national budget; the budget must be conceived of as income and expenditure of the community as a whole and not just income and expenditure for publicly supported projects. Such a budget would estimate the total outlay needed to effect full employment and the expected outlay which would be made in a given period. The deficiencies in the latter as compared to the former would be a concern of government, and government would take steps to facilitate and assure adequate outlay. The basic consideration of such a budget, obviously, would become the manpower and physical resources at a given time.

Although adequate total outlay would not in itself reduce unemployment to the minimum, it would go a long way in that direction and establish a framework in which it would be possible to direct industry and labor so as to reduce materially the frictional aspects of unemployment. We know that the over-all effective demand for goods is the principal limiting factor influencing the volume of employment. Unless and until we are ready to estimate the possible deficiencies in this outlay and plan to compensate for them, we shall face the danger of mass unemployment. If the frictions due to the disposal of new, government-owned plants, the existence of ghost towns, and the shifts in the demand for labor are not too great, we may have a sustained effective demand for goods for some time after reconversion. Once our economy has caught up with the accumulated domestic and foreign demand, we shall face the problem of in-

adequate outlay. This can be met only by machinery for antici-
pating it and by planning to compensate for any deficiencies.

Such a program is not one of government regulation and control; it is a program of government participation. Its basic principles are few: the state has a responsibility for assuring full
employment; in our modern world such employment is not automatic; in order to assure it, the government must be in a position to measure the adequacy of the effective demand and supplement it when necessary; the national budget is conceived of
in terms of the manpower and physical resources of the community. While no one has developed the details of a perfect
approach to this problem, it is important to note that many
economists believe that they have found the key to mass unemployment. The war economy supports their reasoning, and by
applying its principal lesson, we can strive to maintain effective
demand. When we have faced and met this problem, we will be
on our way to Beveridge's goal, full employment in a free society. Other adjustments will be required, but they will do little
to influence the volume of employment unless the total outlay
is sufficient to assure a volume of production which will require
full use of the labor supply.

Maintenance of full employment in a peacetime economy will
require much study and planning. Few competent observers believe that we are prepared to meet this problem. In attacking
physical diseases, we spend hundreds of millions of dollars, and
our scientists take years to discover causes and prescribe treat-
ments and cures. Mass unemployment is the greatest social dis-
ease modern society can contract. Yet we spend relatively little
to diagnose the problem and develop techniques and plans for
eradicating the causes. Once these over-all analyses have been
made, there must be detailed, flexible programs for dealing with
a complex of specific situations which can start the spiral of
unemployment. This is a gigantic task. It requires the best possible technical knowledge, and it requires a large and effective
organization. Our most outstanding recent action to meet this
pressing need has been to abolish the only national agency capable
of dealing with the problem—the National Resources Planning
Board.

In 1944, a plan for full employment was embodied in the Murray-Wagner Full Employment Bill. This statute would give government and private enterprise joint responsibility for maintaining the volume of employment. According to its provisions, the President would submit to the Congress an annual estimate of the volume of spending expected in the nation, and if this was not sufficient to employ the estimated working force, the President would make recommendations as to how the deficiency might be met, including the encouragement of private investment and expenditure. Where and when private activity appeared inadequate to meet the need, a program of public investment and expenditure on local, state and federal levels would be proposed. President Truman has indicated his approval of such legislation. But its enactment was far from assured in the spring of 1945.

Even if the Murray-Wagner Full Employment Bill were passed, we should be far from our goal of jobs for all. Spending is not enough. There are important problems of timing public and private expenditures, deciding upon the source and nature of financing, and planning the location of industry and public works. These and many associated problems require detailed analysis before the maximum benefits can be derived from governmental action. Unless we probe into such issues, post-war dislocations will develop faster than our knowledge of how to meet them.

Once we know more about what ought to be done, we shall have to translate our knowledge into programs, and programs into action. The present tendency toward slogans of free enterprise and private initiative are most misleading and dangerous. They really mean nothing and they can be used, as they have been used in the past, to confuse the issue and delay constructive action. One can certainly agree with Myrdal in fearing that it may be politically impossible to achieve full employment in the United States.

Reconversion will involve many difficult problems. The resulting shifts in the demand for labor will be serious for all workers; Negroes will be affected as a color minority and as workers new to many types of industrial employment. The nature of these adjustments will be described in the next chapter. But it is clear that, regardless of these immediate problems, the status of the Negro as a worker and the state of intergroup relations will be determined primarily by the volume of employment after reconversion. Minorities have a special concern in the creation and maintenance of adequate total outlay to provide full employment.

CHAPTER XV

THE NEGRO WORKER IN RECONVERSION

THE TOTAL volume of employment will set the framework within which the post-war economic status of Negroes will be determined. But there will be another important conditioning factor, the way in which the transition from a war to a peace economy is achieved. The timing of the reconversion, the resulting changes in the directions of the demand for labor, and the experience of minorities during the reconversion will have profound effect upon post-war racial patterns of employment. For groups which are highly visible and which are quickly identified with less desirable types of work, the early patterns of employment in peacetime industries will be crucial. Unless the practice of employing Negroes in a diversity of peacetime industries, firms, and occupations is achieved early in the reconversion, it will be extremely difficult to secure later.

If, during reconversion, a large number of Negroes and other minority groups remain unemployed for any long period, economic forces alone will not facilitate their full utilization in a subsequent recovery. This will follow because a peacetime prosperity will involve a pool of unused labor larger than the level of unemployment during the last years of the European war. If, then, recovery follows a period during which Negroes and other minorities are generally unemployed or restricted to unskilled, service, and heavy occupations and industries, the white worker will develop a vested interest in desirable types of jobs and will again press for community support in eliminating the Negro from competition for these jobs.

We are able to prophesy roughly as to the directions in which there will be shifts in the demand for labor during the reconversion period. In general, workers will move away from industries which have dominated the production of war matériel, and the majority will leave shipbuilding, aircraft, machinery, iron and steel, and federal government. The prewar trend toward employment in service industries will be resumed. Construction will expand, and the number and proportion of workers hired in the building trades will increase, as will employment in domestic service.

A large proportion of Negroes will be among those displaced as a result of the cessation of war production. Almost half of the Negroes in war industries have been concentrated in aircraft, shipbuilding, and iron and steel (including ordnance). Another sizable group have been in government service. Colored workers have been employed primarily in the production branches of the War and Navy Departments and in emergency war agencies of the government, in the newer, government-owned plants, and in other large establishments which will usually close down or be the slowest in reconverting to peacetime production. In addition, large numbers of Negroes have moved into areas where one or two of these industries dominated the community and in which the prospects for peacetime production are extremely small. Because of their distribution in certain war industries and their concentration in single-skilled, semi-skilled and unskilled jobs, many colored workers will not have marketable skills in the peacetime economy. All of these circumstances add up to the probability of extreme job displacement of colored workers during reconversion.

The black worker in aircraft will share much displacement with the white worker. Like their white prototypes, many of the Negro workers are new to the industry and have little experience save that incident to their wartime employment. Because of the widespread breakdown of skills in aircraft, many of its workers have learned but a few operations, most of them will not be readily adaptable to other types of single-skilled and semi-skilled jobs. Because of the glamour of the airplane, a large segment of its war workers have been persons who usually would not be in the labor market; a large proportion of them will probably be forced out of it in peacetime production. Colored workers were pretty well distributed in various production occupations and divisions of some aircraft plants by V-E Day. Although they were often concentrated in the government-owned plants, a representative number were in parent establishments, and it is reasonable to assume that the Negro will emerge as a small part of the industry's labor force, provided we do not have general, mass unemployment. Tens of thousands of colored workers in aircraft during the war, however, will be forced to seek new jobs.

In those shipyards where operations will continue and where the attitude of union officials is favorable or where there are open-shop conditions, some Negroes will remain on the payroll and will probably retain hold on many skilled and semi-skilled occupations, such as welding, shipfitting, machine work, and electrical installation and repair. Unless, however, something is done to assure Negroes' continuing right to work at yards where the union attitude has been unfavorable, they will feel the brunt of extreme displacement. In the spring of 1945, such displacement seemed imminent in the Gulf and the San Francisco bay and Portland areas and in other sections where A. F. of L. craft unions had closed-shop contracts. The separate unions into which Negro shipyard workers were relegated and the work permits under which they were cleared may well be abolished in the post-war period. Under the most favorable circumstances, as many as 100,000 colored workers may be displaced from this industry; many, if not most of them, will be in areas where there is little other industrial activity.

It is almost certain that the Negro iron and steel worker will be in a better occupational position in the post-war period than he occupied prior to hostilities. He has made occupational advancement, and his position in the steel workers' union is more firmly intrenched than ever before. Prior to the defense program, Negroes were generally hired, and they will probably continue to work in many plants where they will remain in new and better occupations as well as in traditional jobs. Their numerical displacement will be less than in aircraft and shipbuilding, because the extent of cut-backs in iron and steel will be less, and Negroes have more seniority in the industry. Nevertheless, scores of thousands of Negroes will be forced to leave this type of production. Many of them, as many of those in shipbuilding, will be suited for construction work.

The occupational and numerical position of the Negro in the automobile industry may be better than his prewar status. During the war, black labor won the right to many types of skilled and semi-skilled work in the Michigan automobile factories. The Negro achieved up-grading in plants like Chrysler, where before World War II he was traditionally employed only as a foundry hand or as a common laborer, and after 1942 he secured production jobs in many firms which previously never employed him. A much larger proportion of Negroes were employed in the wartime production of the principal automobile firms than ever before. The black worker had also intrenched and strengthened his position in the UAW-CIO. Although many individual Negroes will be displaced and down-graded, colored workers as a group should be able to preserve many of their wartime occupational advances, if the economy weathers the strain of the transition from war to peace and *if minorities are not too disproportionately displaced during reconversion by union of seniority*.

The Negro entered electrical and general machinery production during the war. It is doubtful if there will be many colored workers in these types of production by the close of hostilities. Because of the small numerical participation of Negroes in these industries, their post-war unemployment will not be numerically great, but it may involve complete displacement from many firms. In a few of the larger plants, such as Western Electric, and in some areas, such as Philadelphia and New York City, there are indications that Negroes as a group have achieved a permanent place and occupational status.

War production occasioned the employment of millions of people new to the labor market. It also led to the use of many individuals in types of jobs which normally would not be open to them. During the latter phases of the second World War, for example, thousands of colored women entered industrial employment. (At the same time many more thousands, available for such employment, were denied it because of race.) A large number found jobs in government service, where the majority were in clerical capacities. Negro women (and to a lesser degree, Negro men) deserted domestic service and low-paying clerical and teaching jobs. Some went into manufacturing; some found work in the federal agencies; others replaced whites as hotel workers, telegraph messengers, waiters and waitresses, counter girls, and in associated tasks. Some have been satisfactory workers; others have been inefficient or maladjusted to their new work.

The post-war economy will involve the displacement of hundreds of thousands of individual colored workers, and the intensity of this dislocation will be much greater for colored women than for colored men. This will occur largely because of the delayed introduction and incomplete acceptance of Negro women in war production. At the same time practically all Negro (and perhaps white) women in heavy production, such as shipbuilding, iron and steel, and railroad maintenance, will probably be thrown back into the labor market.

Negro women in aircraft, automobiles, and electrical goods will find themselves competing with Negro men and white men and women for a drastically reduced number of jobs. The vast majority of colored female production workers in these and similar industries will be displaced. Some will withdraw from the labor market, but the majority will compete for domestic and other service jobs. A few, who have professional or clerical training, will seek jobs of that type.

Colored women have entered the apparel industry in large numbers. Many of them were power machine operators, and it is highly probable that a large proportion will remain in the industry. This seems to be one branch of manufacturing in which the Negro woman established a firm foothold as a production worker during the war, and the work rotation policy of the garment workers ought to protect Negroes from displacement incident to the application of seniority. Individual colored women will lose their jobs in garment factories, but as a group Negro women will emerge as a more important factor in the industry.

Thousands of Negro women employed in government war agencies will be thrown into the labor market. Some will return to lower paid professional and clerical jobs, such as teaching in the South and typing in Negro institutions and business—displacing the present workers in such jobs. The majority will compete for traditional jobs open to Negro women or will withdraw from the labor market, and this number will be augmented by thousands of colored women who will be released from United States navy yards and arsenals.

Some of the colored men and women who have entered hotel and other types of service jobs will be retained. Their use in such work during the war has conditioned the public to them in areas where Negroes had not been used and has reconditioned the public to them in other areas. Unless there is a breakdown in our economy, many will remain in these jobs. There are, however, too many instances in which these colored workers were poorly selected. As a result of this and certain individual traits, there are many places where their work habits and attitudes have antagonized fellow employees, management, and the public. When there are other workers available, undesirable employees will be summarily dismissed. Where colored workers are involved, they will seldom be replaced by other Negroes, and often the deficiencies of a few will be used as the excuse for firing the whole group.*

One of the most discouraging characteristics of the post-war economy will be the return of Negro women to traditional occupations. This will find its most striking expression in a rapid increase in the number of colored domestic servants. If we have full peacetime employment, there will be an appreciable rise in the demand for servants, and colored women will move back into the kitchen. The increasing number of colored women who will be seeking domestic service jobs will depress the wages and worsen the working conditions in these occupations; the lower the total volume of employment at any given time, the greater

---

* In many establishments and businesses the acceptance of the first Negro workers was delayed until there was no other labor available, and in many of these instances the Negro workers were often unsatisfactory. By the time that color bars were relaxed, the bottom of the manpower barrel was being scraped. Negro and white workers alike were inefficient and often maladapted to mechanical or industrial work. Managements which had dreaded the employment of Negroes, however, saw in the attitudes and production records of the colored workers evidences of the Negro's undesirability. They were looking for objectionable "racial characteristics," and objectionable characteristics appeared in both white and colored workers. Preconceived notions, group identification, and earlier experience had convinced these employers that the undesirable white workers were exceptional; undesirable Negro workers, on the other hand, appeared typical.

the tendencies in this direction. A few of those who return to domestic service will, because of their experience and training, be in a position to seek some of the better types of jobs. The volume of such employment is limited, and the majority of those who seek servants' jobs will be forced to accept the going rates of pay and the established working conditions, or withdraw from the labor market.

Colored men, too, will return to service and other casual employment, but a much larger proportion will stay in industry, and it is safe to assume that Negro males will be accepted as production workers in many plants and industries which will continue to operate in the peace economy. The group will have achieved a degree of occupational advancement, although the majority of its members will remain in unskilled jobs. But a large number of colored men recently up-graded (perhaps the majority) will be forced into lower occupations; many others will be unemployed.

Any type of reconversion will present serious problems to the black worker. He will suffer from a much higher incidence of unemployment than the white worker. The Negro worker will often be displaced from the better jobs he held during the war, and the Negro woman will, for the most part, leave industrial employment. The intensity of these losses and their influence upon the black worker's permanent status in the economy will be determined chiefly by the timing and smoothness of our shift from a war to a peace economy. Seniority provisions, too, will be important.

The Bureau of Labor Statistics has stated that it will take two years after the war for the nation to achieve full employment, and others have noted that the prospects for a smooth transition are far from reassuring. America is fortunate, however, in that it has been able to maintain a larger proportion of its civilian economy than any other principal belligerent. Yet the problems of conversion are great.

The cessation of the European war in the summer of 1945 will enable us to start increasing civilian production before all war production has ceased. This may be a great help. There are, of course, many other factors which will be important. The method of canceling war contracts, the way demobilization of the armed forces is effected, and the criteria which are used to authorize the initiation of additional civilian production by individual establishments will all play significant roles in determining the sort of reconversion we have. But in light of the general desire to be free of governmental regulations, the United States will be fortunate if it can sustain consumer purchasing at sufficiently high levels on the one hand and ward off inflation on the other.

Congress has already given attention to these questions, and the fourth report of the House Special Committee on Post-war Economic Policy and Planning has shown an appreciation of many of the problems. The committee accepted full employment as the goal of post-war economic readjustment. While the group urged opportunity for private initiative and investment to make its full contribution to this end, it specifically stated: "At the same time it is the responsibility of the government to adopt measures for protection against unavoidable economic hazards, especially during the difficult period of transition from production for war to production for peace."

Full employment, according to the committee, will require providing from eight to ten million more jobs than existed in the high peacetime year of 1940. Consequently, somewhere between twelve and fifteen million new civilian jobs will be needed within two years after the defeat of Germany. This is a tremendous task, and the committee felt that unemployment will probably rise during the transitional period, reaching a peak of as many as five million workers even if industry is rapidly expanding. If the expected industrial expansion is sluggish or does not exist, the number unemployed will, of course, rise far above this figure (and probably occasion the displacement of a million Negroes). Any transition will involve a decline in workers' income since labor will be shifting from high-wage war industries to lower-wage non-war industries, and from boom towns to lower-wage areas. Here, again, the Negro will be more adversely affected since few high-wage peacetime jobs will be open to him. The committee placed much reliance upon the unemployment compensation system to tide workers over periods of temporary displacement. But the report specifically noted: "In the event, however, that industry and commerce are unable to reconvert rapidly and expand vigorously, it may be necessary to rely heavily on public-work and relief programs. The nation must be prepared with a program adequate to meet either eventuality."

The most encouraging feature of the report is its realization of the prime importance of an expansion in construction and the probable need for a large program of public works to provide an adequate number of jobs. Quoting experts, the committee noted that it is doubtful if industry can expand civilian construction enough to increase total employment by more than a few hundred thousand workers in the first year after the defeat of Germany. This would not compensate for the loss in public war building, and it would inflict a great hardship upon Negroes who would be displaced in large numbers from heavy industry and for whom construction should offer the greatest peacetime volume of employment. By the end of the war in the Pacific, it was hoped that most of the difficulties would be removed and construction could employ, a year after final victory, about 3,750,000 workers. The committee observed: "The preceding estimates are extremely rough; it is believed, however, that they represent, in general, the most favorable rate of expansion that can realistically be expected. It is clear from these figures that, while the construction industry and its allied materials industries can make an important contribution toward the absorption of demobilized veterans and released war workers, the industry will not be able to expand rapidly enough to absorb a large proportion of those thrown out of work during the reconversion period."

It is recommended that the federal government should lend encouragement and technical assistance to the preparation of plans for a wide range of public works in case continuing large-scale unemployment develops. The program, of course, should be flexible, and to be flexible it must be prepared in advance. The committee recommended federal grants-in-aid to facilitate such planning, but felt that the use of federal funds for financing the programs should be resorted to only if local funds, private investment, and unemployment insurance prove inadequate. And the committee concluded its discussion of public projects with a review of the failure of New Deal spending to create prosperity and with pointed reference to the size of the national debt.

The report also made specific recommendations relative to price and credit controls, taxes, foreign trade and shipping, and agricultural and mining problems. At one place, it stated that price controls over selected products should be continued after the war and that there should be power to restrict consumer credit if such credit would lead to inflationary tendencies.

Some detailed attention has been given to this report because it is, in a measure, a barometer of the official attitude of congressmen towards problems of reconversion. In the first place, it does mark a degree of progress in that a congressional committee with conservative members, such as Hamilton Fish of New York, and with William M. Colmer of Mississippi as chairman, established full employment as a goal and admitted that government has a responsibility to adopt measures for protection against "unavoidable economic hazards." This is a far cry from the traditional attitude of laissez faire which most congressmen espoused a decade or two ago. Also, the analysis of the problems of reconversion is basically sound and generally realistic.

The report is inconsistent and inadequate in its recommendations. In discussing the disposition of industrial facilities which have cost the taxpayers of the nation fifteen billion dollars, the committee was deeply concerned that their sale not upset the national economy. No reference was made in this connection to the importance of securing as large sales price as possible in order to reduce the national debt, nor was there much discussion of the post-war employment capacities of prospective purchasers—a criterion for selecting purchasers that Henry J. Kaiser has suggested. On the other hand, after the committee noted the importance of fostering sound public works to assist in providing employment in the reconversion period and in the post-war era, it was careful to stress local- and state-financed projects as a means of reducing federal expenditures and minimizing the national debt. While it is true that state and local governments should finance these projects wherever they can, it must be realized that many communities do not have adequate funds, and that many others with limited reserves and revenues will not plan boldly and adequately unless they are assured that federal funds will be available where necessary. This will probably be most prevalent in those areas where Negroes will constitute a large proportion of the unemployed.

In dealing with unemployment compensation, the report was much more concerned with "states rights" than with adequate benefits and the human values incident thereto. It was willing to risk the fall in consumer income and effective demand which will come from present inadequate rates in order to preserve such rights. Nor did the committee's report come to grips with the problem of post-war ghost towns. The possible existence of these industrially deserted villages was recognized, but no plans were developed for handling the problems they present.

Any optimism which the over-all soundness of the report may give is quickly destroyed by considering the actions of Congress. In February, 1945, the House of Representatives took its first important action relative to public works for the post-war period. On January 17, 1945, President Roosevelt asked Congress for $78,115,000 for planning public works. Such an appropriation was entirely in accord with the recommendations of the report discussed above. The House cut the figure to $5,000,000, and the United States Conference of Mayors commented on the cut by the House, telling the Senate Appropriations Committee that unless the full amount was reinstated the country was in for another WPA. The mayors wanted to guard against ill-conceived and wasteful temporary measures. They asserted that many cities were ready to spend several billions of local taxpayers' funds for public works as a part of a national re-employment program, but they added that they needed federal funds in order to have the projects ready at the end of the war. Finally, Congress appropriated $17,500,000.

There are many factors which will determine the kind of reconversion we have. Some are military and some are international. But the most important are domestic and can be controlled by the action we take in the United States. The only thing certain about reconversion is its uncertainty. We know, for example, that there is a large accumulated need for consumers' goods, and we know that workers have cash balances and savings. If they elect to spend these funds for consumers' goods, there will be more jobs in the immediate post-war period. And if they decide to invest a sizable proportion of their savings in new houses, the construction industry will expand. Its expansion will offer a larger volume of employment, and all this released purchasing power may lead to a disastrous inflation. If, on the other hand, a large segment of workers do not spend their savings, the volume of employment will decline and there will not be a smooth reconversion.

Action must, therefore, be taken to encourage the spending of accumulated funds and the direction of a large volume of them into housing at the same time that credit and price controls are maintained to guard against inflation. In order to promote the early purchase of goods and the propensity to consume, it is necessary to create a situation in which wage-earners and others have the greatest possible degree of economic security and, at the same time, the minimum of loss in earnings incident to transitional unemployment. In order to encourage people to invest in housing, there must be federal and local legislation, financial inducements through insured loans at low rates of interest, and programs for urban re-development and slum clearance.

Millions of workers will be displaced during the transition from war to peace; if they see no jobs in the near future, or if their incomes are reduced below any reasonable subsistence rates, they will not spend to meet their accumulated needs as freely as has been assumed by those who predict a speedy and smooth reconversion. After V-E Day many people felt that there was no assurance of a speedy transition. This was based upon the sound reasoning that no one had shown how the temporary reconversion unemployment would be terminated. In order to offset this feeling of despair, it is necessary for government at its various levels to prepare permanently to sustain effective demand and to develop flexible plans for public-financed projects to absorb any transitional displacement which threatens to become long-run.

Post-war ghost towns are a serious threat to the reconversion period. If America has a series of depressed areas where thousands of people are without employment and where there is little or no prospect of such employment in the future, the inability of such groups to purchase goods will affect the rest of the country. Such areas are one of the weakest links in our national economy, and unless the populations resident in them at the time of cut-backs are speedily transferred to communities where there are jobs, the spiral of unemployment may be started. It is not only necessary to effect transfers but it is also necessary to make sure that jobs are quickly available for the displaced workers. This, in turn, will be dependent upon the creation of a sufficient volume of post-war employment to absorb the labor supply. And the most important single industry in this connection is construction.

The concentration of Negroes in one-industry towns or their concentration in a single, greatly expanded local industry in a given town, is a serious aspect of the post-war ghost town problem. Long before V-E Day, it was clear that many communities to which a large number of colored workers had moved in response to the demands of war production had no desire to retain this new colored population. Negro migrant workers were usually concentrated in temporary war houses or trailer camps; they had not become a real part of the community, and there was no planning for their future housing or employment. Even if there were not this inhospitable community attitude, the local economy would not absorb them in peacetime. Where there was only a single war industry, as in Ravenna, Ohio, there were no immediate post-war employment prospects for either white or black workers. Where Negroes were concentrated in a single firm, as in Lima, Ohio, there was no prospect of peacetime employment for many of them. The firm involved often will not hire as many workers as it did during peak war production, and in the post-war economy many of its former employees will return from the armed services. Even if other local industries and plants expand in the peace, the established patterns of Negro exclusion will close the doors to colored workers. They will be a stranded, unwanted population.

In those communities where there are single, wartime industries, this is but a part of the whole problem of transferring workers from ghost towns to those places where jobs are available. The United States Employment Service will be required to perform such services, and, in light of its traditional attitudes and practices, extreme care should be taken to see that Negroes and other minorities get a full opportunity for participation at all levels of skill.

In those areas where there is a diversity of industry and where Negroes have been concentrated in a few industries and firms which will close down or contract in the peace economy, steps should be taken to open new types of employment to them. It is in this connection that the efforts of FEPC and others to open jobs for minorities on traction companies become really significant. This situation also points to the need of legislation for a permanent FEPC which would not be restricted to war industries and the importance of having state FEPC's to deal with industries and firms not engaged in interstate commerce.

There is an agricultural problem which is similar to the rise of ghost towns. It is the possible displacement of a million and a half white and Negro farmers and farmhands in the South by machinery. Southern agriculture has long been dominated by cotton production; and cotton production, because of the abundance of cheap labor and the seasonal need for large supplies of labor (at cotton picking time), has been extremely slow to introduce machinery and technological change. But the second World War has greatly modified the situation. The labor requirements of war industries reached down to the southern farms, and, by V-E Day there was an extreme shortage of labor on these farms. At the same time the cotton picker and other forms of machinery will be ready for large-scale production and marketing once the wartime limitations upon their manufacture are removed.

A large number of farm operators in the cotton country were ready to introduce new techniques in 1945. Others will follow suit because of the economies which will result. Those who resist will ultimately be caught between a world market price for cotton much below the current prices and the low cost possibilities of their domestic competitors who have used more effective methods. Many will lose their lands, and they will be replaced by a smaller number of operators who will use a much smaller number of workers. The result will be a displacement of large proportions. Negroes, of course, will constitute a large segment of those who will find no place in southern agriculture. What will happen to these black farm hands and operators, as well as what will happen to their white prototypes, will depend principally upon the volume of employment. Their fate in an economy with from ten to fifteen millions unemployed will be frightful. At best, they will present a serious problem of transition.

In the last analysis, the Negro's fate in the transitional period will be determined largely by what happens in construction. Most displaced colored war workers and veterans will be seeking work in heavy industry. Construction is the only one of such industries which will possibly expand rapidly during the reconversion period. It also has another important feature: it is not concentrated geographically and its expansion will usually be in proportion to the concentration of population. Without a large and flexible program of public works, there will be much unemployment among colored workers during the readjustment period and in the years after the period has been completed.

CHAPTER XVI

SENIORITY—A SPECIAL PROBLEM IN RECONVERSION

No DISCUSSION of the Negro in the post-war era or of Negro-union relations progresses very far without reference to seniority. The fact that by 1945 unions had bargaining contracts covering approximately two-thirds of the workers in manufacturing industries and that in such important types of war production as aluminum, automobiles, non-ferrous metal smelting and refining, shipbuilding, and basic steel over 90 per cent of the workers were under union agreements makes consideration of the subject inevitable. While there is much generalization about seniority and Negro labor, there can be no sound conclusion which will cover all or a majority of possible situations. Seniority, as all devices relating to lay-offs and re-employment, will have different effects in different industries and plants and from one worker to another.

In the simplest terms seniority is preference in employment based upon length of service. It is intended to offer maximum security and most desirable types of work to those who have rendered the longest service. As soon as the skilled workers on railroads had secured recognition and collective bargaining agreements, they pressed for seniority as a means of overcoming favoritism in an industry where employment tenure was interrupted by frequent transfers and lay-offs. The printing trades unions also pressed for seniority early in their development. In both instances seniority served to reduce greatly the number of craftsmen in the labor market. In less stable types of employment, such as building construction, clothing, and coal mining, there is an almost complete absence of seniority provisions in union agreements. Because a large part of the working force in these industries is simultaneously affected by slack work, most unions having jurisdiction in them have preferred work-sharing to seniority arrangements. No doubt the fact that many of the unions involved have traditionally received a large number of semi-skilled and un-trained recruits has also recommended the work rotation plan to them.

The development of work-sharing in coal mining and clothing has some interesting implications for the newer industrial unions. During the reconversion period many of these mass production unions will have a large part of their membership affected by slack work at one time. They, no less than construction, coal min-ing, and clothing, will have a large reserve of unemployed, trained operatives and unskilled workers on their rolls. It may be that in the next few years the desirability of seniority in these unions will be questioned. By V-E Day, however, most unions had accepted and were championing application of seniority in lay-offs and subsequent rehirings. No doubt the problem of the returning veteran, to whom some employers in a sudden burst of patriotism wanted to give job preference, had gone far to dic-tate the widespread acceptance of seniority by the newer unions.

Although there are many types of seniority, the following are the most important: (a) company- or plant-wide seniority under which seniority is computed upon the length of service in the company or the plant, and transfers from job to job within the plant or company have no effect on seniority standing; (b) de-partmental or occupational seniority under which there are sep-arate departmental or occupational seniority lists; (c) various combinations of (a) and (b). In each type of seniority it is cus-tomary to lay off those with the least amount of seniority first and to effect re-employment in reverse order to lay-offs. Such a procedure is in accordance with "strict seniority," the norm around which all seniority agreements are developed.

Were there no union seniority agreements hundreds of thou-sands of Negroes would be displaced from their wartime jobs during the reconversion. This would be true for many reasons. In the first place, in periods of widespread unemployment work-ers new to an industry, a plant, or an occupation are usually let out *as a group* before employees with longer service records. This is a form of employers' seniority. It differs from union sen-iority in that it is open to many exceptions and affords the individual with long work experience no assured job security. For a group, such as Negroes, however, it usually operates to effect general displacement from a new industry when there is widespread unemployment or radical changes in methods of production.

Second, a large proportion of Negro war workers have been concentrated in industries, such as shipbuilding, which will suffer extreme cut-backs in the peace economy. Many shipyards will close down completely, and all workers, white and black alike, will be permanently displaced irrespective of seniority. Similarly, a large number of Negroes have been employed in government-owned and privately operated plants which will either close down permanently or go into other types of production (often under new management). In many instances all wartime employees, regardless of seniority, will be discharged. Many thousands of Negroes attached to ordnance, aircraft, and iron and steel during the war will be included in this group. Finally, a disproportionately large number of colored men and women have been in government establishments—on temporary appointments. Most of these workers will be discharged, and union seniority agreements will not influence this development.

Once it is realized that the bulk of Negro displacement during reconversion will not be occasioned by union seniority alone and would probably occur if there were no widespread application of this seniority, it is possible to consider the influence of union agreements covering lay-offs and re-employment upon the black worker. In some industries and plants, union seniority will accelerate the displacement of colored war workers; in others it will operate to preserve the numerical gains in employment which Negroes have made during the war. For those workers who are fortunate enough to retain jobs in plants where they worked during the war, union seniority will have significant bearing on postwar occupational status. For all workers covered, union seniority will establish objective factors determining job continuity, upgrading or down-grading. The opportunity to retain a job, to remain in a skilled or semi-skilled job or to replace another worker at a lower level of skill will depend upon the worker's position on a seniority list rather than the whim of a foreman or the attitude of management. Under such an arrangement, the important factors are the rules for determining seniority lists, the regulations governing the operation of union seniority and the way management and unions carry out their agreements.

In general, it may be said that three over-all developments will determine the influence of union seniority upon Negro war workers. The first and all-important is the volume of employment. The second is the degree to which servicemen, formerly employed in a given plant, decide to return to their old jobs, and the third is the proportion of women (white) with longer seniority than Negro males who decide to stay on their wartime jobs. All of these are unknowns. It is, however, safe to assume (and fragmentary figures support this) that in a heavy and dirty industry, such as iron and steel, a smaller proportion of veterans will elect to take up their seniority rights than in a cleaner, higher-wage industry, such as automobiles. Also, a larger proportion of veterans and women will elect to use their seniority in a light industry, such as electrical goods, than in a heavy, lower-wage industry, such as meat-packing.

In many instances, however, the returning veteran will not have a chance to exercise his preference for certain types of work. One example will suffice to indicate the nature of this problem. Thousands of young men have been trained for aviation during the war; a large majority would like to remain in the industry. But the predictable post-war employment level of aviation will afford job opportunities for only a small fraction of those who might elect to enter the civilian branch of the industry. Many of those who may want to go into aviation after the war will find no opportunities, and if they have seniority rights in another industry, a large proportion will probably use them. The proportion will depend upon alternative work opportunities, and this will reflect the volume of employment in the nation.

Negroes have just recently been up-graded in some industries and in many plants. In such instances, the type of seniority—plant-wide, departmental, or occupational—will influence the extent to which these occupational gains are maintained. Where Negroes have long been employed in appreciable numbers and have recently been up-graded, plant-wide seniority will usually promote and assure their retention of better jobs, since it will permit them to bid for any and all types of work. In other plants where Negroes were concentrated in a few departments prior to the war and have recently been up-graded to lighter, cleaner, better-paying jobs in other departments, departmental seniority will accelerate their down-grading, since it will restrict their employment to a few types of work, or, if the volume of employment in the plant declines, it may lead to their displacement. In still other plants where Negroes have been recently up-graded, occupational seniority will have a similar effect. In addition, there are special types of seniority, such as the granting of plant-wide seniority to all workers with continuity of employment as of a given date (usually in the 1930's, when there were few Negroes employed) and permitting such employees to use their seniority on a plant-wide basis in selecting any job for which they may be qualified. Where, as is often the case, colored workers were concentrated in only a few types of production jobs and in unskilled work before the war, such agreements will wipe out many of their wartime occupational gains.

An analysis of seniority in the automobile industry of Detroit is instructive. In the first place, in Chapter V, we have described the process of conversion in the industry, and with that background the possibilities of reconversion become more clearly apparent. Second, automobiles present the case of an industry in which there will be intense reconversion problems and unemployment. Finally, the automobile industry stands midway between those types of production in which there will be almost complete permanent shut-down of most plants and those in which production and employment will expand after reconversion; in the automobile industry there will be a decline in payrolls incident to reconversion, but the estimated loss of employees is only 20 per cent of the wartime peak, and the post-war volume of employment is expected to be above any prewar level.

By March, 1945, the 75,000 Negroes employed in automobile plants in Detroit constituted about 15 per cent of all the workers in the principal plants of the industry. The hiring of colored women was delayed until long after Negro men and white women had been accepted, but by the spring of 1945 colored women had entered the industry in sizable numbers. With, and as a necessary condition to this expanded employment of Negroes there came significant occupational advancement. True, Negroes had not achieved equal up-grading opportunities, but there had been sufficient changes in the industry's occupational color patterns to make the preservation of war gains an extremely important and desirable goal to the Negro worker and the Negro community.

The problem was complicated by many factors. At first certain spokesmen for the automobile industry stated that it contemplated employing every available man in the Detroit area for peacetime production. The Detroit City Plan Commission, however, has estimated that after reconversion unemployment in the city may range between 100,000 and 300,000, and interviews with employers in the spring of 1945 indicated that many contemplated sizable declines in payrolls when they returned to peacetime production. It appeared that the big three, General Motors, Chrysler and Ford, would certainly reduce their employment rolls in the peace, although it was impossible to secure an accurate estimate of the extent to which reductions would be made. The Briggs Manufacturing Company had announced a 50 per cent cut in employment after the war, and Packard contemplated a comparable contraction. Hudson contemplated reducing its labor force from 17,000 in March, 1945, to about 13,000 in the post-war period. The Kelsey-Hayes Wheel Company expected a decline from 6,000 to 4,000. A few companies, such as Bohn Aluminum and Brass and Ex-Cell-O, expected to expand in the post-war period. Some of the others, such as Vickers, expected to achieve post-war levels of employment higher than the prewar ones; many of the companies were thinking of returning to 1940 volumes of employment.

As early as the spring of 1945, lay-offs were facing the industry and harassing its employees. Estimates varied as to the extent of the displacement which would follow V-E Day, but most competent observers put the figure between 250,000 and 400,000. On May 15, 1945, Murray Corporation of America, which had employed 11,000 during its wartime peak, reduced its payroll to 5,000. Workers hired as early as 1934 were included among those displaced. Total employment was reduced slightly over 50 per cent; Negro employment was reduced by about the same percentage.

Nowhere is the issue of veterans' treatment under union seniority more alive than in Detroit. Mr. W. Cronin, secretary of the Veterans' Committee of the Automotive War Production Council, speaking for the industry, has already demanded a change in union seniority rules to permit the hiring of servicemen who have never been employed by the industry. He wanted to provide for the employment of an equitable percentage of war veterans in the peacetime, proposing that veterans be placed "at least on equal footing with men and women who have entered the industry since the war began."

The UAW and many other unions had already agreed that all servicemen should be credited with employment seniority for the time they have spent in uniform. But this does not begin for the ex-serviceman without previous work experience in a plant until he gets a job, and it does not permit a newly hired veteran to displace a worker who has acquired seniority through employment in a plant since Pearl Harbor.

With such a sharp difference of opinion on this matter, seniority has become one of the most pressing issues in the automobile industry. The union took the position that if it gave in on this matter, its existence in the industry would be endangered if not lost. On the other hand, the union was conscious of the dangers which would arise if it is maneuvered into a position where it could be blamed for the unemployment of servicemen.

It is in such a complex situation that the problems of Negro displacement and down-grading incident to seniority have arisen. Special treatment for any workers who entered the industry after Pearl Harbor will certainly lead to additional pressure for special treatment for the veteran without past employment status. And, to add more confusion, these two groups are highly competitive; because if there is the type of post-war expansion in the automobile industry which a few prophesy (and many hope for), the new Negro worker and the new white worker will have more chance for a post-war job if the Negro and white veteran without employment experience is not "at least on equal footing" with them.

The six-point transfer agreement set forth the basic seniority principle which will govern employment patterns in the reconversion period. According to this agreement, *the worker transferred out of a peacetime job accumulated seniority in that job regardless of what he did in war production.* In only a few instances were there deviations from this basic principle, as in a small number of plants where labor-management contracts provided that a worker might take his peacetime seniority to his new department.

It may be well to pause and consider what the over-all seniority provision contained in the six-point transfer agreement means to Negro workers. *At the outset it must be realized that it can mean different things depending upon the volume and nature of post-war production.* In instances where a plant will expand in peacetime (an exceptional case in automobiles), such an agreement would limit the total employment and occupational diversification of Negro workers. This would follow because colored workers would accumulate seniority only in those few jobs in which they were employed in the prewar years. Since, however, most Negroes in automobile plants on V-E Day were employed after 1942, most would have no seniority. For those with seniority there would be job rights only in the occupations (usually foundry, janitorial and service) or in those departments where colored workers were employed prior to the war. The situation would, in many respects, be similar to that at the time of conversion to war production (described in Chapter V).

Under conditions of lesser volume of employment in peacetime, the situation is more complex. There would be much displacement, and any type of union seniority (or the absence of union seniority) would involve the discharge of a large number of colored (as well as white) workers. In some instances, where management is favorable to Negroes, the extent of this displacement would be less without union seniority; in other instances, management might seize upon a loose labor market situation as the excuse for dismissing all Negroes or the vast majority of them. Under the six-point transfer agreement a larger number of

Negroes would probably remain on the payroll than under con-ditions of plant-wide seniority, since the older Negro worker would have the right to jobs in occupations and departments which had traditionally been manned by Negroes. The older Negro employees would continue to work in a few departments, but they would lose most if not all of their wartime occupational advancement.

During peacetime production the Chrysler Corporation hired slightly less than 2,000 Negroes—all males; approximately 90 per cent of these were in the Detroit plants. In April, 1945, the cor-poration employed over 18,000 Negroes, and about 10,500 were in Detroit where they made up over 15 per cent of the working force. No Negro women were employed among the 6,000 female workers at Chrysler prior to Pearl Harbor; by April, 1945, there were over 5,000 colored women, who made up 15 per cent of all female workers in Chrysler plants.

By V-E Day, Negro men and women were working in each of the Detroit Chrysler plants in nearly every production capacity and in every unskilled capacity. Some colored men were in skilled jobs. Colored women were engaged principally in aircraft manu-facturing as riveters and kindred assembly operators, in main-tenance as sweepers and cleaners, in truck assembly, and as core-makers in foundry. Negro men, including some who in prewar days were janitors, yard laborers and foundry laborers, were working in many types of machine production, assembly, inspec-tion and maintenance jobs. At Chrysler, as in other automobile companies, the amount of Negro wartime up-grading had de-pended upon the extent that Negroes had pressed for better jobs, that unions had supported their claims, that management believed such up-grading would benefit the company, and that manage-ment had insisted upon up-grading.

At most Chrysler plants it is generally understood that all peacetime employees transferred to wartime occupations accu-mulated seniority in their peacetime jobs. It is also understood that there are and will be considerable variations among Chrysler plants as to the application of union seniority after the war. In addition to the master contract between the company and the Chrysler Department of the international union of UAW-CIO, supplementary agreements have been negotiated between local unions and individual Chrysler plants. One of the most interesting of these covers the Chrysler-Jefferson plant.

Early in May, 1945, officials of the Chrysler-Jefferson local reached a supplementary agreement with management providing that plant-wide seniority will apply to all employees who had seniority prior to January, 1938. Prior to this date few Negroes were in the plant. But the few who were in janitor and laborer capacities may, under the terms of this contract, use their pre-1938 seniority to qualify for any job in the plant for which they have training. As a matter of fact, however, most of the Negroes with long seniority at the Chrysler-Jefferson plant did not seek or secure training for production jobs. Consequently, the majority of the colored workers who have the longest seniority and the greatest opportunity to bid for the better jobs at the plant are not trained to perform these jobs and will not be able to benefit from the up-grading possibility which union seniority affords them.

Under the provisions of this proposed supplementary agreement, a few of the older Negro workers may be much better off occupationally after the war than they were before, and what is more, they may be better off after the war than they were during the war. At the same time, some Negroes hired before 1938 may be displaced since under plant-wide seniority they will be competing with *all* workers hired prior to 1938 rather than only with those workers in the departments where Negroes were traditionally employed in peacetime production. White workers, who under peacetime seniority could not bid for jobs outside their departments, will be able to compete for work as janitors and laborers, and many with long seniority, formerly in jobs for which there may be less demand than in prewar years, may displace individual Negroes from their prewar jobs. Since most of these prewar Negro jobs were unskilled, most whites will be qualified to perform them. The reverse of this, of course, is also true and may result in Negroes' displacing white workers. But since the proportion of Negroes at the Chrysler-Jefferson plant with pre-1938 seniority and the number of post-war jobs they are qualified to perform are small, the net result will not be in the Negro worker's favor.

This supplementary agreement would also mean that all new workers hired during the war period will be re-employed on the basis of seniority and qualifications. Since, however, Negroes were not hired in significant numbers until late 1942, many of them have little seniority and would be in an unfavorable competitive position.

The Briggs Manufacturing Company contemplates a peacetime payroll of 14,000 which is the same size as the employment in January, 1941. At the latter date there were 1,500 Negro workers; in the spring of 1945, when there were 26,000 workers at Briggs, some 5,000 Negroes were employed. Prior to the war, colored workers were used principally as material handlers, body sanders, janitors and laborers. During the war they moved into many new and more desirable classifications.

In the spring of 1945, the company announced its intention to hire over a thousand veterans with less than 90 days' or no seniority, 7,880 workers then on the company rolls with seniority as of May, 1940, or earlier, 610 not then working with the company but with seniority as of or before May, 1940, some 4,300 veterans with seniority, and 255 employees with seniority after May, 1940. Since the majority of Negro war workers were hired after 1942, it is clear that practically none of the 3,500 Negroes hired during the war would have any claim on a post-war job.

Even if the company is not successful in abrogating union seniority rules so as to hire over a thousand new veterans, the majority of new Negro employees will not have enough seniority to qualify for a post-war job. Whereas in some plants, the turnover of new white workers has been so great as to remove many from the seniority rolls and give the Negro a higher place on the lists, it appears that at Briggs the date of entrance for the first Negro war workers is so recent as to remove this as an effective factor. It seems, therefore, that the volume of Negro employment, as the volume of total employment, will be about the same as the prewar level. Since, however, Negroes constituted 10 per cent of the workers at Briggs in 1941, it is doubtful if, even in the absence of seniority, they would be a much larger proportion in peacetime production.

Under the six-point transfer agreement, Negro workers at Briggs would lose most of their wartime occupational gains. This would follow because workers would accumulate seniority in their original classification. There is, however, an additional factor operating to assure this. The officers of the Briggs local were among the first to negotiate a supplementary seniority agreement, an agreement which specifically states that when war work is completed the employee returns to his former classification. This supplementary agreement and the terms of the six-point transfer agreement, if carried out, will assure the loss of most of the Negro's wartime occupational gains.

The Packard Motor Car Company, where management's and union's early passing the buck on matters of Negro up-grading occasioned a veritable crop of hate strikes, has announced that the volume of Negro employment and the occupational opportunities for Negroes will be appreciably better in the post-war period than in the prewar years. In 1940, Packard hired 10,000 workers, of whom less than 4 per cent were colored; these Negroes were concentrated in the foundry. In January, 1945, Packard had 38,000 on its payroll, of whom 17 per cent were Negroes; by March employment had declined to 28,100, and Negroes made up 14 per cent of the total. Colored workers have been employed in many new occupations at Packard during the war.

The company plans to hire 18,000 workers in peacetime production, an increase of 8,000 over pre-war levels. Union seniority agreements in force in the spring of 1945 provided for plant-wide seniority with the privilege to interchange with any similar classification or job in the company. In addition, turnover has been extremely high at Packard during the war (in 1944 the company hired 80,500 workers), so that some wartime colored workers have been able to advance on the seniority lists. Negroes with long seniority (of whom there are less than 400) will be able to maintain their positions in skilled and semi-skilled classifications by keeping wartime jobs or displacing workers on a job for which the colored worker has "the necessary skill and ability to perform."

As a result of this situation, the company has estimated that 1,800, or 10 per cent of its post-war labor force, will be Negroes. This may be over-optimistic, since there are some 8,000 veterans with seniority, and probably two-thirds of them will demand their old jobs. These 5,300 veterans and a larger number of employees with seniority as of 1940 or earlier (of both groups, no more than 4 per cent Negroes can be expected) will fill the bulk of the available jobs. No more than five or six thousand workers with seniority as of 1940 or less will probably be retained. Even with this less optimistic estimate, it appears that plant-wide seniority at Packard, under conditions of a much higher volume of employment than before the war, could result in an appreciable increase in Negro employment and in occupational advancement as compared to the situation which existed in prewar production.

But there is a complicating factor. The reduction of the labor force at Packard to 18,000 will create a very complex situation in which jobs will be abolished, new ones created, and production greatly modified. In order for a worker to bid for a job in peacetime production, he must know where the job is or will be and something of the nature of the process involved. Also, the company will probably attempt to stabilize the working force by insisting that a large volume of these transfers be supported by grievance procedure. Consequently, the individual worker's chance to get a desirable job, even if he has the necessary seniority, will depend largely upon the support he gets from his shop steward or local union officials. The past record of the Packard local in handling Negro-white relations suggests that the Negro's post-war possibilities at Packard may be brighter in theory than in fact.

In the automobile factories of Detroit (and elsewhere) lay-offs and re-employment incident to reconversion will be determined by union seniority agreements. There will be a dispute over the status of the returning veteran, but in the spring of 1945 it seemed that union agreements will not give him equal seniority with the worker hired since Pearl Harbor. In automobiles, as elsewhere, the effect of seniority upon Negroes will differ from plant to plant and from worker to worker; the principal factor determining its influence, and for that matter, the post-war status of black and white labor, is the volume of employment. In general, however, the fate of the Negro worker in automobile production was determined by the six-point transfer agreement which perpetuated the prewar occupational status for most workers in the post-war period.

If only tentative conclusions can be drawn relative to the influence of union seniority upon Negro workers as a whole in the automobile industry, there are no similar limitations relative to Negro women. Female workers are paid the same wages and do similar work as men in automobile plants. Most women are in light and easy jobs, and it can be expected that high seniority males will demand jobs that women have held during the war. The heavier jobs occupied by these men during the war will, in turn, be filled with other men through up-grading as provided by union contracts. Negro women will share the same fate as other women; in addition, Negro women have the least seniority of any group in the automobile industry. Under any form of seniority, they will be largely let out; even if there were no union seniority, this would probably be true in the automobile industry.

The application of union seniority in the meat-packing industry will be beneficial to the Negro. It will operate to sustain the occupational gains colored workers have made in recent years, and it will tend to perpetuate the widespread numerical participation of Negroes in the industry. These results will follow because of the numerical concentration of Negroes in meat-packing, their long record of employment, their occupational distribution, the nature of the labor force which the newer Negro workers have replaced, and the widespread participation of Negroes in the United Packinghouse Workers of America-CIO.

Negroes began entering the northern branch of meat-packing as early as 1881, but it was during the strikes of 1894 and 1904 that they first came in large numbers. World War I, when manpower shortages made packers receptive to employing them, was the occasion for the second large-scale entrance of Negroes; by 1918 colored workers made up 20 per cent of the labor force. In the ensuing years, Negroes, particularly Negro women, lost many jobs, although they remained an important part of the labor force in many centers of meat-packing; by 1930 colored workers constituted slightly over 11 per cent of the total in the industry. During the depression, a large number of unemployed skilled building craftsmen and skilled workers from other industries sought job security in the relatively stable meat-packing industry. Many of these workers, who were white, had, by 1941, acquired from eight to ten years' seniority.

When the war broke out, the majority of the depression recruits to meat-packing left the industry for more desirable and higher paying employment in their usual occupations. In doing this, they forfeited their accumulated seniority. At the same time, the vacancies they created and the new openings in the industry were often filled by colored workers. Widespread wartime employment of Negroes in meat-packing, as elsewhere, was delayed until after 1942, and the use of Negro female war workers to any appreciable degree has been even more recent. As a result of these developments the proportion of Negroes in the industry had about doubled in the period from 1940 to 1945; officials of the United Packinghouse Workers estimate that in the spring of the latter year, from 30 to 35 per cent of all the production workers in the industry were Negroes, and in Chicago the proportion was over 50 per cent.

Since many of these colored men and women had taken the place of workers who had lost seniority, a large proportion of the Negroes in the industry had little to fear from displacement if lay-offs are determined by length of service. In addition, of course, many Negroes had long-time seniority. And selective service, while important, had not called as high a proportion of workers in meat-packing as in most other industries; this had been due principally to the age of workers who elected to remain in the industry and the large number of dependents which the younger men had.

Negroes, while long excluded from certain operations, had achieved a degree of occupational advancement in meat-packing prior to Pearl Harbor. Since that time, there has been additional occupational advancement and new departments and operations have been opened to colored workers. This has been due chiefly to two factors: the manpower needs of the industry, and the aggressive action of the United Packinghouse Workers for equal job opportunities and up-grading for all its members. Few unions have done a better job of education in intergroup relations among its membership; in few unions have Negroes been as active.

The post-war employment prospects in the meat-packing industry are good. Despite wartime expansion, the industry will hardly experience a drastic reconversion. Every indication suggests that the demand for meat will continue for some years to come, and that any serious diminution will be occasioned only by a breakdown of the economy and mass unemployment.

Most meat-packing plants have contracts which call for departmental seniority. A few, such as Swift, have seniority provisions which stipulate that promotions and demotions are to be made on the basis of departmental seniority. Lay-offs, however, are on the basis of plant-wide seniority. Under this arrangement, a higher-paid worker with a longer term of service may displace any other worker (for whose job he is qualified) with less seniority. If, however, the former worker elects not to take a lower-paid or otherwise less desirable job, he may accept the lay-off, and his departmental seniority continues to accumulate.

Union officials estimate that the number of veterans with accumulated seniority in the industry is much smaller than the number of workers with long seniority who have left meat-packing since Pearl Harbor. This fact will combine with the occupational distribution of Negroes, their period of service, and the probable post-war volume of employment to facilitate the continuing participation of Negroes at various levels of skills in the industry. Were there no union seniority in the industry, past experience suggests that general unemployment in other industries, due to reconversion (and possibly due to post-war levels of production), would occasion the displacement of many individual skilled Negroes by whites. This would probably be most prevalent in those departments which had been closed to Negroes until World War II. In the past, hostile, prejudiced, or extremely chauvinistic foremen had often taken the lead in effecting such down-grading. Similar developments and forces would probably lead to a real decline in the number and proportion of Negroes in meat-packing in the post-war period.

Individual Negroes, like individual white workers, will be displaced as the labor market loosens. If union seniority can be maintained in meat-packing, however, such displacement will be determined largely by the length of service and the attitudes and efficiency of the particular worker involved. Union seniority will offer real job protection and occupational status for the mass of Negro workers in the industry. And the United Packinghouse Workers of America have given ample evidence that they are ready and able to translate their non-discrimination statements into fact.

Negroes have long participated in the processing and handling of iron and steel. As in meat-packing, the early mode of entrance to the northern branch of the iron and steel industry was through strike-breaking, then, World War I accelerated the entrance of black labor into the industry. The proportion of Negroes in blast furnaces and steel rolling mills increased from 4.5 per cent in 1910 to 8.5 per cent in 1930.

From the start, the iron and steel industry has established "Negro jobs" and "white jobs." The former, of course, were the heavier, dirtier and lower-paid. This racial occupational system was generally accepted in the North as well as in the South; yet despite its existence, iron and steel as a heavy, dirty, hot industry probably had a larger proportion of Negro skilled workers than any other major type of manufacturing in the United States in 1930. In most instances, skilled Negroes were restricted to certain plants and to a limited number of departments in these plants.

During the depression of the 1930's, there was a great decline in the output of steel. Unemployment was extremely intense in this capital goods industry, and although in the earlier phase of the depression Negroes retained their relative proportion of employment, the proportion of colored workers in skilled trades was quickly and materially reduced. The greatest displacement of skilled Negro workers was in the North and West. Later there was disproportionately intense displacement of Negroes from the industry at all occupational levels, so that by 1940, colored workers constituted only 5.5 per cent of the workers.

Not reflected in these census data was the fact that although many Negroes were in the southern, middle Atlantic, and middle western branches of the industry, numerous plants hired either no Negroes or only an extremely small number in service and laboring capacities. This was most striking in Pennsylvania, Ohio, Indiana, and Illinois. Within a given steel corporation, it was not uncommon for certain plants to employ ten per cent Negroes or more while other plants used few if any colored laborers.

Early wartime expansions in Negro employment in iron and steel were concentrated in traditional occupations in firms which had used Negroes in the past. Ordnance, which was a rapidly expanding branch of the industry, afforded Negro men and women production jobs from the start, chiefly in new war plants. As the labor market became tighter, additional steel plants opened unskilled and semi-skilled jobs to Negroes. By the summer of 1942, the labor market developments and the non-discriminatory executive orders were accelerating the process, and about 7 per cent of those employed by iron and steel (including ordnance) were Negroes. A year later over 11 per cent of the workers in iron and steel were Negroes, as were 7.5 per cent of those in ordnance. At the beginning of 1945, the corresponding figures were 11.5 per cent and 9.6.

When, in 1936, the Steel Workers Organizing Committee started the campaign out of which the United Steel Workers of America-CIO emerged, it realized that Negroes would have to be fully included if the new organization were to succeed. Negro response was, in general, about the same as white, and large numbers of colored workers embraced unionism for the first time. Little progress, however, was made in securing up-grading for Negroes until 1942. This was due principally to two factors: the traditional acceptance of certain types of jobs for Negroes, with the resulting exclusion of colored workers from certain departments, and the general acceptance of departmental seniority by the new union. When, however, economic forces required a modification of the color occupational patterns, the United Steel Workers sometimes accelerated the process and secured up-grading for Negroes on the basis of their seniority. Thus, within departments where Negroes had worked in the past, the union successfully pressed for their up-grading; in departments and plants from which Negroes had long been excluded, the union occasionally joined government in urging the acceptance of Negroes, or in some cases it took the initiative. The union has also been effective in overcoming the opposition of white workers to the entrance of Negroes into better types or new areas of work.

In iron and steel, as in many other types of production, the Negro achieved numerical and occupational advancement during the period 1940-45. Because of the strong tradition of restricting Negroes to certain departments and occupations and the importance of long established plants in the total output of the industry (as contrasted to concentration of production in new plants in ordnance), the degree of up-grading has not been as great in steel as in many other war industries. Tradition had kept the Negro out of many jobs he might have filled and had the right to occupy in the prewar period; this same factor made his wartime occupational progress slow as compared to the rapid strides he has made in other industries. Despite this fact, however, there is ample evidence that the Negro worker has entered new types of work, new plants, and new departments during World War II.

A distinction should be made between iron and steel and ordnance. As a relatively new branch of the industry, ordnance was not hampered by racial traditions and could, as it did, hire a a sizable proportion of Negroes in new production jobs. This relatively favorable racial occupational pattern was accelerated by the fact that much of ordnance was carried on in government establishments, and a large proportion of the remainder was in government-owned and privately operated plants, where it was less difficult to enforce federal non-discriminatory policies. Production of ordnance will be drastically reduced in the peacetime economy. The bulk of workers, black and white, male and female, will be displaced, and union seniority will have little influence upon the status of the Negro who will be let out, regardless of the existence or absence of union agreements covering lay-offs and re-employment.

In the iron and steel industry, exclusive of ordnance, such will not be the case. Union seniority will often protect and perpetuate the recent gains of Negroes. Both management and union officials expect most of the established iron and steel plants to maintain or expand their prewar payrolls. The return to the 40-hour week will encourage such a development. In many instances, there may be some contraction from wartime levels, although the extent will vary from plant to plant. Where there are significant readjustments incident to reconversion, they are expected to be accomplished in a gradual manner. At the same time, steel is not a particularly attractive industry, and there has been tremendous turnover. Many white workers who entered the industry during the war quickly moved into other lighter and cleaner work. Negroes, too, moved in and out of steel, but since the more desirable industries were less hospitable to them, a larger proportion of colored workers remained in iron and steel. Those who did so have, obviously, accumulated seniority, and the departure of whites who were employed earlier advanced many colored workers on seniority lists.

A large number of white and Negro steel workers entered the armed services. Of these a fairly large proportion of the whites will look for other work and will not seek to exercise their job rights in iron and steel if they can get jobs in other fields. Negro veterans, on the other hand, will probably return to steel mills in relatively larger numbers. When they come back, they will find that some of the jobs to which they had a right before the war (and in which they could not get placements) have been opened to Negroes.

Although there is some plant-wide seniority in iron and steel, most union contracts are on the basis of departmental seniority. In those plants where Negroes were introduced into the labor force during the war, they were usually concentrated in the least desirable departments. Whites previously employed in such work often moved to other types of employment and consequently lost seniority in iron and steel. Even the white veteran who had seniority in these departments will often not choose to take it up if he can find any other kind of work. As a result of these circumstances, the Negro worker new to certain iron and steel plants will find job security in the application of union seniority.

In those plants where Negroes achieved promotion within given departments during the war, the prevalent union seniority agreements will give job security and occupational status to the older Negro worker. He will have long seniority, and for the first time this seniority will carry with it the right to more desirable jobs.

Where Negroes have entered new departments and where they have the better jobs in these departments, departmental seniority may lead to their displacement. If there is a combination of plant-wide and departmental seniority, a worker so displaced may secure a job in another part of the plant. If there is no provision for such transfer, he may be displaced from the plant. His loss of a permanent job in the industry is highly probable in instances where his new job is desirable. The chief danger to him is the white veteran who has accumulated seniority in the department and elects to use it.

In addition to the types of situations covered by the three industries described above, there will be another important category. It includes those types of production such as electrical equipment, engines and turbines, machinery, and scientific instruments, where Negro employment was negligible before the war, and in which wartime gains have been made. Without resorting to detailed analysis, it can be concluded that, in general, union seniority, regardless of type, will accelerate the displacement of colored workers and reduce, if not destroy, their occupational gains.

The generalization on the unfavorable influence of union seniority upon Negroes in these industries is based upon two factors: the newness of Negroes to the industry, and the competition of white women and returning veterans. In almost all of these branches of production few if any Negroes were hired prior to the war; those who were on the payroll were in laboring and service capacities. Colored workers, therefore, except the few who had prewar job status, cannot accumulate much seniority. At the same time these industries greatly preferred women to Negroes, and in most plants white women have more seniority than Negro men. And a larger proportion of white veterans from these industries will elect to use their accumulated seniority.

For the most part these industries will contract in the peace. There will, therefore, be a much smaller number of jobs than workers with seniority. A larger proportion of women will want to stay in many of these industries than in heavy or dirty production. Negroes, as a group, will have the shortest length of service. They will be the first laid off, and it is doubtful if on an industry-wide basis they will be able to achieve rehiring. In their case, union seniority will assure and accelerate a development which economic factors would occasion to a large degree.

The simplest solution to the seniority problem as it affects Negroes may seem to be the adjustment of the rules in those instances where injustice will result. Seniority lists and an estimate of post-war employment levels indicate the locale of such developments. And there is much to be said in favor of the end result. There are adjustments in seniority to permit the continuing employment of shop stewards and other union officials. Since the Negro's gains in some industries and many plants have been very recent, strict seniority would in many instances erase all or many of these gains. In such situations it is not the Negroes' fault that they are concentrated at the bottom of the seniority lists. A union which has expended much energy and effort to achieve the integration of Negroes certainly stands to lose, if under its own seniority rules all colored workers are displaced, or the vast majority are relegated to the lowest-paid jobs. For there are grave dangers to unions in mass production industries if Negro members are thrown out of work as a group and remain idle and anti-union in the labor market.

Although there is much merit to the argument for seniority adjustment, it is too simple. As a general rule, group-adjusted seniority is like hot ice cream; it is not consistent with the basic principles of the concept. Although adjustments in seniority may be desirable *where they can be achieved with the full understanding and support of white and Negro membership and where the Negro workers realize and fully accept the temporary nature of the arrangement,* as a practical matter, there are few unions which can or will take this step. In this connection it cannot be stressed too much that if there are adjustments in seniority for any group, and the rank and file of union members do not understand and approve the move, there will be resentment against the preferred group. If it happens to be composed of Negroes, those who have strong feelings about seniority (and the unions have been stressing its importance for some time) will be joined by those who are anti-Negro in opposing the move. The result will be intense anti-Negro sentiment in the union.

After all, union officials are elected. During World War II, only a very small fraction of the membership attended meetings and participated actively in union affairs. In many locals the proportion of Negroes among this minority of active members was small. This has two important implications. In few unions is there any machinery to reach the bulk of members and explain why group adjustments in seniority may be desirable for the union; in an even smaller number of unions are the Negro members active enough to give adequate political support (votes) to union officials who might try to effect such adjustments. Then, too, there is the ever-present pressure for relaxing seniority rules so as to give hiring preference to veterans with no job experience. Many unionists argue honestly, and with much logic to their position, that once group adjustments are made in seniority, there will be pressures for so many adjustments in so many directions that the whole system will break down.

Most Negro workers in war plants had from one to three years' seniority in the spring of 1945. Most women in war work had slightly more seniority than colored males, and there were a large number of veterans and potential veterans with at least four years' seniority. At the same time there were a vast number of young and desirable veterans who had no seniority but who will be attractive to employers as individual workers and as a group which can be used to weaken labor unions. Seniority adjustments for Negroes, if widespread, would probably become the basis for a drive to effect preferential employment for veterans without previous seniority. Many of the same arguments that are advanced in favor of special treatment for Negroes could be applied to veterans, and certainly a proposal for adjustments in favor of ex-servicemen would receive much more public support. If, however, such a development should occur, and if in its wake unions were destroyed, it seems likely that much of the resentment against the destruction of these unions would be transferred from the veteran to the Negro.

Philip Murray, president of CIO, has set forth his organization's opposition to relaxations in union seniority agreements. In discussing this problem as it affects Negroes, he has rightly emphasized the fact that only in an expanding post-war economy can Negro workers hope for job opportunities and occupational status. Mr. Murray has pointed out that seniority eliminates favoritism in lay-offs, rehiring, and up-grading, while its relaxation would create anti-Negro and anti-union attitudes on the part of white workers and "transfer the burden of discriminatory hiring policies of management to the labor movement, where it does not belong." Mr. Murray added, "If seniority principles are not equitably and justly applied, the remedy is to make it work, not destroy the vehicle which is the prime guarantee against discrimination within industry which is government by labor industry contracts."

In certain industries and plants where post-war production will reqire an equal or smaller number of workers than did war production, the union seniority problems of the Negro worker are a part of a larger issue. It is a conflict of interest between the older workers who have long departmental and plant seniority and the newer workers who have little tenure. Where, for example, there are supplementary agreements giving the older men plant-wide seniority, with the right to displace other workers in any department, the down-grading of most of the younger men is inevitable. But in many plants, the younger workers are numerically strong enough to defeat such agreements. Apparently, they have not been active in union affairs in large numbers; once their job status becomes involved they may become active. The younger white and Negro workers who are displaced or down-graded by union seniority may yet get together on their common problems. The acceptance of supplementary seniority agreements affords a ready mechanism for effecting modifications in situations which present a threat to their future interests, and it would be the type of remedy suggested by Mr. Murray in instances where the principles of seniority are "not equitably and justly applied." In the case of both groups, however, this will involve infinitely more union activity than has typified them in the period of war production.

In the spring of 1945 union problems of seniority were just beginning to appear. Even at that date it was clear that they would present great difficulties. While it seemed that no appreciable relaxations in seniority can or will be made by unions during reconversion, it is possible that some relaxations may ultimately be required by events. In some mass production industries it is difficult to see how union strength and union contracts can be maintained if large reserves of experienced workers remain on the labor market at the same time that their former fellow-workers remain in full employment. No doubt the membership which is employed will favor the termination of seniority after a short lay-off period. This may precipitate another political battle within the union if it is proposed at a time when the laid-off workers are still affiliated in large numbers. Even if there is no appreciable opposition, it is difficult to see how the union will be able to retain the loyalty and support of members who have no seniority, i.e., right to a job; and in mass production industries, it is extremely dangerous for unions to permit a large number of qualified workers in the labor market to be unaffiliated or anti-union.

The Negro is important in this picture because, seniority or no seniority, it will be difficult to convince him or the community from which he comes that he has not been discriminated against. It will be an exceptional employer who will not reply to his quest for work with the factual statement that union seniority regulations occasioned his dismissal. The same situation, without the complicating factor of race and color, will exist in relation to white workers similarly laid off. These men and women—black and white alike—will form a dissatisfied pool of labor. Many of them will not look kindly at the unions. All of them will be a source of weakness to organized labor.

CHAPTER XVII

WHAT TO DO

THE NEGRO worker made significant gains between 1942 and 1945. He secured more jobs at better wages and in a more diversified occupational and industrial pattern than ever before. He was beginning to participate as a real part of the American labor force, and his membership in unions increased to a remarkable degree. These gains were due primarily to two factors: the existence of full employment, and the application of a federal policy of fair employment practices.

Long before V-E Day, it was clear that the nation faced the possibility of long-term mass unemployment in the post-war period. This was a threat to all workers and to labor unions; it loomed as a major catastrophe for the black worker who, despite wartime gains, was far from integrated into American industry. Negroes were among the first to experience displacement due to cut-backs, and it was obvious that as transitional unemployment mounted, they would feel its effects with disproportionate intensity. By the spring of 1945, the application of union seniority in lay-offs was often accelerating and intensifying the displacement of colored workers.

The only effective attack upon mass unemployment is to plan and act to assure jobs for all; the best safeguards against intense and prolonged suffering incident to transitional displacement are adequate unemployment benefits and action to secure full employment as soon as possible; the surest way to minimize individual and group displacement due to seniority is to provide work opportunities for all. Each of these basic economic post-war problems will be influenced markedly by the over-all economic condition of the nation; an adequate volume of employment emerges as the most effective approach to all of them.

Full employment will not solve all of the problems of management, labor, or minorities; nor will it remove all of the occasions for intergroup tensions and conflicts. It will, however, create an economic situation in which racial competition for jobs will be reduced, management can continue to utilize minority groups' workers in higher levels of employment, and labor unions can extend their programs of education for intergroup understanding. Full employment will create an economic and social framework in which one of the basic causes of group antagonisms can be dealt with effectively.

Full employment means more than jobs. It has been indicated above that even if we are able to effect a smooth reconversion, there is the possibility of a deficiency in consumer demand soon after the war is over. In order to offset this, some economists have advocated the development of well-conceived public works, more adequate social security, and expanded cultural advantages. The people who would benefit from the resulting facilities and services are those who are most directly concerned in intergroup problems, low-income white and Negro families.

In a society with greater economic security and the prospect of continuing job opportunities, the working people would be more prone to concentrate upon the real economic and social problems which affect them. They would have less motivation, and eventually, less inclination to keep their competitors down as a means of securing a larger segment of an inadequate volume of employment and services. The Negro too would share in this greater security. At the same time he would develop a greater sense of belonging since he would have a chance to earn a living and an opportunity to benefit from a larger total supply of housing, education, health services, and recreational and leisure-time facilities. It is only in a setting such as this that the recent economic gains for color minorities can be consolidated and expanded; it is only in such a social and economic setting that America can hope to make real progress in solving its race problem. For color tensions arise from job competition, inadequate housing, inferior education and other public services, and feelings of not belonging. They are nurtured by general and individual insecurity, and in periods of widespread social disorganization they offer ready and welcome ammunition for demagogues.

Regardless of what is done to assure full employment and a smooth reconversion, the transition from a war- to a peacetime economy will involve a large volume of temporary unemployment. This, in turn, will mean the dislocation of a vast number of colored workers and the loss of occupational advancement. There will be competition for too few jobs as long as this unemployment exists, and the color line will be the location of many strained and tense situations. Each of these will require special treatment if the possibilities of conflict are to be minimized. At the same time, there must be some over-all approach aimed at meeting the national aspects of the problem. The most significant result which can be achieved when there are severe job dislocations is the creation of a feeling on the part of all groups that America is prepared to meet its post-war problems and that reconversion dislocations are to be of temporary duration.

Color minorities need more. They need tangible evidence that their nation, their state, and their community are all prepared to encourage and secure fair employment practices. The federal government, hesitantly and belatedly, gave such evidence through the creation of FEPC, and that wartime agency has become a symbol to Negro Americans. Its abolition, or the denial of necessary jurisdiction and sanctions to assure its peacetime effectiveness, will occasion great disillusionment among Negroes. This disillusionment will have its economic bases in the extreme job displacement which will occur, and it will have its psychological bases in the frustrations which will follow from Negroes' losing a symbol of security.

In the early war years Negroes were not fully employed even when the available local supply of white labor had been absorbed. This was particularly true where new industries, firms and occupations were involved. In the transition to peacetime production, Negroes will be displaced from many desirable types of work. Even if the demand for labor subsequently increases, they will not automatically go back into equally desirable types of employment. At the same time industries and establishments which have never hired many Negroes will expand in the peace. Unless, therefore, there is machinery to see that Negroes as a group hold on to some of their wartime employment gains, and unless this machinery starts to effect Negro participation in new types of work early in reconversion, the post-war prospects for colored workers are dark.

Traditionally prejudiced labor unions will revert to old practices unless there is some federal or state agency constantly pushing them out of these practices. Those unions which are progressive will act more quickly and decisively to enforce announced non-discriminatory policies if they have the prodding of fair employment legislation to justify their action to a questioning (and sometimes hostile) membership.

America—black and white alike—has little understanding of what a federal policy and machinery for fair employment practices can do. Obviously, it will not create any larger volume of jobs, and, obviously, unless there is enough work to go around, some will be without employment. Economically, then, fair employment practices will serve only to divide more equitably such work as is available at any given time. This will not eradicate racial and group competition for too few jobs; it will not mitigate white opposition and hostility toward Negroes' having work while some whites are permanently idle. It will, however, provide a legal and official basis for employer and union action to give minorities a larger and more equitable share of the existing work; it will bring some recalcitrant employers and unions in line; it will protect those employers and unions which want to be fair from being pressed to absorb a disproportionately large segment of the available Negro labor supply. And it will, for a time, sustain the morale of black America and its belief in American democracy.

A federal program for fair employment practices will do the latter because it will maintain a symbol and perform significant functions. If a continuing FEPC succeeded only in establishing equal employment opportunities for Negroes in the federal agencies, it would be extremely significant as a precedent to private industry and as a source of hope and confidence to Negroes. A permanent FEPC, with powers of enforcement, will do this and more. It will extend the New Deal successes in securing equitable employment for minorities on public-financed construction, and such public works will be extremely important during a smooth reconversion and a peacetime economy of full employment. A federal statute requiring fair employment practices in industries engaged in interstate commerce would offer the assistance to progressive unions outlined above, and it would result in greater diversification of minorities' employment. Most important, it would be the one possible effective machinery to assure minorities a chance to preserve some of their recent occupational gains.

Racial employment patterns established during the reconversion period will have significant influence upon the post-war employment prospects for colored citizens. The demand for labor will shift during reconversion, and there is every indication that most of the industries destined to expand do not and have not employed many colored workers. The concentration of gains in Negro employment in a few war industries and in a relatively small number of individual plants has further complicated the issue. All of these circumstances re-enforce the need for federal, state and local action to assure fair employment practices.

The war opened many new types of training to Negroes. Most of this has been in occupations essential to the prosecution of the war; some will be important in the peace. In the post-war economy, however, the volume of trade schooling will decline. The Negro will, nevertheless, need additional preparation if he is to be a participating segment in the trained labor supply of the nation.

Prior to Pearl Harbor, there had been an extreme shortage of young Negro artisans in the construction industry. This was due, in part, to the fact that during the depression few men entered the building trades crafts; it was also due to the fact that the number of Negro apprentices had been steadily declining for a generation. In addition, the increasing importance of the mechanical trades in construction had reduced the proportion of Negro artisans in the industry since colored workers were generally excluded from these newer occupations. In the post-war period the demand for building mechanics will increase appreciably. Unless, however, younger Negroes are given the chance and encouraged to prepare themselves for this work, the prewar trend toward a decline in Negro construction craftsmen will be continued.

At the same time, the Negro will face a work-world in which labor unions will be more important than they were prior to the second World War. If he is to maintain a place in the future economy, he must be conditioned to participate in labor unions, and events in the earlier phases of reconversion have indicated that his participation has been woefully inadequate in many local situations. This will place a new responsibility upon the trade school which prepares him and upon the vocational guidance agency which gives him counsel. The Negro community itself must be prepared to orient the black worker to participate in and to understand organized labor.

Agencies and individuals concerned with the training and placement of Negroes must give more attention to the directions which the demand for labor will take. An example of new employment possibilities is afforded by considering housing. Certainly in the post-war period we shall build a large number of houses for low- and medium-income families; many of these will be in multiple unit projects, and a large segment of them will be occupied by Negroes. These large housing projects will have to be managed and maintained. For the most part, there are today few individuals prepared to perform efficiently either of these functions; they are, however, occupations in which the Negro, if trained, can find professional employment.

In our larger cities, it is possible that the mistress and servant relationship in domestic service will be displaced by an employer-employee relationship. There is, for example, no reason why the cleaning of apartments and small homes cannot be so organized as to permit its being done on contract. Such an approach will require organization of the service and will involve the substitution of wage-earners for the traditional individual servant. The Negro, as the accepted domestic worker, can and should take an active part in the organization, operation and execution of this new expression of a traditional occupation.

Three measures are of crucial importance on the federal level. The first is legislation and planning to assure full employment.

The second is legislation and administrative machinery to achieve a smooth and quick reconversion. The third is federal legislation for a permanent FEPC with sanctions for enforcement.

While it is true that any one state is relatively ineffectual in securing full employment by itself, there is no such relative impotence in regard to the assurance of fair employment practices. Already New York has passed a law creating a state FEPC with enforcement powers. Indiana's legislature labored long and brought forth a legislative mouse—a FEPC with no powers of enforcement, which says in effect that it is naughty to discriminate. New Jersey has a law against discrimination in employment. Pennsylvania had an excellent bill in the 1945 session of its legislature, but it failed to enact it. Similar legislation was pending in a dozen or more states in the spring of 1945, and its enactment was a first step towards meeting the pressing post-war economic problems of intergroup relations.

The state FEPC has certain areas of operation which are peculiarly its own. As has been noted, there will be a shift in employment to service industries and the distributive trades. The number and proportion of persons employed in public and semi-public utilities will also probably increase in the peace. None of these significant branches of industry can be reached by a federal fair employment agency, which of necessity will be restricted to firms engaged in interstate commerce; none of them has traditionally hired a large number of non-whites; nor has any of them used Negroes in clerical capacities, or often on skilled jobs. State legislation and machinery for securing fair employment practices are necessary if colored workers are to share in these expanding industries.

At the same time, the state has many employees, and seldom do Negroes have an equal chance to join this growing corps of civil servants. It is important that private enterprise be inspired to democratic employment practices through the example of government at all levels. The state will set such patterns only if there is a legislative basis for them.

Next to the federal government, the local community and its government have the greatest opportunity to contribute to the establishment of full employment. After all, the incidence, the cost, and the dangers of mass unemployment initially fall upon the local community. Certainly the disastrous results from racial conflict affect the local community more than any other geographic unit.

Few communities had, by V-E Day, become fully conscious of what widespread unemployment would mean to them. Most war centers with inflated populations still were indulging in wistful hoping (and believing) that the swollen labor supply would evaporate or move back home. Few, however, were prepared to investigate where and how these workers would move. As a result, few areas with large numbers of migrant workers were concerned about the national volume of employment or adequate plans to move men to available jobs.

The first responsibility of a local community is to recognize that failure to plan for enough jobs to engage the local labor supply (either at home or in another area) will involve serious economic, social and morale costs to the community. (Such failures are, of course, terribly dangerous to the economy as a whole since they may represent the first phase of a spiral of national unemployment.) Minority groups are directly concerned with prompt local action to secure an adequate volume of employment. For as long as there are large numbers of unemployed workers in the local labor market, economic problems are generally distorted into group antagonisms, and the community escapes facing and taking action upon a basic issue.

There are two principal sources of employment in any area: privately financed industry (including agriculture) and government-financed projects and activities. Every inducement should be given to private enterprise to supply work for all. When and where it cannot do the whole job, as it admits in almost every community, there must be advanced planning for programs of public works and associated developments. Post-war activities of this nature will largely be in response to local initiative, and we cannot hope for full employment unless that initiative is forthcoming. Local planning for full employment is fundamental to jobs for all; jobs for all are fundamental to economic opportunities for minorities and intergroup understanding.

On the local level, as on the state and federal levels, there must be provisions for equitable distribution of the available jobs. The first place to attack this problem is in the municipal agencies where patterns of fair employment practices should be established. In recent years several scores of official mayors' interracial committees have been formed. The establishment of democratic racial employment in city government is one of the first projects to which they should give attention.

The experiences of the PWA and, more recently, the experiences of public housing have shown that Negroes do not automatically enjoy equal work opportunities on public-financed construction projects. Craft unions have often been the principal impediment. It is important, therefore, for local governments to establish fair policies and machinery to enforce such policies on public works. First, there needs to be a city ordinance prohibiting racial discrimination. Then, the labor unions should be brought together with the contracting agency of the city government in order that they can know in advance the city's position on this matter. Finally, some responsible official or agency in the city administration must be charged with the duty of seeing that contractors and labor unions follow announced statements of policy.

It is difficult to be optimistic about the future prospects for full employment and racial understanding. In the spring of 1945, the nation was approaching the post-war period and there was little machinery to plan for an adequate volume of employment. Important legislation was pending in Congress, but its passage was not at all certain. More alarming was the fact that there was no effective and active over-all planning machinery on the federal level. And full employment requires such machinery, for legislation alone is inadequate.

There was no assurance that adequate controls will be maintained during the period of transition from war to peace, although there seemed to be an increasing realization of the desirability of such controls. The danger, of course, was that the situation may get out of hand before there is effective action to set up machinery to minimize the intensity of unemployment during reconversion and to sustain purchasing power at the same time that inflation is guarded against.

In the latter part of May, 1945, the Senate Education and Labor Committee voted to send the fair employment practice legislation to the floor of the Senate; there it faced the threat of a filibuster by southern senators. In addition, the life of the wartime FEPC was endangered by adverse House action on the 1946 budget for the agency, and Senate action on an appropriation for the agency gave rise to a short filibuster in which the Senators from Mississippi vied in filling the air with attacks upon Negroes.

On the local level, there was little to give encouragement. Where cities had established machinery to consider post-war planning, in almost every instance the volume of jobs contemplated was inadequate to assure full employment. Municipal planning, no less than industrial planning, had assumed that the other fellow would take up any apparent slack. In race relations, the trend was in the same direction. After the Detroit race riot of 1943, scores of cities established mayors' and citizens' committees on race or intergroup relations. These cities were frightened, and they wanted to prevent local riots. It soon became apparent that riot prevention was not enough and that the only significant steps were those which attempted to deal with the basic causes of intergroup tensions and conflicts, and employment is a principal one of these. But most local committees had shied away from these basic issues; and, when the summer of 1944 passed without a serious racial clash, most intergroup committees were content to sit and wait for another crisis.

These are familiar developments in the United States. They do not, of course, mean that the employment needs of the post-war period will not be met. They do indicate that we had not prepared ourselves by V-E Day to deal with the inevitable problems of the future. It is possible that as critical situations face us, we will be ready to act. It is unfortunate, however, that such action will be hasty and not as effective as that which is carefully planned and based upon study and competent research.

The Negro is dedicated to fight for the right to work. In doing this he is simply expressing a universal desire to survive. The danger ahead is that his fight to work and that of his white prototype may occur in a society with not enough jobs to go around and result in racial conflict. In the past this has often happened, and there is every reason to believe that it may typify the postwar period. In the United States, it's work or fight on the color line.

SELECTED BIBLIOGRAPHY

"Analysis of Veterans' Seniority Proposals," *Briggs Assembler*, December, 1944, pp. 12-13.

Bailer, Lloyd H., "The Negro Automobile Worker," *Journal of Political Economy*, October, 1943, pp. 415-28.

Beveridge, William H., *Full Employment in a Free Society* (Norton, 1945). 429 pp.

Branson, Herman, "The Training of Negroes for War Industries in World War II," *Journal of Negro Education*, summer number, 1943, pp. 376-85.

Brown, Earl, and Leighton, George R., *The Negro and the War* (Public Affairs Committee, Inc., 1942). 32 pp.

Brown, Ina Corinne, *Socio-Economic Approach to Educational Problems* (Government Printing Office, 1942). 166 pp. Volume I of the National Survey of the Higher Education of Negroes of the U. S. Office of Education.

Caliver, Ambrose, "Office of Education Services to Negroes," *Education for Victory* (U. S. Office of Education, Federal Security Agency, February 20, 1945), pp. 19-24.

Cayton, Horace R., and Mitchell, George S., *Black Workers and the New Unions* (University of North Carolina Press, 1939). 473 pp.

Cohn, David L., "How the South Feels," *The Atlantic Monthly*, January, 1944, pp. 47-51.

Cooper, Lyle, *Reasons for the United Packinghouse Workers of America Favoring the Creation by Congress of a Permanent Fair Employment Practice Commission, as Provided in S. 101* (Chicago: UPWA, 1945). 15 pp. (mimeographed).

Davis, John A., *How Management Can Integrate Negroes in War Industries* (New York State Committee on Discrimination in Employment, 1942). 42 pp.

—— "The Negro Outlook Today," *Survey Graphic*, November, 1942, pp. 500-3, 562-3.

Demobilization and Readjustment (National Resources Planning Board, 1943). 106 pp. Report of the Conference on Post-war Readjustment of Civilian and Military Personnel.

Economic Base of Detroit (Detroit: City Plan Commission, 1944). 53 pp.

Economic Problems of the Reconversion Period (Government Printing Office, 1944). 79 pp. Fourth Report of the House Special Committee on Post-war Economic Policy and Planning.

Edwards, Alba M., *A Social-Economic Grouping of the Gainful Workers of the United States* (Government Printing Office, 1938). 264 pp.

Employment of Negroes as Platform Operators in the Local Transit Industry (Committee on Fair Employment Practice, 1945). 4 pp.

Employment Security Review (Washington: Social Security Board). July, 1942, the entire issue.

"Extent of Collective Bargaining and Union Status, January, 1945," *Monthly Labor Review*, April, 1945, pp. 816-22.

FEPC: How It Operates (Government Printing Office, 1944). 19 pp. A pamphlet of the Committee on Fair Employment Practice.

Feldman, Herman, "The Technique of Introducing Negroes into the Plant," *Personnel* (American Management Association, September, 1942), pp. 461-6.

"Found: A Million Manpower," *Modern Industry*, May 15, 1942, pp. 28-31.

Franklin, Charles L., *The Negro Labor Unionist of New York* (Columbia University Press, 1936). 415 pp.

Frazier, E. Franklin, *The Negro Family in the United States* (University of Chicago Press, 1939). 686 pp.

Fuller, Helen, "Controls after Victory," *The New Republic*, April 9, 1945, pp. 472-3.

Furcolowe, Charles, "The Truth About Negro Labor," *Forbes'*, December 1, 1942, pp. 8-9.

Gosnell, Harold F., "Symbols of National Solidarity," *Annals of the American Academy of Political and Social Science*, September, 1942, pp. 157-61.

Granger, Lester B., "Barriers to Negro War Employment," *Annals of the American Academy of Political and Social Science*, September, 1942, pp. 72-80.

—— "Negroes and War Production," *Survey Graphic*, November, 1942, pp. 469-71, 543-4.

—— Sobel, Louis H., and Wilkinson, William H., *Toward Job Adjustment* (Welfare Council of New York City, 1941). 78 pp.

"Half a Million Workers," *Fortune*, March, 1941, p. 96 et seq.

Handbook of American Trade-Unions (Government Printing Office, 1936). 340 pp. Bulletin No. 618 of the Bureau of Labor Statistics, U. S. Department of Labor.

Hansen, Alvin H., *Full Recovery or Stagnation?* (Norton, 1938). 350 pp.

—— "Wanted: Ten Million Jobs," *The Atlantic Monthly*, September, 1943, pp. 65-9.

Harbison, Frederick H., *Seniority Policies and Procedures as Developed Through Collective Bargaining* (Princeton University, 1941). 63 pp.

—— *Seniority Problems During Demobilization and Reconversion* (Princeton University, 1944). 31 pp.

Haynes, George E., *The Negro at Work During the World War and During Reconstruction* (Government Printing Office, 1921). 144 pp.

Hearings Before Select Committee Investigating National Defense Migration (Government Printing Office, 1941). 34 parts. Report of Tolan Committee.

Henderson, Elmer W., *The Employment of Negroes in the Federal Government* (Committee on Fair Employment Practice, 1943), 7 pp. (mimeographed).

Herbst, Alma, *The Negro in the Slaughtering and Meat-Packing Industry in Chicago* (Houghton Mifflin, 1932). 182 pp.

Johnson, Charles S., *Patterns of Negro Segregation* (Harper, 1943). 332 pp.

―――― *The Economic Status of Negroes* (Fisk University Press, 1933). 53 pp.

Johnston, Eric A., "We Must Have Steadier Jobs," *The Saturday Evening Post*, March 31, 1945, p. 11 et seq.

Keynes, John Maynard, *The General Theory of Employment, Interest and Money* (Harcourt, Brace, 1936). 403 pp.

Kirkpatrick, Forrest H., "Color in the Production Line," *International Quarterly*, summer, 1942, pp. 25-7, 46.

Lasseter, D. B., "The Impact of the War on the South and Implications for Postwar Developments," *Social Forces*, October, 1944, pp. 20-6.

Lee, A. M., and Humphrey, N. D., *Race Riot* (New York: The Dryden Press, 1943). 143 pp.

Lewis, Edward, "We Tackled the Unions—and Won," *Opportunity*, May, 1940, pp. 138-40.

Locke, Alain, "The Unfinished Business of Democracy," *Survey Graphic*, November, 1942, pp. 455-9.

Manpower: One-Tenth of a Nation (Government Printing Office, 1942). 15 pp. A pamphlet of the War Manpower Commission.

Marshall, Thurgood, "Negro Status in the Boilermakers Union," *Crisis*, March, 1944, pp. 77-8.

McWilliams, Carey, *Brothers Under the Skin* (Little, Brown, 1943). 325 pp.

Minorities in Defense (Government Printing Office, 1941). 19 pp. A pamphlet issued by the Committee on Fair Employment Practice and the Labor Division of Office of Production Management.

Monthly Survey of Events and Trends in Race Relations (Fisk University). All issues.

Murray, Philip, "CIO Head Opposes Seniority Revision," *The Chicago Defender*, January 27, 1945.

―――― *C.I.O. Re-employment Plan* (Washington: Congress of Industrial Organizations, 1945). 29 pp.

Myrdal, Gunnar, *An American Dilemma* (Harper, 1944). 2 vols., 1483 pp.

―――― "Is American Business Deluding Itself?" *The Atlantic Monthly*, November, 1944, pp. 51-8.

Negro Workers After the War (National Negro Congress, 1945). 23 pp. A pamphlet.

Negro Workers and the National Defense Program (Bureau of Employment Security, Social Security Board, 1941). 21 pp.

Northrup, Herbert R., "The Negro and the United Mine Workers of America," *Southern Economic Journal*, April, 1943, pp. 313-26.

―――― "Organized Labor and Negro Workers," *Journal of Political Economy*, June, 1943, pp. 206-21.

―――― *Organized Labor and the Negro* (Harper, 1944). 312 pp.

Odum, Howard W., *Race and Rumors of Race* (University of North Carolina Press, 1943). 245 pp.

Ransom, Leon A., "Combatting Discrimination in the Employment of Negroes in War Industries and Government Agencies," *Journal of Negro Education*, summer number, 1943, pp. 405-16.

Reddick, L. D., and Others, "The Negro in the North During Wartime," *Journal of Educational Sociology*, January, 1944, the entire issue.

Reid, Ira DeA., *Negro Membership in American Labor Unions* (National Urban League, 1930). 175 pp.

Report on Employment of Negro Workers in Construction of USHA-Aided Projects (United States Housing Authority, 1941). 8 pp. A mimeographed report.

Sancton, Thomas "Trouble in Dixie," *The New Republic*, January 4, 1943, pp. 11-14; January 11, 1943, pp. 50-1; January 18, 1943, pp. 81-3.

—— "Something's Happened to the Negro," *The New Republic*, February 8, 1943, pp. 175-9.

—— "The Race Riots," *The New Republic*, July 5, 1943, pp. 9-13.

"Seniority Provisions in Union Agreements," *Monthly Labor Review*, May, 1941, pp. 1167-77.

Slichter, Sumner H., "Jobs After the War," *The Atlantic Monthly*, October, 1944, pp. 87-91.

Spero, Sterling D., and Harris, Abram L., *The Black Worker* (Columbia University Press, 1931). 509 pp.

Sterner, Richard, *The Negro's Share* (Harper, 1943). 433 pp.

Survey of Employment Prospects for Negroes in Armament Industries (Bureau of Employment Security, Social Security Board, 1941). 7 pp.

The Construction Industry in the United States (United States Department of Labor, 1944). 149 pp. Bulletin No. 786 of the United States Bureau of Labor Statistics.

"The Negro's War," *Fortune*, June, 1942, p. 77 et seq.

The Negro Worker (American Management Association, 1942), 32 pp.

The Wartime Employment of Negroes in the Federal Government (Committee on Fair Employment Practice, 1945). 65 pp. (mimeographed).

Thompson, Charles H., "The American Negro in World War I and World War II," *Journal of Negro Education*, summer number, 1943, pp. 263-7.

—— ed., "The Position of the Negro in the American Social Order," *Journal of Negro Education*, July, 1939, the entire issue.

"War and Post-War Trends in the Employment of Negroes," *Monthly Labor Review*, January, 1945, pp. 1-5.

Weaver, Robert C., "A Wage Differential Based on Race," *Crisis*, August, 1934, pp. 236-8.

—— "An Experiment in Negro Labor," *Opportunity*, October, 1936, pp. 295-8.

—— "Defense Industries and the Negro," *Annals of the American Academy of Political and Social Science*, September, 1942, pp. 60-6.

—— "Detroit and Negro Skill," *Phylon*, second quarter, 1943, pp. 131-43.

—— "Economic Factors in Negro Migration-Past and Present," *Social Forces*, October, 1939, pp. 90-101.

—— "Federal Aid, Local Control, and Negro Participation," *Journal of Negro Education*, January, 1942, pp. 47-59.

—— "Negro Employment in the Aircraft Industry," *Quarterly Journal of Economics*, August, 1945, pp. 597-625.

—— "Racial Employment Trends in National Defense," *Phylon*, fourth quarter, 1941, pp. 337-58; first quarter, 1942, pp. 22-30.

—— "Recent Events in Negro Union Relationships," *Journal of Political Economy*, September, 1944, pp. 234-49.

Weaver, Robert C., "The Defense Program and the Negro," *Opportunity*, November, 1940, pp. 324-27.

—— "The Employment of Negroes in United States War Industries," *International Labour Review*, August, 1944, pp. 141-59.

—— "The Employment of the Negro in War Industries," *Journal of Negro Education*, summer number, 1943, pp. 386-96.

—— "The Negro in a Program of Public Housing," *Opportunity*, July, 1938, pp. 1-6.

—— "The Negro Comes of Age in Industry," *The Atlantic Monthly*, September, 1943, pp. 54-59.

—— "The Negro Veteran," *Annals of the American Academy of Political and Social Science*, March, 1945, pp. 127-32.

—— *The Urban Negro Worker in the United States, 1925-36* (Government Printing Office, 1939). 87 pp. Volume II. *Male Negro Skilled Workers in the United States, 1930-36.*

—— "Training Negroes for Occupational Opportunities," *Journal of Negro Education*, October, 1938, pp. 486-97.

—— "With the Negro's Help," *The Atlantic Monthly*, June, 1942, pp. 696-707.

—— and Weckler, Joseph E., *Negro Platform Workers* (American Council on Race Relations, 1945). 48 pp.

Wesley, Charles H., *Negro Labor in the United States, 1850-1925* (Vanguard Press, 1927). 343 pp.

Westmoreland, Edgar P., ed., *Report of Southern Regional Conference for Negro Teacher Trainers and Assistant State Supervisors of War Production Training and Trade and Industrial Education* (U. S. Office of Education, 1944). 86 pp. (mimeographed).

Wilkerson, Doxey A., *Special Problems of Negro Education* (Government Printing Office, 1939). 170 pp. Staff Study No. 12 of the Advisory Committee on Education.

Wolfe, French E., *Admission to American Trade Unions* (Johns Hopkins University Press, 1912). 181 pp.

INDEX

A. C. Spark Plug Co., 64, 76

American Federation of Labor (A. F. of L.), 223-31; action to combat discrimination, 176, 223-8; building construction department, 35-6, 216; metal trades department, 35-7, 219, 225-6, 229; racial policies, 215-6, 218; racial practices, 37, 217-9

Aeronautical Products, Inc., 64, 76

Aircraft industry, 15, 36, 37-8, 109-30, 194, 221-2, 267-8; barriers to Negro employment, 36, 109-18; post-war employment prospects, 267-8; utilization of Negroes, 124-30

Alabama, 51-3

Alabama Shipbuilding and Drydock Co., 37

Allison Division of General Motors, 114-15

American Management Association, 16, 195-6, 212-13, 216

Apprenticeship, 20-21

Aptitude tests, 48

Armed forces, segregation in, ii

Army, see War Department

Arsenals, 21

Atlanta, Georgia, 29, 86, 127

Automobile, Aircraft and Agricultural Implement Workers of America, United, see UAW-CIO

Automobile industry, 7, 15, 32-3, 61-77, 194, 269, 285-94

Auxiliary unions, 35, 128, 217-8, 224-5, 228-31; definition, 218

Baltimore, Maryland, 22, 30, 84-5, 87, 140, 201-2

Baltimore Sun, 22-3

Barriers to Negro employment, 16-27, 31-2, 35-7, 40; in World War II, 19-27, 63-70, 83-8, 99-102, 108, 109-18, 207-11, 224-6, 298-9

Beaumont, Texas, riot in, iii

Bell Aircraft Corp., 111-3, 125, 127

Bethlehem Steel Corp., 33-4, 36, 223, 229

Beveridge, Sir William, 107 footnote, 262, 263

Birmingham, Alabama, 51, 87

Boeing Aircraft Company, 36, 116-17, 216, 226

Bohn Aluminum and Brass Corp., 286

Boilermakers, Iron Shipbuilders, Welders and Helpers of America, International Brotherhood of, 217, 218, 224-30

Boom towns, 25

Border states, 41

Brewer Drydock Co., 39

Brewster Aeronautical Corp., 113

Bricklayers, Masons and Plasterers' International Union of America, 5

Briggs Manufacturing Co., 64, 70, 76-7, 286, 291-2

Brown and Sharpe Manufacturing Co., 39

Buffalo, New York, 34, 70, 111-3

Buick Division of General Motors Corp., 64-5, 75

Bureau of Employment Security, 23-4, 110

Cadillac Motors Division of General Motors Corp., 64

California Shipbuilding Co., 224

Carpenters, 5, 12, 28-32; displacement of Negroes, 97-8, 99

Charleston, South Carolina, 5, 23, 54-5

Chevrolet Motor Division of General Motors Corp., 64, 76

Date Due